Metaphor in Hopkins

Metaphor in Hopkins

by

Robert Boyle, S.J.

Chapel Hill
THE UNIVERSITY OF NORTH CAROLINA PRESS

COPYRIGHT © 1960, 1961 BY
THE UNIVERSITY OF NORTH CAROLINA PRESS
Manufactured in the United States of America

PRINTED BY THE SEEMAN PRINTERY, INC., DURHAM, N. C.

THIS BOOK WAS DIGITALLY PRINTED.

Matribus tribus—

Mariae

Societati

Agneti

hoc opus indignum

D D D

R B

Imprimi potest
    Joseph P. Fisher, S.J.
    Provincialis
    Provinciae Missourianae

Nihil obstat
    George C. Tolman, C.M., S.T.D.
    Censor Deputatus

Imprimatur
    ✠ Urban J. Vehr, D.D.
    Archiepiscopus Denveriensis
    die 27a Martii, 1961

Preface

The purpose of my study is twofold: to set forth a method of criticism and to apply that method to certain of Hopkins' poems. One principal conclusion to which I come is that Hopkins' mind (like, it seems to me, every profound artist's mind) finds its fullest expression in metaphor. My effort to express my understanding of metaphor, somewhat different from and wider than the traditional definitions of the word, occupies much of my attention in this work.

For what is good in this study, I owe much to many people. Most of all I express gratitude to Raymond Schoder, S.J., and to W. H. Gardner, both admirable scholars. If I seem to disagree with them often, it is because I take for granted the vast areas of agreement and the splendid insights they have shared with me, Father Schoder in long hours of discussion and Mr. Gardner in his volumes of criticism. To Cleanth Brooks, who with friendly and expert skill directed the doctoral dissertation from which this book developed; to Hopkins critics cited in this work and many not cited; to many of my former and present colleagues at Regis College, notably David Hoene, Donald Klene, John Teeling, S.J.; to D. A. Bischoff, S.J., who generously shared with me his extensive knowledge of Hopkins' manuscripts; to Mrs. Evelyn Gribben, who brings typing close to the conditions of the fine arts; finally, and most of all, to my Superiors in the Society of Jesus—to all these I express my indebtedness and gratitude.

I must also record here my thanks to the Regis College Faculty Publications Endowment Fund for aid in the publication of this book and to the Ford Foundation for a grant under its program for assisting American university presses in the publication of works in the humanities and the social sciences.

The text upon which my study is based is the third edition of *Poems of Gerard Manley Hopkins,* edited by W. H. Gardner (New York: Oxford, 1948). I follow the numbers given to the poems in this edition, which is referred to throughout as *Poems*. For textual variations, I have depended upon the knowledge and MS copies of Father Bischoff, who has checked for me all extant copies of the texts I use. I refer to the other standard works in the following abbreviated forms:

1. *The Letters of Gerard Manley Hopkins to Robert Bridges*, edited by Claude Colleer Abbott (London: Oxford, 1935), as *Letters 1*.
2. *The Correspondence of Gerard Manley Hopkins and Richard Watson Dixon*, edited by Claude Colleer Abbott (London: Oxford, 1935), as *Letters 2*.
3. *Further Letters of Gerard Manley Hopkins*, edited by Claude Colleer Abbott (2d ed.; London: Oxford, 1956), as *Letters 3*.
4. *The Journals and Papers of Gerard Manley Hopkins*, edited by Humphry House (London: Oxford, 1959), as *Journals*.
5. *The Sermons and Devotional Writings of Gerard Manley Hopkins*, edited by Christopher Devlin, S.J. (London: Oxford, 1959), as *Sermons*.
6. W. H. Gardner's *Gerard Manley Hopkins (1844-1889), A Study of Poetic Idiosyncrasy in Relation to Poetic Tradition* (2 vols.; New Haven: Yale, 1948), as *Gardner 1* and *2*.
7. John Pick's *Gerard Manley Hopkins, Priest and Poet* (London: Oxford, 1942), as *Pick*.

The Scriptural quotations are taken from the translations of Ronald A. Knox (*The Holy Bible* [New York: Sheed and Ward, 1956]) and of James A. Kleist, S.J., and Joseph L. Lilly, C.M. (*The New Testament* [Milwaukee: Bruce Publishing Co., 1954]).

The present chapter 9, in somewhat different form, appeared originally as "Hopkins' Imagery: the Thread for the Maze," in *Thought*, 35 (Spring, 1960), 57-90.

For the merit of the Index, Sister Mary Lucy King, O.S.F., who made it, deserves great thanks.

Contents

	PAGE
Preface	vii
Introduction	xi
Chapter 1: The Heroic Breast	3
Chapter 2: God's Grandeur	25
Chapter 3: The Shekinah	45
Chapter 4: The Vital Candle	71
Chapter 5: Peace	111
Chapter 6: That Small Commonweal	125
Chapter 7: The Valley of the Shadow	145
Chapter 8: The Good Earth	162
Chapter 9: The Thread for the Maze	172
Notes	207
Select Bibliography	221
Index	227

Introduction

> And still th'abysses infinite
> Surround the peak from which we gaze.
> Deep calls to deep and blackest night
> Giddies the soul with blinding daze
> That dares to cast its searching sight
> On being's dread and vacant maze.
>
> "Nondum," *Poems,* No. 22, stanza 5

Hopkins' mature poems express, almost without exception, some facet of divine life in human beings. His vision of reality focused most clearly on the operation of Christ's life stemming from the center of the Trinity, divinizing the hearts of acquiescent humans, reaching even to animals, birds, trees, the good earth itself.

Hopkins' imagery points to this divine activity, and his most interesting and complex metaphors and similes reveal their ultimate natures and functions, I believe, only in this light. The principal aim of this study, in fact, is to reveal as the unifying and vitalizing factor in Hopkins' mature imagery his underlying view of divine life flowing into the heart and acts of the just man.

By the term "imagery" I wish to refer exclusively to metaphor and simile. An analysis of one important image in a unified poem will, according to my theory, offer a good basis for a critical evaluation of the total poem. Sometimes, as in the second poem I consider, one image cannot successfully be isolated from companion images. But in general my effort will be to isolate and dissect an image and then to consider its function in the organic whole. The application of this critical method to Hopkins' poems will, I trust, test its efficiency.

Metaphor and simile, in my theory, are essentially different.[1] For practical purposes, however, they may be approached as if they were composed of the same elements. As I shall explain at greater length in my final chapter and as, I trust, will become more evident from the examples I offer, an image may be defined as the comparison of two unlike objects on the basis of a likeness *in* each one. Thus two nouns, signifying the two unlike objects, and an adjective or a verb, signifying the quality or the act found in each object, will make up every image.

For example, Hopkins' early "Nondum" contains the following stanza:

> We see the glories of the earth
> But not the hand that wrought them all:
> Night to a myriad worlds gives birth,
> Yet like a lighted empty hall
> Where stands no host at door or hearth
> Vacant creation's lamps appal.
>
> (*Poems,* No. 22, stanza 2)

The stars are compared to lamps, and here they share an act—giving light in a vast space—and at least two qualities—suggesting the causality of a living host and the mysterious and sinister absence of that host.

Metaphor, which is far more a specifically poetic proposition than is simile, states identity rather than comparison. Hopkins' artistic mind, as I shall endeavor to show, sought out metaphor as its favorite means of expression. The predicate noun of the metaphorical proposition is seen as existing *in* the being. The *being,* note, is not expressed by the noun alone, but by the subject plus "is." When Hopkins says, for example, that "the mind is a mother of immortal song,"[2] he states that the nature, "a mother," exists in and by the being, "the mind is." Here the two nouns signifying the unlike objects are "mind" and "mother." The "is" signifies the existence of the subject "the mind," and in this total being the alien nature, "mother," is conceived to operate. This new being, the mind-mother, produces a song-child through long gestation and perhaps difficult birth. This living process cannot begin without the insemination of reality, the dynamic union between reality and the knowing mind.

Another and more subtle metaphorical process in Hopkins' poetry may be isolated and observed in his rhythm. Metaphorical rhythm results when the sound patterns of the speech imitate the sound patterns, the motions, the qualities, and the acts of the thing signified by the speech—or, in some cases, of something other than the thing signified.

Meter and rhythm will be considered in this study as forms of metaphor. Meter, of course, is a set or formally organized rhythm which can be charted apart from any particular sounds, e.g.:

$$\cup / \mid \cup / \mid \cup / \mid \cup / \mid \cup /$$

Accompanying these formal verse rhythms are various speech rhythms, which come into being because of particular sounds and sound combinations, stresses, etc.:

> Of mán's fírst disobédience, and the frúit. . . .
>
> *(Paradise Lost,* I, 1)

> . . . And, like a forester, the groves may tread,
> Even till the eastern gate, all fiery-red,
> Opening on Neptune with fair blessed beams,
> Túrns ínto yéllow góld his sált gréen stréams.
>
> *(Midsummer Night's Dream,* III, ii)

The great poets manipulate the rhythms of their language to express the rhythm of the object of which they speak or to express the rhythms they feel within themselves as their response to those objects, or to do both. For example, in the following choice image from *Troilus and Cressida,* I, iii, Shakespeare expresses with speech rhythm (which is inextricably compounded of accent, quantity, vowel sounds, consonant stops and prolongations of sound, silences, etc.) more of the ignominious gulp with which the temerarious little boats disappear than any abstract *meaning* could possibly do:

> With due observance of thy godlike seat,
> Great Agamemnon, Nestor shall apply
> Thy latest words. In the reproof of chance
> Lies the true proof of men: the sea being smooth,
> How many shallow bauble boats dare sail
> Upon her patient breast, making their way
> With those of nobler bulk!
> But let the ruffian Boreas once enrage
> The gentle Thetis, and anon behold
> The strong-ribb'd bark through liquid mountains cut,
> Bounding between the two moist elements,
> Like Perseus' horse: where's then the saucy boat,

> Whose weak untimber'd sides but even now
> Co-rivall'd greatness? either to harbour fled,
> Or made a toast for Neptune.

Milton expresses the wrangle between Adam and Eve most vividly by the wrangle between formal meter and speech rhythm in the last line of Book IX of *Paradise Lost*:

> Thus they in mutual accusation spent
> The fruitless hours, but neither self-condemning,
> And of their vain contest appear'd no end.

The metrical conflict in that last line, with the conventional verse accent playing against the real speech accent in different musical times (what Hopkins calls counterpoint) can be crudely indicated thus:

And of their vain contest appear'd no end.

Speech accents are indicated by the solid accent marks; verse accents, by the broken ones. The time of the verse accent is indicated by the bars above the poetry; the time of the speech accent, by the musical analogy below it.

Hopkins is aiming at a similar effect of conflict in the heavy syncopation of the last line of "Spelt from Sibyl's Leaves." The accent is syncopated, but since the sprung rhythm does not admit the conventional verse accent and the musical time built on that bar or foot, and thus excludes the counterpoint, the musical bars coincide—i.e., only one musical *time* is involved. Here, then, the interaction is between Hopkins' sprung accent and the speech accent in the same musical time:

... thoughts against thoughts in groans grind.

Again, the rhythms of the object dictate the rhythms of Milton's language describing Satan's flight through the abyss of chaos. The rhythms in this language are a "metaphor" of the rhythms of the actual Satan struggling in the fumes and emptiness of the wild abyss:

> At last his Sail-broad Vans
> He spreads for flight, and in the surging smoke
> Uplifted spurns the ground, thence many a League
> As in a cloudy Chair ascending rides
> Audacious, but that seat soon failing, meets
> A vast vacuity: all unawares
> Flutt'ring his pennons vain plumb down he drops
> Ten thousand fadom deep, and to this hour
> Down had been falling, had not by ill chance
> The strong rebuff of some tumultuous cloud
> Instinct with Fire and Nitre hurried him
> As many miles aloft: that fury stay'd,
> Quencht in a Boggy *Syrtis,* neither Sea,
> Nor good dry Land: nigh founder'd on he fares,
> Treading the crude consistence, half on foot,
> Half flying; behoves him now both Oar and Sail.
>
> (*Paradise Lost,* II, 927-42)

Note that subordinate speech rhythms and the sounds themselves imitate other things: the "vast vacuity," in its open-mouthed repetition of the long vowel and in its plethora of vowels, imitates the thing of which it speaks;[8] the rising, falling, and logaoedic rhythms and the onomatopoetic sounds themselves express the tumultuous deep and its varying elements while they remain part of the larger imitation of Satan's own rhythm.

It is a similar complex of metaphorical rhythms which often dictates the structure of Hopkins' verse and, therefore, of the imagery included in that verse. A full understanding of any of his images means that the meter of the whole and the accompanying rhythms are, as much as may be, understood, or at least are acknowledged.

That Hopkins practiced this art of metaphorical rhythms is evident from any casual examination of his work. The early prize-poem, "The Escorial," written when he was fifteen, foreshadows his skill in using rhythms and sound:

> But from the mountain glens in autumn late
> Adown the clattering gullies swept the rain;
> The driving storm at hour of vespers beat
> Upon the mould'ring terraces amain;
> The Altar-tapers flar'd in gusts; in vain
> Louder the monks dron'd out Gregorians slow;
> Afar in corridors with painèd strain

Doors slamm'd to the blasts continually; more low,
Then pass'd the wind, and sobb'd with mountain-echo'd woe.

(Poems, No. 1, stanza 13)

Here the fifth and sixth lines contrast admirably, working together to express rhythmically the two events they signify. And rhythmically expressive is the juxtaposition of two strong accents, "Doors slamm'd," a hint of the vital element in sprung rhythm (in which the meter is set up beforehand only in regard to the number of beats, not in regard to the number of syllables, and hence can serve more freely as a metaphoric rhythm).

In "A Vision of Mermaids," No. 2, Hopkins indicates how well he has learned from Milton to reproduce in the rising movement of the verbal rhythm and in the aptness of sound the motions and the sounds of the object itself:

Some, diving merrily, downward drove, and gleam'd
With arm and fin; the argent bubbles stream'd
Airwards, disturb'd; and the scarce troubled sea
Gurgled, where they had sunk, melodiously.
Others with fingers white would comb among
The drenchèd hair of slabby weeds that swung
Swimming. . . .

"The argent bubbles streamed" expresses in its rising movement the rise of the bubbles, with the flowing line emphasized in the lengthened vowel of "streamed." The rising movement stops in "airwards," to be replaced by the rocking movement of "airwards, disturb'd," which in its sound echoes the small bursting of the bubbles on the rocking surface. Hopkins was instructed by his master Milton in the secrets of "apt numbers." And the rhythms imitating the motion and feel of those "slabby weeds" may well owe something to the ears of a Ghost and of a Caesar:

. . . the fat weed
That roots itself in ease on Lethe wharf. . . .

(Hamlet, I, v)

. . . This common body,
Like to a vagabond flag upon the stream,
Goes to and back, lackeying the varying tide,
To rot itself with motion.

(Antony and Cleopatra, I, iv)

INTRODUCTION   xvii

Hopkins' rhythmic skill is mastered and "realized on paper" (*Letters* 2, p. 14) fully for the first time in *The Wreck of the Deutschland*, where the following stanza, the meter (or repeated beat or "measure" of rhythm) of which imitates primarily the motion of the sea, expresses in its various rhythms also the motion of the choppy waves, the gusts of the strong wind, and above all the spirals (small, larger, largest: "wiry, white-fiery, and whirlwind-swivellèd") of the snow sweeping past the ship on its long spinning descent into the sea:

>   Into the snows she sweeps,
>   Hurling the haven behind,
>   The Deutschland, on Sunday; and so the sky keeps,
>   For the infinite air is unkind,
>   And the sea flint-flake, black-backed in the regular blow,
>   Sitting Eastnortheast, in cursed quarter, the wind;
>   Wiry and white-fiery and whirlwind-swivellèd snow
>   Spins to the widow-making unchilding unfathering deeps.
>
>   (*Poems*, No. 28, stanza 13)

This stanza, remotely like the stanza of Milton's Nativity Ode, builds with rise and fall from the opening two-stress (three-stress in Part II) to the closing six-stress line, and the cumulative motion seems to me like that of the ocean or of the ship in the ocean. In the first part of the poem, the poet himself is rocked by this powerful rhythm which bursts its stanzaic bounds between the climactic seventh and eighth stanzas, and he is buffeted (as the rhythms and the sounds express) in stanza 8 as the nun is buffeted in stanza 19. That God Himself is this ocean Hopkins states in stanza 32, and he makes sufficiently clear that the ocean that swings and buffets (and kills) the ship and the nun is ultimately the same ocean that swings and buffets (and spares) the poet.

How subtle the expression of reality through rhythm and sound (inclusive, of course, of meaning, but not altogether dependent upon meaning) can be is perhaps better shown in the following stanza, which expresses the accident and the plight of the ship:

>   She drove in the dark to leeward,
>   She struck—not a reef or a rock
>   But the combs of a smother of sand: night drew her
>   Dead to the Kentish Knock;

> And she beat the bank down with her bows and the ride of
>   her keel:
> The breakers rolled on her beam with ruinous shock;
>   And canvas and compass, the whorl and the wheel
> Idle for ever to waft her or wind her with, these she endured.
>
> (Stanza 14)

In the captain's report of the accident, we read the following: "The ship touched the sand twice slightly before she became fixed."[4] The testimony of the captain and of other survivors also indicates that those on board had no suspicion of the nearness of the sand bar and that they did not know what the ship was striking until she stuck. Hopkins has expressed those two touches on the sand through the rhythm and sound of his language. The shock of her totally unexpected striking on some unknown substance is expressed in the dash after the verb and the two questioning touches in "reef" and "rock" with the hovering pause after each; and the final convincing penetration into the deadly, smothering sand, by the rush and finality of the third line with its expressive sibilants.

This consideration of the function of Hopkins' rhythms and sounds gives the clue to Hopkins' meaning when he told Bridges that he sometimes sought higher values than *immediate* clarity: "Obscurity I do and will try to avoid so far as is consistent with excellences higher than clearness at a first reading. This question of obscurity we will some time speak of but not now. As for affectation I do not believe I am guilty of it: you should point out instances, but as long as mere novelty and boldness strikes you as affectation your criticism strikes me as—as water of the Lower Isis" (*Letters 1*, p. 54). In order to understand Hopkins' images fully and to perceive the reasons which justify his novelties and boldness, it is not enough to consider merely the significations of his words and predications. The dictates of meter, rhythms, and sound must also receive full consideration. If *meaning* had been Hopkins' prime consideration, he would have composed very differently. As he wrote to Bridges nearly ten years after the above quotation:

But however that reminds me that one thing I am now resolved on, it is to prefix short prose *arguments* to some of my pieces. These too will expose me to carping, but I do not mind. Epic and drama and ballad and many, most, things should be at once intelligible; but everything need not and cannot be. Plainly if it is possible to express a subtle and recondite thought on a subtle and recondite subject in a subtle and recondite way and with great felicity and perfection, in the end, something must be sacrificed, with so trying a task, in the process, and this may be the being at once, nay perhaps even the being without explanation at all, intelligible. Neither, in the same light, does it seem to me a real objection (though this one I hope not to lay myself open to) that the argument should be even longer than the piece; for the merit of the work may lie for one thing in its terseness. It is like a mate which may be given, one way only, in three moves; otherwise, various ways, in many.

(*Letters 1*, pp. 265-66)

In this study of Hopkins' mature imagery, by which I mean metaphor and simile, I will consider the individual words which make up the image, then the predication which forms the individual image and orders the words, and then the total context (in so far as that is feasible) which determines the choice of these words in that order.

I have chosen eight significant images which have a vital influence in eight important poems and which further express eight themes pervasive in Hopkins' mature work. The theme of the divine life in human beings flows through these images from its source in the interior life of God to its ultimate activity in the good earth. The images indicate too, though roughly, the chronological deepening of this vision in Hopkins' mind.

The images are:

1. . . . lovely-felicitous Providence
Finger of a tender of, O of a feathery delicacy, the breast of the
   Maiden could obey so, be a bell to, ring of it, and
Startle the poor sheep back!

(*The Wreck of the Deutschland, Poems*,
No. 28, stanza 31, composed in 1876)

2. It will flame out, like shining from shook foil. . . .

("God's Grandeur," *Poems*, No. 31,
composed in 1877)

3. Mary Immaculate,
Merely a woman, yet
Whose presence, power is
Great as no goddess's
Was deemèd, dreamèd; who
This one work has to do—

> Let all God's glory through,
> God's glory which would go
> Through her and from her flow
> Off, and no way but so.
>
> > ("The Blessed Virgin compared to the Air we
> > Breathe," *Poems*, No. 60, composed in 1883)

4.
> My heart in hiding
> Stirred for a bird,—the achieve of, the mastery of the thing!
>
> > ("The Windhover: To Christ our Lord,"
> > *Poems*, No. 36, composed in 1877)

5.
> And so he does leave Patience exquisite,
> That plumes to Peace thereafter.
>
> > ("Peace," *Poems*, No. 46, composed in 1879)

6.
> Óur tale, O óur oracle! Lét life, wáned, ah lét life wind
> Off hér once skéined stained véined varíety upon, áll on twó
> spools. . . .
>
> > ("Spelt from Sibyl's Leaves," *Poems,*
> > No. 62, composed about 1885)

7.
> I cast for comfort I can no more get
> By groping round my comfortless, than blind
> Eyes in their dark can day or thirst can find
> Thirst's all-in-all in all a world of wet.
>
> > ("My own heart. . . ," *Poems*, No. 71,
> > composed about 1885)

8.
> Earth, sweet Earth, sweet landscape, with leavès throng
> And louchèd low grass, heaven that dost appeal
> To, with no tongue to plead, no heart to feel;
> That canst but only be, but dost that long—. . . .
>
> > ("Ribblesdale," *Poems*, No. 58,
> > composed in 1882)

The important markings and corrections in the various manuscripts are for the most part indicated in the careful annotations of Bridges and of Gardner in *Poems*. On pp. 202-3 Bridges indicates the MS sources, which are four: A, Bridges' own collection of Hopkins' autographs and Bridges' copies of other poems; B, Bridges' copies of poems from A, with Hopkins' additions and corrections; D, Canon Dixon's collection in letters from Hopkins; and H, the posthumous papers that were sent to Bridges after Hopkins' death. Father Bischoff, in his article, "The Manuscripts of Gerard Manley Hopkins," *Thought*, 26 (Winter, 1951), pp. 551-80, gives a more recent account of the MSS, and is preparing a revision of his own account to bring the matter further up to date. The following relevant markings and changes in the MSS of my eight texts have been sent to me by Father Bischoff: In A the following markings occur:

Finger of a tender of, O of a feathery delicacy, the breast of the

Maiden could swing with, be musical of it and

Startle the poor sheep back! is the shipwrack then a harvest,

does tempest carry the grain for Thee?

Hopkins himself has crossed out "swing with it, be musical of it and" and substituted above it, "obey so, be a bell to, ring of it, and"

In my third image, the only markings are in A, as follows:

This one work has to do—
Let God, God's greatness, through,
God's greatness, which would go
Through her, and only so.

That second line is canceled and the present reading written in Bridges' hand. In B the present reading is unmarked.

In the line which follows my second image, H offers the interesting variant, "Goes gathering, like the ooze of oil," and the fifth line of the poem in both A and H reads, "Generations have hard trod, have hard trod."

In the H MS the seventh image reads:

I grope for comfort I can no more get
By casting round my comfortless. . . .

The present reading appears in H in a marginal note.

Also in H, the following variant for the last line of my eighth image appears:

That canst but only be—still be it, be it long,

and the line which follows then reads,

Be it out, this being, why well thou dost that; strong. . . .

How exacting we may be with Hopkins' imagery in regard to his words and predications (to say nothing of the crowning glory of his work, his "apt Numbers, fit quantity of Syllables, and the sense variously drawn out from one Verse into another"), we may gather both from the ideals underlying his criticism of others and from his own discussion of his work, of which the following explanation of his Purcell sonnet (No. 45) is a satisfactory sample. Hopkins' craftsmanlike scrutiny of his words, apparent in almost everything he wrote, is stressed here too:

The sonnet on Purcell means this: 1-4. I hope Purcell is not damned for being a Protestant, because I love his genius. 5-8. And that not so much for gifts he shares, even though it shd. be in higher measure, with other musicians as for his own individuality. 9-14. So that while he is aiming only at impressing me his hearer with the meaning in hand I am looking out meanwhile for his specific, his individual markings and mottlings, 'the sakes of him.' It is as when a bird thinking only of soaring spreads its wings: a beholder may happen then to have his attention drawn by the act to the plumage displayed.—In particular, the first lines mean: May Purcell, O may he have died a good death and that soul which I love so much and which breathes or stirs so unmistakeably in his works have parted from the body and passed away, centuries since though I frame the wish, in peace with God! so that the heavy condemnation under which he outwardly or nominally lay for being out of the true Church may in consequence of his good intentions have been reversed. 'Low lays him' is merely 'lays him low,' that is, strikes him heavily, weighs upon him. (I daresay this will strike you as more professional than you had anticipated.) It is somewhat dismaying to find I am so unintelligible though, especially in one of my very best pieces. 'Listed,' by the by, is 'enlisted.' 'Sakes' is hazardous: about that point I was more bent on saying my say than on being understood in it. The 'moonmarks' belong to the image only of course, not to the application; I mean not detailedly: I was thinking of a bird's quill feathers. One thing disquiets me: *I meant* 'fair fall' to mean *fair (fortune be)* fall; it has since struck me that perhaps 'fair' is an adjective proper and in the predicate and can only be used in cases like 'fair fall the day,' that is, *may the day fall, turn out, fair*. My line will yield a sense that way indeed, but I never meant it so. Do you know any passage decisive on this?

(January 4, 1883, *Letters I*, pp. 170-1)

Some four years earlier, when he had sent the sonnet to Bridges, Hopkins had explained fully the word *sakes*:

Sake is a word I find it convenient to use: I did not know when I did so first that it is common in German, in the form *sach*.[5] It is the *sake* of 'for the sake of,' *forsake, namesake, keepsake*. I mean by it the being a thing has outside itself, as a voice by its echo, a face by its reflection, a body by its shadow, a man by his name, fame, or memory, *and also* that in the thing by virtue of which especially it has this being abroad, and that is something distinctive, marked, specifically or individually speaking, as for a voice and echo clearness; for a reflected image light, brightness; for a shadow-casting body bulk; for a man genius, great achievements, amiability, and so on. In this case it is, as the sonnet says, distinctive quality in genius.

(May 26, 1879, *Letters 1*, p. 83)

Word-casting for a role in a Hopkins' line is no casual affair.

Hopkins' equally meticulous way with an image could be extensively illustrated outside his poetry, too, but for my purposes I choose this illustration of the grappling of his mind with an image:

> Now this is the artist's most essential quality, masterly execution; it is a kind of male gift and especially marks off men from women, the begetting one's thought on paper, or verse, on whatever the matter is; the life must be conveyed into the work and be displayed there, not suggested as having been in the artist's mind: otherwise the product is one of those hen's-eggs that are good to eat and look just like live ones but never hatch (I think they are called wind eggs: I believe most eggs for breakfast *are* wind eggs and none the worse for it).—Now it is too bad of me to have compared Burne Jones's beautiful and original works to wind-eggs; moreover on better consideration it strikes me that the mastery I speak of is not so much the male quality in the mind as a puberty in the life of that quality. The male quality is the creative gift, which he markedly has. But plainly, while artists may differ indefinitely in the degree and kind or variety of their natural gifts, all shd., as artists, have come, at all events shd. in time come, to the puberty, the manhood of those gifts: that should be common to all, above it the gifts may differ.

(June 30, 1886, *Letters 2*, p. 133)

With such care to examine all facets of his imagery, Hopkins is likely to give us images that will bear (and require) a great deal of careful examination on our part.

An amusing example of Hopkins' willingness to accept all the implications of an image appears in a letter written to Bridges in reply to his evidently rather harsh criticism of the beloved *Deutschland* (Bridges had said that he would not for any money read it again—cf. *Letters 1*, p. 46). Hopkins tells him that with some effort he

> would have got more weathered to the style and its features—not really odd. Now they say that vessels sailing from the port of London will take (perhaps it should be / used once to take) Thames water for the voyage: it

was foul and stunk at first as the ship worked but by degrees casting its filth was in a few days very pure and sweet and wholesomer and better than any water in the world. However that may be, it is true to my purpose. When a new thing, such as my ventures in the Deutschland are, is presented us our first criticisms are not our truest, best, most homefelt, or most lasting but what come easiest on the instant. They are barbarous and like what the ignorant and the ruck say. This was so with you. The Deutschland on her first run worked very much and unsettled you, thickening and clouding your mind with vulgar mudbottom and common sewage (I see that I am going it with the image) and just then unhappily you *drew off* your criticisms all stinking (a necessity now of the image) and bilgy, whereas if you had let your thoughts cast themselves they would have been clearer in themselves and more to my taste too. I did not heed them therefore, perceiving they were a first drawing-off.

(May 13, 1878, *Letters 1*, pp. 50-51)

Finally, rhythm was supremely the object of Hopkins' study and solicitude, as the indexes to his *Letters* and *Notebooks,* the "Preface" to his poems, and above all the poems themselves will suggest. This postscript to a letter to Bridges will testify well enough here to Hopkins' attention to rhythm in his poetry: "To do the Eurydice any kind of justice you must not slovenly read it with the eyes but with your ears, as if the paper were declaiming it at you. For instance the line 'she had come from a cruise training seamen' read without stress and declaim is mere Lloyd's Shipping Intelligence; properly read it is quite a different thing. Stress is the life of it" (May 21, 1878, *Letters 1*, pp. 51-52).

The eight images above, if they will render up their imagistic treasures and carry us besides into the elements of word, predication, and rhythm (inclusive of its components), and if they will bring to light the expressed and implied themes which they involve, may become for us eight peaks from which we can cast our searching sight over what has sometimes been, even for competent critics, the "dread and vacant maze" of Hopkins' mature poetry.

Metaphor in Hopkins

CHAPTER 1

The Heroic Breast

che l'essere del mondo, e l'esser mio,
  la morte ch' Ei sostenne perch' io viva,
  e quel che spera ogni fedel com' io,

con la predetta conoscenza viva,
  tratto m' hanno del mar dell' amor torto,
  e del diritto m' han posto alla riva.
                          Paradiso, XXVI

To give God glory and that by sacrifice, sacrifice offered in the barren wilderness outside of God, as the children of Israel were led into the wilderness to offer sacrifice. This sacrifice and this outward procession is a consequence and shadow of the procession of the Trinity, from which mystery sacrifice takes its rise....
                          Sermons, p. 197

> ... lovely-felicitous Providence
> Finger of a tender of, O of a feathery delicacy, the breast of the
>   Maiden could obey so, be a bell to, ring of it, and
> Startle the poor sheep back!
> *The Wreck of the Deutschland, Poems,* No. 28, stanza 31

The concern of Providence here is not the maiden but the other passengers, "the rest of them." They seem, at first glance, a deserted and comfortless flock. But actually, as our image makes clear, God is using the cry of the nun as a means of gathering His flock back into the fold. The Comforter, the Finger of God (both terms applied to the Holy Ghost) touches the nun in two ways: as He touched the poet in Part I of the poem, bringing him to assent to God's mastery, to share in the Sacrifice; and as an instrument to call others to that same assent, to a share in that same Sacrifice.

The divine Finger which touched Hopkins in stanza 1 almost unmade him, driving his heart "hard at bay" so that it was forced to cry out either "yes" or "no." He said "yes," bowing to God's mastery, and found that the God Who had wrung his heart was actually its "Father and fondler," that He exercised His mastery only in order to give His divine life to His son through that assenting *yes* of the human will. The same Providence touched the nun through "wrecking and storm," and found the complete and unwavering assent of the martyr from her, expressed in her great cry. But while she was crying only to "divine ears," He was using her cry to reach the ears of His wandering sheep. A church bell, when it sounds out its peals, simply "speaks itself," acts its own nature; but the man who rings it intends that sound to reach the ears of the faithful and call them to the Sacrifice. So here the nun speaks only what is in her, the Word to Whom she is joined in perfect faith and love; but Providence, the Good Shepherd, swings His bell not only for her own sake but for his scattered flock.

The brawling and beating of the romping, brutal waves come from that same Finger, which masters "the sway of the sea." It is that motion which swings throughout the poem, and for the most part it is neither tender nor delicate. It is the physical power through which God wrings His rebel, through which He drives the malice of man to the point where it must stand and accept God or reject Him. But the Finger which swings the waves also touches the spirit. "... it can penetrate deeper than any two-edged sword, reaching the very division between soul and spirit, between joints and marrow, quick to distinguish every thought and design in our hearts" (Hebrews, 4:12). In this touch it is "of a tender, ... of a feathery delicacy." When His poising, balancing palms sway the waves before bringing them, as Christ once did in the storm on Lake Gennesareth (Matthew, 8:24-27), "to a poise, to a pane" by His divine power, the physical and external effect is analogous to the inner sway and balancing of the will. He so swayed the wills of the apostles in "the weather of Gennesareth" (stanza 26) and found them wanting in faith. He so sways the poet in Part I and the nun in Part II and finds them responsive. In our image He calls to the spirits of His sheep, startling them from their "comfortless unconfessed" state with the call to confess Him as the poet did in stanza 2, as the nun did in the previous stanzas, so that they too may be comforted by having Him "for the pain, for the patience," by having Him wafted out to them from the "Glow, glory in thunder." It is this spiritual touch which is "lovely-felicitous" and "feathery," that last word implying that in this spiritual activity it is not as it was in the physical activity of stanza 12:

> O Father, not under thy feathers nor ever as guessing
> The goal was a shoal, of a fourth the doom to be drowned. . . .[1]

The feathers of the Comforter, the Divine Dove, are stretched out, our image implies, for those who will return, and through the voice of the nun He startles them to urge them back. Their wills are free, and even driven at bay, they can persist in malice and rejection if they choose, they can be unrepentant prodigals. But their Father is yearning for them to return, ready for them, calling them. It is the deep emotional impact of the word "feathery" in this context that motivates the interruption of the "O" in the line, in so far as the meaning and not the sound pattern is in question. Hopkins begins to say, "Finger of a tender—that is to say, of a feathery delicacy," and the feelings roused by the approaching "feathery" cause him to interrupt the last phrase with the interjection and thus to throw special emphasis on the expressive adjective.

The breast-bell metaphor can be grasped only in relation to the central fact of the whole poem, the Sacrifice of Christ. The various elements of our metaphor, otherwise irreconcilable, meet and are fused in the call of sinners to the Sacrifice of the Lamb. In Part I, the poet describes his own storm before the altar, his flight to the heart of the Host, the Victim, and his consequent rise on the wings of the Dove, or his and the Dove's wings. The martyred virgins in stanza 22 are lettered with the mark of the Lamb: "Do not lay waste land or sea or wood, until we have put a seal on the foreheads of those who serve our God. . . . The Lamb, who dwells where the throne is, will be their shepherd, leading them out to the springs whose water is life; and God will wipe away every tear from their eyes" (Apocalypse, 7:3 and 17). Through sharing in the sacrifice of the Lamb, Who is also the Shepherd of those sheep who are washed white in His blood, the flock comes to the waters of life. That great Sacrifice, effected on Calvary (the "voel" of stanza 4),[2] is extended throughout time and space in the Mass, where the Host, the same Victim, still offers Himself and His flock with Him. Hopkins joins the Host on the altar in Part I and thereafter comprehends the mystery of which St. Paul constantly speaks, of Christ present in the universe, victorious over sin and death. The unchancelled nuns find Him in the storm, bringing them to sacrifice, and their wills pierce straight through pain and death to join with the Lamb,[3] the straight wills (the Scriptural "heart right" and "single eye" of stanza 29 from Matthew, 6:21-23) as unwavering in the blast as the beacon of light from a lighthouse tower, like the beam of "Heraclitean Fire" (*Poems*, No. 72):

> Across my foundering deck shone
> A beacon, an eternal beam.

This light breaking from the loving, faithful, "crimson cresseted" heart of the nun is, as the following line and the final line of the poem make clear, the divine Light of Whom John speaks in the opening lines of his gospel, the Word Himself, made flesh to be sacrificed for us. The Mass and the Sacrifice of Calvary are one, and it is for this reason that the bell which summons the hearers to the altar is heard by sheep, because they are the flock who must be led to life by the Lamb, the Victim, and the Shepherd.

Hopkins considers that the other passengers are "poor sheep" and that they are "comfortless unconfessed" in seeming at least, whereas the "tall nun" is in heaven with Christ, a virgin-martyr, one of those who "are the Lamb's attendants, wherever he goes" (Apocalypse, 14:4). The reasons for the assumption of their unhappy spiritual state are, among others, that as passengers on the Deutschland they are perhaps victims of the Dantean "beast of the waste wood" of stanza 20, who in Hopkins' eyes is a scatterer of the sheep of Christ in the two Deutschlands, "double a desperate name," i.e., country and ship; in that case they would never have had the chance to join with the Host on the altar, as the nuns certainly had, even though now unchancelled and away from their altar; in any case, they are sinners like all of us and sheep requiring a pastor to help them. In this aspect of their need, "unconfessed" can refer to sacramental confession and the absolution which the pastor gives in the name of the Supreme Pastor, Christ; primarily, however, I believe the word refers to that confession which, as in the Confession of St. Augustine, as in the confession of the poet in stanza 2, is assent to Christ, a submission to His mastery, a following of Him even to complete self-sacrifice.

Further, the situation of the nun, as cast out from her country because of her faith and her religious status, and the evidence of her complete assent to God's will which Hopkins finds in her cry, indicate that she has followed the Lamb, has for His sake borne the pain in patience. The newspaper accounts of the wreck give no such heartening evidence in regard to the other passengers. They indicate rather that the others were in extreme distress, some even throwing themselves in despair into the sea or attempting suicide in other ways. Hence the contrast which Hopkins posits in our image between the nun and the other passengers is not without foundation. The nun, like Simon Peter, recognizes the eternal Word through faith and love and gives evidence of rejoicing already in His triumph over sin and death in her; the others, apparently wandering like lost sheep and shaken and sifted like wheat, seem unable or unwilling to find their Shepherd or to be stored in the heavenly barns.

The nun in our image stands in relation to the other passengers as Simon Peter and the Blessed Virgin stand in relation to all men. She gives a demonstration of profound faith, as Peter did (Matthew, 16:15-18), and is therefore called by Hopkins in stanza 29, as Simon was by Christ, a rock—the nun is, appropriately, a Roman rock, the Tarpeian rock, unaffected by the blasts of the storm outside, of weak and evil nature, or of Satan inside. She shines out like a beacon with the "heart's light" Who enlightens every man coming into life, as she guides others as Peter the Shepherd did (John, 21:16-17), offering them by her example support in faith. She is in this last like Peter in a way that prepares for the grain image that immediately follows our own image and that builds, like our bell image, on the violent motion of the sea. Christ pictures His followers as being, like Job, given into the power of Satan, as these passengers are caught and battered externally by sand and water, internally by the weakness and the malice of their human wills and the temptings of the Enemy.

But Peter in his faith will offer a support, as the nun here offers a support: "And the Lord said, Simon, Simon, behold, Satan has claimed power over you all, so that he can sift you like wheat: but I have prayed for thee, that thy faith may not fail; when, after a while, thou hast come back to me, it is for thee to be the support of thy brethren" (Luke, 22:31-32).

It is in giving forth the Word that the nun is like the Blessed Virgin. In stanza 30 Hopkins refers to Jesus as the flame and light of the heart, the light which shines from the beacon, the nun's heart, in the last line of the previous stanza and in the following lines. He is the Son of the Virgin Mary, the maid; and He is also the Son, in an analogous sense, of this maid, the nun. The feast which followed the night of the storm in which the nun gave Him that glory which only a martyr can give was the Feast of the Immaculate Conception, December 8, in which the Church celebrates Mary's own conception in her mother's womb as free from any stain of sin. Her nature was prepared to be the instrument of sharing with God our human nature. She could then conceive and bring forth the eternal Word. To be so conceived, and to conceive the Word as Mary did, are both done, finished, in the past, and will not be done again. But the nun also is a mother of the Word, as are all of His faithful followers, and like Mary she brings Him forth in spirit. And as Mary gave Him to the world, so the nun in our image offers Him to the other passengers.

The address to the Word in the final two lines of stanza 30,

> But here was heart-throe, birth of a brain,
> Word, that heard and kept thee and uttered thee outright,

is obviously a close paraphrase of Luke, 11:27-8: "When he spoke thus, a woman in the multitude said to him aloud, Blessed is the womb that bore thee, the breast which thou hast sucked. And he answered, Shall we not say, Blessed are those who hear the word of God, and keep it?"

The words of another English author, Bede, on the text have an illuminating relation to Hopkins' image. This passage of Bede is found in the *Roman Breviary,* Lectio 9 of the *Commune Festorum Beatae Mariae Virginis,* and hence was certainly most familiar to Hopkins: "Quinimmo beati qui audiunt verbum Dei et custodiunt. Pulchre Salvator attestationi mulieris annuit, non eam tantummodo quae Verbum Dei corporaliter generare meruerat, sed et omnes qui idem Verbum spiritaliter auditu fidei concipere, et boni operis custodia vel in suo vel in proximorum corde parere et quasi alere studuerint, asseverans esse beatos; quia, et eadem Dei Genitrix, et inde quidem beata, quia Verbi incarnandi ministra facta est temporalis; sed inde multo beatior, quia ejusdem semper amandi custos manebat aeterna."*

Bede uses imagery identical in many respects to that of Hopkins —imagery familiar in the Catholic tradition and in fact included in the name "Word," which is normally the "conception" of a spirit's knowing ("birth of a brain") effected through love ("corde parere"—"heart-throe"). That the Word enters into the soul of a Christian through the ear, "omnes qui idem Verbum spiritaliter auditu fidei concipere," gives an image which Hopkins employs with extraordinary subtlety and power in "The Blessed Virgin compared to the Air we Breathe," as we shall see in my third chapter. Bede's traditional comparison here of every Christian with Mary is, up to a point, the same as Hopkins' comparison of the nun with Mary in stanza 30 of *Deutschland*. Bede points out that Mary has a double relation to the Word: first, to the *Verbum incarnandum,* the Word-to-be-made-flesh, which relation is peculiar to Mary; second, to the *Verbum amandum,* the Word-to-be-loved, brought forth in the heart, which relation she has in common with every other Christian. And this last is so glorious—a fact which "The Windhover" states too, as chapter 4 will set forth—that it outshines the first. Mary as "keeping" the Word always ("custos Verbi amandi") is more blessed than Mary as handmaid of the Lord.

Hopkins' comparisons of the nun with Peter and with Mary not only express the nun's attainment of Christ and her complete union with Him, but prepare us for her work as Christ's instrument in our image, as both Peter and Mary are Christ's instruments in the Church. God works through Peter and through Mary to guide His sheep and to bring His grain home to His barns, and here the nun shares their work. She does it by speaking what is in her, by bringing forth, uttering outright, the Word to whose Heart she too has fled with a fling of the heart, like Hopkins in stanza 3. She casts forth, as in stanza 34, the flame which is "Jesu, heart's light," and, as in stanza 35, "our heart's charity's hearth's fire."

* Indeed blessed are those who hear the word of God and keep it. Beautifully the Saviour acknowledged the confession of the woman, asserting to be blessed not only her who merited to bring forth bodily the Word of God, but also all those who spiritually, by the hearing of faith, conceive that same Word and strive through the keeping of good works to bring Him forth and (as it were) nourish Him both in their own hearts and in the hearts of their neighbors. This follows because this same Mother of God is indeed blessed in that she was made to be the temporal handmaid to the Word-to-be-made-flesh; but she is much more blessed because she remains the eternal keeper of the Word-to-be-loved forever.

There is a vast difference, obviously, between both the scope of the nun's activity and the quality of her apostolic work, and the scope and quality of the work of Peter and Mary. The nun is not appointed to preach the Word to the whole world, nor is she chosen from among women to bring the Word-made-flesh into His universe. She is very much like the bell of No. 57; she simply "selves":

> ... each hung bell's
> Bow swung finds tongue to fling out broad its name;
> Each mortal thing does one thing and the same:
> Deals out that being indoors each one dwells;
> Selves—goes itself; *myself* it speaks and spells;
> Crying *Whát I dó is me: for that I came.*

And, since she is one with Christ, like the "just man" of the sestet of No. 57, the name she flings out like the flame that bursts from her heart is not only her own but that of her "new self and nobler me," Christ. The Word Who is born of her "heart-throe" in divine charity finds tongue in her cry and rings out to the ears of His sheep. Her breast which holds heart and lungs is swung physically by the Finger of God swaying the waves, is swung spiritually by the Finger of God calling forth her complete and unselfish confession of the Word. The Word breaks from her heart, aimed at divine ears by her, aimed at His flock's ears by Him. The one Word breaks from her, as many words, the words of this poem which sound in our ears, break from the heart of the poet in stanza 18.

The rhythm tells us that the nun is a hung bell, a big bell, which is pushed into motion by the sway of the Finger of God, gathering speed and force until it clangs out its message in the final line of the stanza. That rhythm would indicate that we are not dealing with a sheep bell, one of "the narrow bells" of which Hopkins wrote in his early fragment, No. 87, even if the meaning did not make that clear. How different the rhythm of

> His sheep seem'd to come from it as they stept,
> One and then one, along their walks, and kept
> Their changing feet in flicker all the time
> And to their feet the narrow bells gave rhyme

from that of our image. Furthermore, the finger of the shepherd does not ring a sheep bell, and those bells rather give a warning to the shepherd than to the sheep. The breast of the maiden is another type of bell, obedient to the purpose of the One Who is ringing it, although she does not know, probably, what that purpose is. She merely intends to express her faith and love, but He intends also to warn and to call His sheep.

Since she is on a ship and swaying with the waves, it would appear possible that she is a ship's bell or a buoy-bell. But again, the function of such a bell is difficult to reconcile with what the bell of our image does—obedient to the Finger of God it rings out the power and presence of that Finger, and it startles sheep back. This startling of sheep back is immediately aligned with harvesting the grain and bringing it home, so that it seems clear that the sheep are brought back to safety, or at least called and frightened back, by the sound of the bell. A ship's bell gives signals and might indicate the presence of the captain to frightened passengers, but why should it startle them? And when they got back, perhaps to the center of the ship, how would they be better off? And a buoy-bell simply warns or gives a point of measurement. If ships were conceived of as sheep, they might be said to be startled back from a danger spot by such a bell, but the image would be a peculiar one here, and there is a much more satisfactory solution.

The solution of Mr. Gardner—and he is the only critic who has dealt with this complex, difficult, and centrally important image—is by no means satisfactory. Listing certain "metaphysical" images of Hopkins, Mr. Gardner states that in our image Hopkins compares "a nun faced with death to an electric bell" (*Gardner 1*, p. 189). It appeared to me from that description, his only remark on the particular point, that Mr. Gardner was picturing one of the two breasts of the nun, that he pictured a finger lightly touching the nipple of one breast as if it were the push button of an electric bell, and that the resultant shrill sound was what startled the other passengers. I could see reasons for his arriving at such an *outré* reading: the electrical contact between God and creature is a favorite image with Hopkins, as we shall have further occasion to see; "electrical horror" is mentioned in stanza 27; the lightness of the touch is contrasted to the power of the result. But to term the image thus read a "metaphysical" one hardly does away with the overwhelming difficulties of a peculiarly unpleasant intimacy attributed to God, of a lack of connection between the "bell" and the sound it makes, of the absence of any conceivable reason for God's finger touching the nun's breast, etc. Mr. Gardner's reading suffers, in my opinion, from a trouble so basic that it is the source of the majority of critical errors and squabbles—word trouble. He takes the word "breast" to mean "mammary gland" rather than "chest cavity," and from this determination on his part derives his reading, which destroys the image and to some extent warps the development of the poem. He might have been alerted by the fact that the Word the nun rings out breaks from her heart, or even by Herbert's lines which he earlier (*1*, p. 171) quotes:

> Poets have wrong'd poore storms: such dayes are best,
> They purge the aire without; within, the breast.

The metaphor perhaps defeats Mr. Gardner because he does not grasp with sufficient vividness the spiritual situation in which the metaphorical fusion takes place, bringing all these disparate elements into an organic unity. The physical situation he does grasp, but I judge that he does not fully grasp the Catholic view which Hopkins' metaphor expresses and in the light of which alone it is intelligible and powerful—that the Word Who lives by faith in the heart of the nun is also the Lamb of Calvary and of Catholic altars, and at the same time the Shepherd Who calls His flock to the living waters through a share in His Sacrifice. Thus God's all-powerful touch—which almost unmade the poet in stanza 1, which sways the sea (and *thus* pushes this bell)—is light but effective on the delicate but powerful heart of the nun; her reaction is not only her own but also that of the Word with Whom she is joined; and her expression of her complete self-sacrifice in joining His great Sacrifice is a warning and a call to the others who have not joined.

The two liturgical hymns from the Common of Virgins in the Breviary exercise an influence on the imagery of the whole poem, and in particular on the passage we are especially considering. The first of these, a hymn ascribed to St. Ambrose, reads as follows:

> Jesu, corona Virginum,
> Quem Mater illa concipit
> Quae sola Virgo parturit,
> Haec vota clemens accipe:
>
> Qui pergis inter lilia,
> Septus choreis Virginum,
> Sponsus decorus gloria
> Sponsisque reddens praemia.

> Quocumque tendis, Virgines
> Sequuntur, atque laudibus
> Post te canentes cursitant,
> Hymnosque dulces personant;
>
> Te deprecamur supplices,
> Nostris ut addas sensibus
> Nescire prorsus omnia
> Corruptionis vulnera.*

The comparison in the first stanza between Mary and other virgins in relation to Jesus, the lilies and the spouse from the Canticle of Canticles in the second stanza, the virgins who follow the Lamb wherever he goes from Apocalypse, 14:4, in the third stanza, and the comparison between the virgins and the rest of us sinners implied in the last stanza—all of these have obvious similarities to the images of the *Deutschland*, and particularly to stanzas 21 and 22, and to 30 and 31.

The second hymn, an eighth-century anonymous composition, has even more pointed reference to our passage. I give the form proper to virgin-martyrs:

> Virginis Proles Opifexque Matris,
> Virgo quem gessit, peperitque Virgo;
> Virginis partos canimus decora
>   Morte triumphos.
>
> Haec enim palmae duplicis beata
> Sorte, dum gestit fragilem domare
> Corporis sexum, domuit cruentum
>   Caede tyrannum.
>
> Unde nec mortem, nec amica mortis
> Mille poenarum genera expavescens,
> Sanguine effuso meruit serenum
>   Scandere caelum.

---

* Jesus, Crown of virgins, Whom that mother conceived who alone brought forth as a virgin, graciously accept these prayers: You who go forth among the lilies, surrounded by choirs of virgins, a Bridegroom adorned with glory, dispensing rewards to brides. Wherever You go, virgins follow, and with praise singing after You they make their way and sing out sweet hymns. We humbly pray that You grant that our souls have nothing whatever to do with wounds of corruption.

> Hujus oratu, Deus alme, nobis
> Debitas poenas scelerum remitte;
> Ut tibi puro resonemus almum
> Pectore carmen.*

The Virgin of the first two lines of stanza 1 is Mary, Mother of Jesus; the virgin of line 3 is the saint whose feast is being celebrated. The "womb-life grey" of the Creator and His birth—"manger, maiden's knee" of stanza 7 of *Deutschland* and "maid's son" of stanza 30—are compared in the hymn, as in stanza 30 of *Deutschland*, with the bringing forth of Him by the glorious death of this other virgin. No doubt the "partos triumphos" of the hymn may be read "the triumphs obtained" (as Dom Matthew Britt, O.S.B., does read it in his invaluable *The Hymns of the Breviary and Missal* [New York: Benziger, 1952], p. 377), but the birth image is the basic meaning of "partos" and the comparison of the two "bringing forths," Mary's and this virgin's, could be missed only in an inadequate translation. "The triumphs brought forth" or "new born" would be better here than "obtained."

The two palms of stanza 2 of the hymn recall the "poising palms" of Hopkins' stanza 21, though the words refer to different (but related) objects. The two palms of the hymn are the reward of chastity, whereby the virgin triumphed over her own frail body, and the reward of martyrdom, whereby she triumphed over the bloody tyrant. The palms are bestowed by Christ "beata sorte," which suggests His attitude and action in the *Deutschland*. There too He weighs, chooses for this high sacrifice by eternal predestination, triumphs in the nun, and bestows the reward.

The "amica mortis" of stanza 3 of the hymn, the things associated with this cruel death, recall the list of Death's embodiments in stanza 11 of the *Deutschland*. The fearlessness of the virgin recalls the nun as she is in stanza 17, "a lioness." And the implied contrast in the hymn between the wild cruelty of earth and the "caelum serenum" suggests the contrast seen in stanzas 19 and 23 of the poem.

* Offspring of a virgin and the Maker of your mother, Whom a virgin bore in her womb and a virgin brought forth, we sing the virgin's triumphs brought forth by a glorious death. For this virgin was blessed by lot of a twofold palm; while she strove to master the frail sex of her body, she overcame the tyrant red with slaughter. Hence, dreading neither death nor the things of death, the thousand kinds of torture, she, having poured forth her blood, merited to ascend to a serene heaven. At her prayer, gracious God, wipe out the punishment due us for our sins, that we may ring out to You from a pure breast a loving song.

Most suggestive for our image is this last stanza of the hymn, with its prayer that through the virgin's intercession God may forgive the just punishment due to our sins, so that we ("like her" is implied) may with a pure breast ring out a loving song. In our image, the nun with pure and courageous breast does ring out a loving song, she swings with and is musical of the Finger of God which is giving her motion both physically and spiritually, she obeys, is a bell, and in her selfless song of love reflects the infinite love of the Sacrificed.

From the bell-shaped chest cavity, the *pectus resonans,* then, Christians are exhorted to ring out the power and glory of the King as shown in his martyrs. This is precisely what the nun does here. And since she is rung by the Pastor and since He intends her peal as call to the Sacrifice, it is most appropriate that she be a church bell and specifically a sacring bell, which not only calls to Mass but especially in England was rung at the Consecration of the Mass (the renewal of the Great Sacrifice) and again at the Communion (the union between the Paschal Lamb and His co-victim). The sacring bell does not startle the faithful flock, but it will startle the sinning of the heedless flock, the "poor sheep." In *King Henry VIII,* Surrey speaks of this effect when he says to Wolsey, "I'll startle you Worse than the sacring bell, when the brown wench Lay kissing in your arms, lord cardinal" (III, ii, 294-96). The picture of Wolsey sinning and startled in his sin by the call and the implied warning and threat of the sacring bell is parallel in many ways to Hopkins' picture of the poor harried sheep on the Deutschland startled by the call and warning of the bell *they* hear. The Martyr-Master who draws forth this sound from His chosen co-victim is also the Shepherd of those sheep, as well as the Hunter, the Orion, of man's wolfish malice. The same bell which expresses the faith, love, and complete self-sacrifice of the nun is also a call to the sheep who hear it, and for that matter could be a warning, too, to any wild beasts who might be "dogged in den" thereabouts. Our image implies the presence of beasts in implying the danger which threatens the "poor sheep."

The other passengers are sheep because they too are destined for a share in the Sacrifice along with the Lamb of God, the *Agnus Dei,* if they will assent, and because they are harried and abject and cut off from their Shepherd. The importance of Luther's presence in stanza 20 is emphasized here if one realizes that in Hopkins' view Luther is responsible both for the casting out of the nuns from the land which could produce so beautiful a flower as Gertrude the Virgin (the lover of the Heart of Christ and child, like Luther, of the Catholic Church, the New Eve) and for the cutting off of these sheep from their true Pastor, the successor of Simon Peter. Whether one agrees that such is Luther's role in the real world is of vital importance in determining one's attitude toward reality, but it is beside the point in determining one's understanding of this poem. The role Hopkins assigns to Luther is certainly the one he plays in this poem, and to grasp the poem one must perceive him as the waster of the garden and the harrier of the flock.

An eminent critic of Hopkins' work once told me that he considers the shift of image from sheep to harvest as "sudden and violent." To Hopkins it was not so, because it is based on the imagery which Christ used in expressing precisely the subject of our image. This is, as is evident, the extrinsic basis of our image and the one which follows it. The *intrinsic* connection between the images exists, I believe, in the motion expressed by the rhythm. The same motion that rings the bell also harvests or threshes the grain, and the blasts which wreck the ship are also instruments for achieving the spiritual threshing and for blowing Peter's ship with its cargo of grain home to God's barns. But the extrinsic connection rises from the mind of Christ as reflected in Matthew's Gospel. The words of our stanza, "pity of the rest of them," are the signal for the full heart of Hopkins to relieve its pressure not in sweet words expressive of the nun's achievement but in a bitterer direction—and then his thought shifts as he remembers the images of Christ, Who felt deep and profound pity for men and women in a similar comfortless, unconfessed situation: "One day the sight of the masses touched his heart, for they were bruised and battered down—just like sheep that have no shepherd. It was on this occasion that he said to his disciples: 'The harvest is plentiful; but the laborers are few. Therefore, pray the Owner of the harvest to send out laborers to do his harvesting'" (Matthew, 9:36-38). He is their Shepherd, and He is watching. He sent His disciples out to His sheep, as Luke stresses in presenting the same images: "After these incidents, the Lord appointed another group, seventy-two in all, and sent them out two by two to go ahead of him to every town and place which he intended to visit personally. He said to them: 'The harvest is plentiful, but the laborers are few. Pray the Owner of the harvest, therefore, to send out laborers to do his harvesting. Go now; but mind: I am sending you out like lambs among a pack of wolves'" (Luke, 10:1-3). His lambs on the Deutschland are harried by the cruel elements, by the heresies of Luther and others, by the effects of Adam's sin deep in their natures, by all the attacks of the world, the flesh, and the devil, but they are not alone and without their Pastor, because His voice rings out to them in the voice of the nun, as His voice sounded in the world in the voices of His apostles. They are comforted in her voice by Him, startled back from their self-bent to the one Word, the true Lamb, and carried home (perhaps) on the sacrificial altar of the shipwreck.

The following two stanzas carry on this thought of God's mastery over the souls of men, though so delicately does He invade and move the recesses of the spirit that He no more disturbs or destroys the free choice of the human will than air, as Hopkins states in a later, magnificently precise image to express the same idea, disturbs or destroys the long fur or "flix" on a snowflake:

> Wild air . . . goes home betwixt
> The fleeciest frailest-flixed
> Snowflake. . . .
> ("The Blessed Virgin compared to the Air we Breathe,"
> *Poems*, No. 60)

This is the tender and feathery delicacy of God's touch on the human will, the human heart. And the following stanzas, which like the closing stanzas of the first part of the poem celebrate the Pauline mastery of God, the victory of Christ over death and above all over sin, "man's malice," echo also the passages of Paul which comprise so large a part of the liturgy celebrating the Sacred Heart of Jesus. The love of Christ which reaches out to the apparently most abandoned of His sheep, to "the-last-breath penitent spirits," and snatches them back to the flock, this love which glides lower than His own death and the dark in His passion (this has nothing whatever to do with Purgatory, as Gardner thinks—Hopkins is speaking of Christ's *rescue* operations) in order to purchase mercy for the lingerers as well as for the listeners, this love of the "heart-fleshed" Miracle begotten when the flame of the Holy Ghost overshadowed Mary—this is the love which rings out in our image and which echoes Paul's words to the Ephesians, chosen by the Church for the Mass of the Sacred Heart:

With this in mind, then, I fall on my knees to the Father of our Lord Jesus Christ, that Father from whom all fatherhood in heaven and on earth takes its title. May he, out of the rich treasury of his glory, strengthen you through his spirit with a power that reaches your innermost being. May

Christ find a dwelling-place, through faith, in your hearts; may your lives be rooted in love, founded on love. May you and all the saints be enabled to measure, in all its breadth and length and height and depth, the love of Christ, to know what passes knowledge. May you be filled with all the completion God has to give. He whose power is at work in us is powerful enough, and more than powerful enough, to carry out his purpose beyond all our hopes and dreams; may he be glorified in the Church, and in Christ Jesus, to the last generation of eternity.

(Ephesians, 3:14-21)

The poet's sense of and response to the rhythms of the sea and the ship, of the alarm and huddling back of the sheep, and, above all of the motion and sound of the bell, are the factors which, to my ear, determine the structure of rhythms and sounds in our image. The rhythm created by the repeated "of," the pause and swoop of sound, the irregular swings of phrase, build up to the strong regular rocking of the last line. The general rhythm in our image, as throughout the poem, is the sway of the ship in the sea, and here the growing motion of the sea in a rising wind. The same rhythm suggests the irregular starting and the final definite rocking of a big bell. That Hopkins has such a motion in view is indicated not only by this rhythm and the text, but also by the original text of the B MS. There is no manuscript of the poem extant in Hopkins' writing (the only one was destroyed in the last war), but in the B MS in Bridges' hand the original lines read:

> ... the breast of the
> Maiden could swing with, be musical of it and
> Startle the poor sheep back!

Hopkins himself crossed out those words and wrote above them the present text.

Our image also suggests, it seems to me, in its rhythms and its vowel and consonantal patterns (especially the run-over rhymes of "the breast of the M" with "rest of them" and "fessed of them," and "ring of it, and S" with "Providence") the fright and huddling of the sheep.

Before Mr. Gardner's work appeared, I was accustomed to reading the last line of stanza 31 with the stress on the word "back." It seemed to me that the meaning demanded such stress, since the main thought appeared to be that the sheep were stopped by the bell, not that these people were sheep. To stress "sheep" appears to carry the idea that the creatures startled back were sheep rather than something else, and I adverted to no such contrast. Thus I was surprised and puzzled by the marking which Mr. Gardner gives the line on page 8 of the third edition of *Poems*:

> ′ x x x   ′ x   x x   ′ x   x x ′ x
> Startle the poor sheep back! is the shipwreck then a harvest,
> x ′   x x x   ′   x   x
> does tempest carry the grain for thee?

In the A MS, which is a copy made by Bridges from Hopkins' autograph, the stress marks are as Mr. Gardner has indicated them. This is no absolute proof that Hopkins so intended the stresses, since Bridges sometimes interpreted "the intention of the rhythm" (Bridges' Preface, *Poems*, p. 203) himself, and any reader of Hopkins' letters to Bridges will be likely to hold Bridges' interpretations in the matter suspect. However, since the marks *may* be transcribed from Hopkins' own MS, and since Bridges' opinion in any case is worthy of consideration, the markings swayed my first conviction.

Further consideration of Mr. Gardner's really excellent exposition of the Welsh influences in Hopkins' verse, and particularly of Hopkins' use of *cynghanedd*,[4] convinced me that most probably "sheep back" was to balance in stress as in sound with "shipwreck" and that my favored reading did not correspond with the music of Hopkins' line. As my ear became accustomed to this rhythm, I came to perceive the meaning which aligns our image most profoundly with the main theme of the poem and which I had missed before. A vigorous and vital rhythm can do this, it seems to me, justly, since while it is true that the meaning determines the rhythm, the determined rhythm can reveal the meaning.

The strength and swing of the beat, owing in part to the *cynghanedd*, and the gradual *diminuendo* in vowels from the high point in "sheep," cut off there by the "p," with a lessening in "ship" and a lengthening in "har-" and "temp-" and "grain," drawn out as these are by their consonants, recalled to my mind the very similar build-up of the bell of No. 57 that we have previously considered,

> . . . each hung bell's
> Bow swung finds tongue to fling out broad its name,

where the iron beat of "hung, swung, tongue" changes in "fling" and spreads out over the countryside in "broad" and the nasal-lengthened "name." The bell of our image is a more excitable bell perhaps, its rhythm is not so big and so peaceful, but it is doing the same work.

Its sound is caught up in the blasts of wind and cannot spread as does the sound of the bell in Sonnet 57, but it too manages to swing and be musical in its own way.[5]

The perception of meaning which came to me through the great, expressive beat on the word "sheep" was that here, as elsewhere in the poem, Hopkins is comparing the courage and single-eyed vision of the nun to the fearfulness and lack of vision of others. The poem opens with a description of his own fear and lack of vision; we are told that even the faithful waver, the faithless fable and miss; the pitiful plight of the victims of the storm and wreck is dramatically contrasted with the nun as lioness, prophetess, bell. So here, I perceived, Hopkins in stressing sheep is once again pointing out that these others, the evidence seems to indicate, are *not* lions and prophets and bells. They could be, if they had faith and love as the nun does, but they are not. They do not ring out a joyous word of welcome and acceptance; they need to be rung *to*. They do not *meet* Christ and understand; they are in the position of Hopkins in stanza 3, "where, where was a, where was a place?" They are not bells, as the nun is a bell, but they are sheep, poor sheep needing to hear the voice of their Good Shepherd, lambs needing to be called to the Sacrifice which opens upon the waters of life. This emphasis on their situation as harried and bruised and as called to the altar justifies the stress on "sheep" and reveals, too, the relation of the other passengers to the general theme of a sharing of Christ's victory over death and sin through a sharing of His Sacrifice. And in the last comforting image of our stanza the other passengers merge with the nun in being His grain.

The image we have been especially considering, then, expresses a theme vitally important in this poem as in others of Hopkins' mature poems—the Pauline revelation we saw above, that Providence arranges for His children "all the completion God has to give." At the end of "In the Valley of the Elway," No. 40, we hear Hopkins praying to the "Father and fondler of heart thou hast wrung" to sway His poising palms considerately for the Welsh wanderers:

> God, lover of souls, swaying considerate scales,
> Complete thy creature dear O where it fails,
>   Being mighty a master, being a father and fond.

The foot of the Good Shepherd, Who keeps His sheep always in view, echoes in the last line of "The Lantern out of Doors," No. 34:

Christ minds; Christ's interest, what to avow or amend
There, éyes them, heart wánts, care háunts, foot fóllows kínd,
Their ránsom, théir rescue, ánd first, fást, last friénd.

Those doomed to drowning on the Deutschland are most of all sheep for their *thoughts*, which are startled back from a concern with the outer wind and water to an attention to the inner Christ. This is the bias of a similar image in No. 65, one of the great desolation sonnets:

My cries heave, herds-long; huddle in a main, a chief
Woe, world-sorrow. . . .

These poor sheep, his anguished cries, find no Comforter or comforting, no relief brought by Mary Immaculate, in the wildly wringing tempests in his soul. But the sheep on the Deutschland do find a Comforter Whose loud bell startles them back from plunging over the "cliffs of fall" of despair.

That the sheep are safely folded and the grain safely stored is stated, about the grain, in "The Starlight Night," No. 32, where Hopkins sees the glorious stars as the outer wall of Christ's barn:

These are indeed the barn; withindoors house
The shocks. This piece-bright paling shuts the spouse
  Christ home, Christ and his mother and all his hallows.

The sheep folded in God's mercy appear in the last lines of "The Blessed Virgin compared to the Air we Breathe," No. 60, where Mary, like the nun in our image, is the instrument of bringing the sheep of Christ home to their fold:

World-mothering air, air wild,
Wound with thee, in thee isled,
Fold home, fast fold thy child.

The deepest meaning of our image lies in its expression of the deepest meaning of the poem, which in turn attempts to express something of the profoundest mystery and central truth of the Catholic faith —God's sharing of the inner life of the Trinity with His creature, through the Incarnation and Sacrifice of Christ. This sharing in God's life, which Catholics signify by "divine grace," is achieved through sharing in Christ's Sacrifice, and it is to this divine life that the bell of our image calls the sheep. Hopkins clarifies his notion and throws light upon the depths of our image in this quotation from his spiritual writings:

Why did the Son of God go thus forth from the Father not only in the eternal and intrinsic procession of the Trinity but also by an extrinsic and less than eternal, let us say aeonian one?—To give God glory and that by Sacrifice, Sacrifice offered in the barren wilderness outside of God, as the children of Israel were led into the wilderness to offer sacrifice. . . . The sacrifice would be the Eucharist, and that the victim might be truly victim like, like motionless, helpless, or lifeless, it must be in matter. Then the Blessed Virgin was intended or predestined to minister that matter. And here then was that mystery of the woman clothed with the sun which appeared in heaven. She followed Christ the nearest, following the sacrificial lamb 'whithersoever he went.'

In going forth to do sacrifice Christ went not alone but created angels to be his company, lambs to follow him the Lamb, the flower of the flock, 'whithersoever he went,' that is to say, first to the hill of sacrifice, then after that back to God, to beatitude. They were to take part in the sacrifice and he was to redeem them all, that is to say / for the sake of the Lamb of God who was God himself God would accept the whole flock. . . . Christ then like a good shepherd led the way. . . .

(Sermons, p. 197)

The procession of the Word in eternity and in time, a truth basic and vitally influential in Hopkins' mature imagery, is developed by Hopkins' German contemporary, the powerful and original theologian Matthias Scheeben, in terms which, like Hopkins' words quoted above, stress the flow of divine life from the center of the Trinity into us through Christ (and Mary, as Hopkins notes and Scheeben most thoroughly develops in his Mariology):

In what does the supernatural organism of the mysteries of Christianity consist? In this, that the mystery of the Godhead, the inner communication of the divine nature, prolongs and reproduces itself exteriorly. It is projected into the outside world so far as the Son of God assumes a created, human nature, and imparts to it, in His person and as belonging to Him, the substantial union and unity that He Himself has with His Father. Not only this one human nature, however, but the whole human race, is to enter into closest union with God. To bring this union about, the Son of God, made man, unites Himself to us in His humanity in the most intimate, substantial fashion, to form one body with us, as He Himself is one Spirit with His Father. And as He Himself has the same nature and life as the Father, by virtue of His spiritual oneness of essence with the Father, so by His ineffable union of body with us He wishes to make us share in His divine nature, and to pour out upon us the grace and life that He has received in their entire fullness from the Father and has communicated to His humanity. Thus by a prolongation of His eternal procession from the Father, the Son of God goes forth from the Father and enters into the human race as a real member thereof. As a result, we enter into a most perfect union of continuity with the Father, the ultimate source of divine life. Consequently there is formed in us a perfect replica of the unity of God's Son with the Father. Thus our participation in the divine nature and divine life becomes a reproduction of the fellowship in nature and life which the Son of God has with His Father, as their supreme, substantial oneness requires.

(The Mysteries of Christianity, trans. Cyril Vollert, S.J. [St. Louis: Herder, 1946], p. 481)

Hopkins' association of Christ the Host (the Eucharist), the Sacrificial Lamb Who is Shepherd leading His flock back into the bosom of the Father to an eternal sharing in the life of the Trinity, with His creatures who are all to take part in the sacrifice, reveals the prime aspect under which the passengers on the Deutschland are sheep. They are called by God to join in the great Sacrifice in union with the Lamb and eucharistic Victim. Hopkins states the idea even more clearly in explaining to Bridges the significance of the Corpus Christi procession:

But the procession has more meaning and mystery than this: it represents the process of the Incarnation and the world's redemption. As Christ went forth from the bosom of the Father as the Lamb of God and eucharistic victim to die upon the altar of the cross for the world's ransom; then rising returned leading the procession of the flock redeemed / so in this ceremony his body *in statu victimali* is carried to the Altar of Repose as it is called and back to the tabernacle at the high altar, which will represent the bosom of the godhead. The procession out may represent the cooperation of the angels, or of the patriarchs and prophets, the return the Church Catholic from Christ's death to the end of time.

(June 16, 1882, Letters I, p. 149)

"The procession out" is the "though felt before" of stanza 7 of *Deutschland*; "the return," the "though in high flood yet" and indeed the whole situation of Hopkins, the nun, the other passengers, and all Christians and men. Those who cooperate with the Victim and get *back* into the procession are comforted and saved; those who refuse, wander and are lost.

This giving of divine life is expressed in the stanzas which follow our image in the majestic picture of God throned behind death, a Pauline picture, and in the Johannine picture of the life-giving shower which closes stanza 34. Here is expressed the true nature of the Word that the nun rings out: the kind King, royally reclaiming his own flock. The storm and wreck in its *spiritual* essence is not the fierce lightning of fire hard-hurled which John, the Son-of-Thunder, wanted Christ to call down on the unfriendly Samaritans, when Christ told him, "The Son of Man has come to save men's lives, not to destroy them" (Luke, 9:54-56). It is a shower of the water of eternal life, water which poured from the Sacred Heart on the altar of the cross, from the Hero of Calvary Whose image hangs over every Catholic altar and to Whom all men must come sooner or later (cf. stanza 8). It is life-giving water, as in the concluding stanza of the poem life-giving light and warmth are asked for from our Day-star Christ, the fire of divine life for our human hearts. The bell of our image calls the sheep to the bosom of the Father, to that sharing of God's own life which is infinitely greater than the gift of human life, "of breath and bread," and to which we are called by "God's finger touching the very vein of personality, which nothing else can reach. . . ." (*Sermons*, p. 158).

A grasp of this complex but perfectly balanced and deeply expressive metaphor brings us into the core of Hopkins' masterpiece. From the solid basis of this image, the whole tremendously complex poem, with its structure of thought and imagery and sound and rhythms, can be brought into focus. Without a grasp of it or with a wrong grasp, our understanding of Hopkins' development of his vision, his insight into the nun's function as the instrument of the Good Shepherd Who guards every one of His sheep and brings them, by a sharing of His Sacrifice, to the water of life, is at least dark, and probably warped. The detailed study of one important image in the closely meshed, perfectly integrated work of a profound and subtle mind can throw much light. And this image touches the theme most influential in the mind and the work of Hopkins—the divine life which pours out from the inner activity of the Trinity upon His creation. In the image to which we turn in the following chapter, the literal sharing of the divine life to which Christ's sheep are called is shadowed forth both in the difficulties and in the triumph of others of God's living and glorious creatures.

CHAPTER 2

God's Grandeur

The world is charged with the grandeur of God.
　It will flame out, like shining from shook foil;
　It gathers to a greatness, like the ooze of oil
Crushed. Why do men then now not reck his rod?
Generations have trod, have trod, have trod;
　And all is seared with trade; bleared, smeared with toil;
　And wears man's smudge and shares man's smell: the soil
Is bare now, nor can foot feel, being shod.

And for all this, nature is never spent;
　There lives the dearest freshness deep down things;
And though the last lights off the black West went
　Oh, morning, at the brown brink eastward, springs—
Because the Holy Ghost over the bent
　World broods with warm breast and with ah! bright wings.
　　　　　　　"God's Grandeur," *Poems*, No. 31

　The spirit of the Lord fills the whole world....
　　　　　　　　　　　　　Wisdom, 1:7

Like a jewel the vault of heaven is set above us; the sight of it is glory made visible. Plain to our view is the sun's passage as it shines out, a very masterpiece of his workmanship, who is the most High. How it burns up the earth at noon-day! How fierce its glow, beyond all endurance! Tend thou the furnace, heat is thy daily portion; yet three times hotter the sun, as it burns up the hill-side, scorching all with its fiery breath, blinding men's eyes with its glare. Swiftly it speeds on its course, to do the bidding of the Lord, its glorious maker.
　　　　　　　　　　　Ecclesiasticus, 43:1-5

　Then thou sendest forth thy spirit, and there is fresh creation.
　　　　　　　　　　　　　Psalms, 103:30

> It will flame out, like shining from shook foil. . . .
> "God's Grandeur," *Poems*, No. 31

The "it" in our image refers to "grandeur." Grandeur expresses eminence, magnificence, and sublimity, and those in huge and colossal proportions. The grandeur in question is that of God, so that there is no limit whatever to it, either extensively or intensively. Hence the question at once arises: Why the trivial simile, the comparison of cosmic and infinite grandeur with the reflection of light from a sheet of gold foil shaken by the hand?

That the "foil" refers to gold foil is not immediately evident from a consideration of this line alone. The comparison could involve, as some have thought, a fencer's foil, flashing in the sun, if one considered this line apart from its predecessor. However, in the first line of the poem, with the electrical image carried in the verb "charged," there is a preparation for the introduction of moving gold foil as a revelation of God's grandeur.

At the time the sonnet was written, Faraday's celebrated "ice-pail" experiment was standard laboratory practice to determine both the presence and the force of the electric charge in a metal sphere. The ball suspended from a silk thread was lowered into the gold-leaf electroscope, and the gold foil would move in proportion to the intensity of the charge. Thus the presence of this mysterious power which filled the metal ball and was quite invisible, unattainable except by the revelation of the moving foil, became evident and even measureable. The further fact that a flash could be induced under proper conditions may have helped to lead to our image of a sheet of gold leaf flashing back the light of the sun. The electrical flash of lightning, important in the theophanies of Scripture, when the power and presence of God shone forth, is associated with this flashing from the foil, as the A MS's "lightning" in place of "shining" indicates and as Hopkins makes clear in explaining the image to Bridges:

I protest, and with indignation, at your saying I was driven to the same image. With more truth might it be said that my sonnet might have been written expressly for the image's sake. But the image is not the same as yours and I do not mean by foil set-off at all; I mean foil in its sense of leaf or tinsel, and no other word whatever will give the effect I want. Shaken goldfoil gives off broad glares like sheet lightning and also, and this is true of nothing else, owing to its zigzag dints and creasings and network of small many cornered facets, a sort of fork lightning too.

(January 4, 1883, *Letters I*, pp. 168-69)

The figure of lightning, as *Deutschland* amply illustrates, makes a good symbol of God's punishing and threatening rod of authority, and in any use it carries with it at least the potential of danger and destruction. For example, when Christ uses the image to express the unmistakable Second Coming—"As the lightning starts in the east and blazes its way to the west, so it will be with the advent of the Son of Man" (Matthew, 24:27)—the element of threat to some is clearly involved.

Hopkins does not want a figure that will imply threat of danger, since this poem deals with life-giving flame rather than with judging or purging flame. Yet he wants an image which will both tie up with the revelation of a mysterious, pervading force[1] and give a visible manifestation of the majesty and beauty of God. The flame of lightning would do both of these. Two sections from Hopkins' *Journals* will show his observation of lightning and other points of interest for our image:

July 8—After much rain, some thunder, and no summer as yet, the river swollen and golden and, where charged with air, like ropes and hills of melting candy, there was this day a thunderstorm on a greater scale—huge rocky clouds lit with livid light, hail and rain that flooded the garden, and thunder ringing and echoing round like brass, so that there is in a manner earwitness to the χαλκεον οὐρανόν. The lightning seemed to me white like a flash from a lookingglass but Mr. Lentaigne in the afternoon noticed it rose-coloured and lilac. I noticed two kinds of flash but I am not sure that sometimes there were not the two together from different points of the same cloud or starting from the same point different ways—one a straight stroke, broad like a stroke with chalk and liquid, as if the blade of an oar just stripped open a ribbon scar in smooth water and it caught the light; the other narrow and wire-like, like the splitting of a rock and danced down-along in a thousand jags. I noticed this too, that there was a perceptible interval between the blaze and first inset of the flash and its score in the sky and that that seemed to be first of all laid in a bright confusion and then uttered by a tongue of brightness (what is strange) running up from the ground to the cloud, not the other way.

(Journals, p. 212)

The appearance of the river, "charged with air," is suggestive of the image which follows ours in "God's Grandeur," but for our image, besides the description of the lightning itself, it seems to me significant that Hopkins pictures the flash to be "uttered by a tongue of brightness." The flame which shines from the world in our image is not unrelated, as we shall see, to other Pentecostal tongues of flames which once "uttered" the grandeur of God.

In another description of lightning, Hopkins notes a change which has points of resemblance to the change of flame in the poem:

Thunderstorm in the evening, first booming in gong-sounds, as at Aosta, as if high up and so not reechoed from the hills; the lightning very slender and nimble and as if playing very near but after supper it was so bright and terrible some people said they had never seen its like. People were killed, but in other parts of the country it was more violent than with us. Flashes lacing two clouds above or the cloud and the earth started upon the eyes in live veins of rincing or riddling liquid white, inched and jagged as if it were the shivering of a bright riband string which had once been kept bound round a blade and danced back into its pleatings. Several strong thrills of light followed the flash but a grey smother of darkness blotted the eyes if they had seen the fork, also dull furry thickened scapes of it were left in them.

(*Journals*, pp. 233-34)

The lightning at first is a playful and charming sight, but it changes in character to become bright, terrible, and killing. In the poem, similarly, the flame which is, and should be, lovely and revealing of grandeur becomes through abuse searing and killing.

Lightning can be lovely in Hopkins' imagery. We have seen in stanza 5 of *Deutschland* the "Glow, glory in thunder" which utters Christ. In "Spring" (No. 33), the

> . . . thrush
> Through the echoing timber does so rinse and wring
> The ear, it strikes like lightnings to hear him sing. . . .

But part of the force of those images comes from the pressure of the lightning's suppressed qualities of danger.

In our image, Hopkins wants a figure which will express the flaming quality of God's grandeur as revealed in the world and will not carry with it any suspicion of threat or danger. He wants it to do what "Pied Beauty" (No. 37) does, to express the glory and the beauty of the unchanging God in the flash of creatures who reflect His glory and beauty, without any reference to the malice of man which deflects and warps His light. Hence lightning will not serve, since by its suggestion of death and destruction it brings in at least an implication of malice and sin, of God's grandeur smeared and smudged. We are God's looking glass, Hopkins states in his retreat sermon, but if we sin "We are deep in dust or our silver gone or we are broken or, worst of all, we misshape his face and make God's image hideous" (*Sermons*, p. 240). Other creatures, which cannot sin, always reflect God's glory and beauty—"the thunder speaks of his terror" (*Sermons*, p. 239)—unless they are prevented from so doing by malicious man. They retain, in so far as man permits it, the "cheer and charm of earth's past prime" (No. 35) and to the limit of their finite capacity reflect the infinite beauty of their Creator.

The world as a good creature reflecting and revealing God's grandeur—this is the subject which must be imaged in our passage. And since the attention is centered on the finite creature, the image may and should be a small one. The Source of the grandeur which the world reflects and is saturated with is infinite and requires (and will receive) a huge image. But the world itself, in relation to the Source of grandeur, is small, insignificant, though dear, as we shall have occasion to observe in a later chapter. Hence our image should be brilliant, harmless, and may be small. The gold foil, gleaming and flashing in the sunlight, is a thoroughly expressive image of the finite world, gleaming and flashing in the glory of God's majesty.

Reflection of light in terms of gold foil appears twice in the *Journals*. Here a consideration of the different degrees in reflection of light from snow leads to further examples of reflection, stressing and making bright the shape of eyes or the face of the schoolboy:

Where the snow lies as in a field the damasking of white light and silvery shade may be watched indeed till brightness and glare is all lost in a perplexity of shadow and in the whitest of things the sense of white is lost, but at a shorter gaze I see two degrees in it—the darker, facing the sky, and the lighter in the tiny cliffs or scarps where the snow is broken or raised into ridges, these catching the sun perhaps or at all events more directly hitting the eye and gilded with an arch brightness, like the sweat in the moist hollow between the eyebrows and the eyelids on a hot day or in the way the light of a taper Tommy was screening with his hand the other morning in the dark refectory struck out the same shells of the eyes and the cleft of the nostrils and the flat of the chin and tufts on the cheeks in gay leaves of gold.

(Pp. 228-29)

In another passage, a square yellow field—recalling the "Landscape plotted and pieced—fold, fallow, and plough" of "Pied Beauty" (No. 37)—catches the light and "throws up" or gives contrast to a black and green elm tree: "July 23—... beautiful blushing yellow in the straw of the uncut ryefields. . . . One field I saw from the balcony of the house behind an elmtree, which it threw up, like a square of pale goldleaf, as it might be, catching the light" (p. 249). The gold foil of our image is more active than this field, but performs the same function of catching the light. Thus it offers an analogy to the lovely revelation of God in His creatures.

In "The Sea and the Skylark" (No. 35) Hopkins makes use of the moon as a timeless witness to the grandeur of God rung out in those two creatures throughout time, like Keats's Nightingale. Hopkins is referring there, I believe, to Psalm 88:36-38: "Pledged stands my inviolable word, I will never be false to David; his posterity shall continue for ever, his royalty, too, shall last on in my presence like the sun; like the moon's eternal orb, that bears witness in heaven unalterable." In "God's Grandeur," it is the sun, the familiar symbol of God in Scripture, which gives force to our image of the foil, to the image of oil which follows, and of course to the enormous image which closes the poem. Scripture offers a rich background for this imagery. For example, the opening of Psalm 18:

See how the skies proclaim God's glory, how the vault of heaven betrays his craftsmanship! Each day echoes its secret to the next, each night passes on to the next its revelation of knowledge; no word, no accent of theirs that does not make itself heard, till their utterance fills every land, till their message reaches the ends of the world. In these, he has made a pavilion for the sun, which comes out as a bridegroom comes from his bed, and exults like some great runner who sees the track before him. Here, at one end of heaven, is its starting-place, and its course reaches to the other; none can escape its burning heat. The Lord's perfect law, how it brings the soul back to life!

There is God revealed in His creatures, and especially in the sun, whose rays and warmth reach masterfully to all living beings. St. Paul, with a different emphasis, states that God can be known through His creatures, and that men should, even with such natural revelation alone, "reck His rod": "The knowledge of God is clear to their minds; God himself has made it clear to them; from the foundations of the world men have caught sight of his invisible nature, his eternal power and his divineness, as they are known through his creatures. Thus there is no excuse for them; although they had the knowledge of God, they did not honour him or give thanks to him as God . . ." (Romans, 1:10-21). The flame of our image is like another Scriptural revelatory flame: "And here the Lord revealed himself through a flame that rose up from the midst of a bush; it seemed that the bush was alight, yet did not burn. Here is a great sight, said Moses, I must go up and see more of it, a bush that does not waste by burning. But now, as he saw him coming up to look closer, the Lord called to him from the midst of the bush, Moses, Moses; and when he answered, I am here, at thy command, he was told, Do not come nearer; rather take the shoes from thy feet, thou art standing on holy ground" (Exodus, 3:2-5). In later lines of our poem we find the generations of men ignoring the flame that reveals God, trampling on the world and living things, bushes and all, that might reveal Him, profaning with shod feet what should be holy ground, not bare soil. The flame in the bush, like the flame in our image, is a revealing and not a destructive flame, shining in the "blackest night" of "being's dread and vacant maze," as we saw in "Nondum," to guide men to God, "Where seek thee with unsandalled feet" (No. 22).

Our image shares a sentence with the next image of the poem and is closely allied to it. This close alliance between the two images will, I trust, justify giving the second as much attention as I have given the first, with the hope that further light will thus be cast on the image with which this chapter specifically deals, and, consequently, on the whole sonnet. In this second, allied image Hopkins speaks of the "ooze" which "gathers to a greatness." The popular conception of electricity as a fluid may have had a background influence on this image too, for electricity was thought to gather upon one over-full body before flowing to another in which a deficiency of the "fluid" created a vacancy. At any rate, our image speaks of an *ooze* of oil which gathers, and oil oozes from the body in which, like God's grandeur, it is hidden, potentially beautiful, powerful, serviceable. The shining from the foil indicates a surface reflection; the oil which oozes from the olive is intrinsic to the olive, hidden within, saturating without revealing its presence, as the grandeur of God saturates the world. This seems to me the main point of the image—that something hidden, beautiful, and wonderfully powerful is revealed. Hence I conclude that the picture here is of oil oozing from an olive and of the particles of that ooze drawn together (by "electrical" force?) and gathering in a great drop, rather than of oil oozing from a press and gathering in a pool. Either picture seems to me possible, but the first appears to me far preferable.

If the picture were to be taken as identical with that of the crushed oil in Hopkins' early poem, "A Soliloquy of One of the Spies left in the Wilderness" (*Poems*, No. 5), in which cool feet indicate the comfort of Egypt (unlike the shod and trampling feet of our poem) and the wine and oil indicate in familiar Scriptural fashion the plenty of Egypt, then a press and a pool would be most likely:

> Give us the tale of bricks as heretofore;
> To knead with cool feet the clay juicy soil.
> Who tread the grapes are splay'd with stripes of gore,
>   And they who crush the oil
> Are spatter'd.

Or if one were to accept the whole picture presented by the *Journals* and *Sermons* in closely similar imagery for precisely the same idea, one would, I think, picture a pool of oil: "All things therefore are charged with love, are charged with God and if we know how to touch them give off sparks and take fire, yield drops and flow . . ." (*Sermons*, p. 195). There we have the world charged with God, the electrical spark from touch, the flame which results, and drops resulting in flow; thus the "greatness" of our poem would be a pool of oil, a gathering of drops, if more than one drop were pictured.

My reasons for thinking that the yield of which our image treats is one drop, the gathering of ooze from an olive which is at least partly visible rather than the gathering of ooze from the cracks of a press, are not conclusive, taken separately, but seem to me persuasive if taken together. In the first place, as I have said, it seems to me that the idea in this poem is that the beauty and power is hidden within the olive and can be brought out without a press at all, e.g., by the pressure of the fingers or the palms. Furthermore, the "finest oil" of the Scriptures, which was used for the Tabernacle lamps and for anointing, was crushed by gentle hand pressure or in a mortar, so that the oil would be clear with as little of the flesh of the olive as possible in it.

This oozing of oil can reasonably be related, too, to the bloody sweat of Christ in the garden of Gethsemane. The name of the garden means "oil-press," and Hopkins adverts to the connection in his early "Barnfloor and Winepress" (*Poems*, No. 18):

> Terrible fruit was on the tree
> In the acre of Gethsemane;
> For us by Calvary's distress
> The wine was rackèd from the press;
> Now in our altar-vessels stored
> Is the sweet Vintage of our Lord.

The oil of Gethsemane can readily flow into the wine of the Eucharist of Calvary, since oil and wine are closely associated in Scriptural imagery. At any rate, a connection between the oil and the drops of Christ's blood would make a concentration on one drop more significant. Patristic literature dwells on the truth that one drop of Christ's blood would have sufficed to save numberless worlds, yet He poured out all. It is such imagery that gives background to Hopkins' image in another portion of the notes quoted above (from *Sermons*, p. 194): "Suppose God showed us in a vision the whole world enclosed first in a drop of water, allowing everything to be seen in its native colours; then the same in a drop of Christ's blood, by which everything whatever was turned to scarlet, keeping nevertheless mounted in the scarlet its own colour too...." One drop of oil, too, might reflect the whole world, and it would give things a smooth and gleaming light that could well figure the glory of God. And one such drop can well be called "a greatness," both in relation to the particles of the ooze which compose it and in relation to the revelation it makes.

In any case, drop or pool, the oil is closely allied to the revealing flame and the golden light of the previous image, for it is such clear oil that God demanded to feed the flame which revealed His presence in the gold-gleaming Tabernacle: "And the Lord said to Moses, Bid the sons of Israel bring thee oil of the olive, pure and clear, to feed at all times the lamps before the veil, where the ark bears record of me in the tabernacle that attests my covenant. Aaron shall set them there to burn before the Lord from evening to morning; a rite you shall observe continually, age after age. They shall be set there always in the Lord's presence, on the lamp-stand that is of pure gold" (Leviticus, 24:2-4). This text and imagery was (or could have been) impressed on the poet's mind every time he entered the chapel or church, since the light which witnesses to the presence of God in the Catholic tabernacle, attesting the New Covenant, is fed by the oil of the olive (or beeswax, by concession I suppose) in obedience to this command from God. The *Codex Juris Canonici* is explicit: "Coram tabernaculo, in quo sanctissimum Sacramentum asservatur, una saltem lampas diu noctuque continenter luceat, nutrienda oleo olivarum vel cera apum . . ." (Canon 1271). This oil is crushed for the glory of God and uses its power of giving light in order to reveal His grandeur and bring men to adore Him, to "reck his rod."

In another way, too, the oil is similar to the gold leaf, reflecting, not as a flash but in a smooth, liquid way, the light of the sun. That oil is intimately related in Hopkins' mind with the light of sunrise and sunset can be abundantly illustrated from the *Journals* and from the *Poems*:

April 22—But such a lovely damasking in the sky as today I never felt before. The blue was charged with simple instress, the higher, zenith sky earnest and frowning, lower more light and sweet. High up again, breathing through woolly coats of cloud or on the quains and branches of the flying pieces it was the true exchange of crimson, nearer the earth/ against the sun / it was turquoise, and in the opposite southwestern bay below the sun it was like clear oil but just as full of color. . . .

(*Journals*, p. 207)

Westward under the sun the heights and groves in Richmond Park looked like dusty velvet being all flushed into a piece by the thick-hoary golden light which slanted towards me over them.

(P. 192)

[The cloud] was anointed with warm brassy glow. . . .

(P. 212)

At sunset [the sky] gathered downwards and as the light then bathed it from below the fine ribbings and long brindled jetties dripping with fiery bronze had the look of being smeared by some blade which had a little flattened and richly mulled what it was drawn across.

(P. 216)

. . . the sun below in a golden mess.

(P. 237)

In his early "Winter with the Gulf Stream" (*Poems*, No. 3), Hopkins describes the sunset:

> A gold-water Pactolus frets
>
> Its brindled wharves and yellow brim,
> The waxen colours weep and run. . . .

In "The Alchemist in the City" (No. 10), the poor scientist, frustrated in his search for the "not to be discover'd gold," dreams of finding a distant spot:

> There on a long and squarèd height
> After the sunset I would lie,
> And pierce the yellow waxen light
> With free long looking ere I die.

The healing "oil of gladness" flows in "Easter Communion" (No. 13), without reference to color. But in "Spelt from Sibyl's Leaves" (No.

62), Hopkins returns to the picture of the yellow light, as in a horn lantern, clinging to the west: "Her fond yellow hornlight wound to the west...." This resembles the early "A Voice from the World" (No. 77), "When lily-yellow is the west," and both recall two passages from the *Journals*: "In the sunset all was big and there was a world of swollen cloud holding the yellow-rose light like a lamp . . ." (p. 201), and "Bright sunset: all the sky hung with tall tossed clouds, in the west with strong printing glass edges, westward lamping with tipsy bufflight, the colour of yellow roses" (p. 236). All this concern with the waxen yellow light is, I think, in the background of the oil image. No doubt if one pushes the image to its limit and decides Hopkins refers to a drop clinging to the surface of the olive, the yellow color will go, since unrefined oil is normally not yellow. The gleam and gloss and the powers of lighting, healing, and anointing remain, but the color will change. This may have been what Hopkins had in mind. In a remarkable description of a peacock's train in the *Journals,* he describes the dark spot in the eye of the train as ". . . then within all a sluggish corner drop of black or purple oil" (p. 210). But in "God's Grandeur," at least as I picture it, the oil is golden like the foil. Without being able to prove it except by pointing to such comparisons as the yellow field with the gold leaf and such autumn scenes as "A Spanish chestnut and two elms in the grounds seem to fill the air up with an equable clear ochre . . ." (*Journals*, p. 189), I have nevertheless always supposed that Hopkins had in mind the yellows of autumn, creeping over the greens of summer and revealing a new glory. The yellow flash from the autumn leaves and the yellow ooze of color would parallel the flash from the golden foil and the ooze of yellow over the olive. But this is my own elaboration of the image, which makes me happy but may not please others. It may be ignored, I think, without loss to the poem, though it seems to me to enhance Hopkins' images.

The two images are small, one a tiny flashing, the other a tiny gathering, to express a pervading grandeur. The grandeur itself is not small, but the world that receives it is tiny in relation to the source of the grandeur. Now, however, as the poem progresses, the world grows. We now see it in relation not to God and to the sun, but in relation to rebellious and contumacious man. Instead of recognizing the authority of God's majesty and grandeur in nature, as St. Paul says he should, by honoring and caring for "the growing green" as the lovely and revelatory creation of God, man tramples it in his contempt for and ignorance of his and its Creator. The world is now a big place, literally a stamping ground for generations of shod feet. And the flame from creatures which should reveal God is from greed abused so that it sears the earth, and the oil which should bear witness to God is smeared on the earth, and the smudge of smoke and the smell of sweat (not the sweet ointments of the Spouse of the Canticle of Canticles, of Christ the Anointed One, of anointed men) wipe out the evidence of God's grandeur.

This description of the destruction of nature's beauty should not be taken as an indictment of the industrial practices in England and the world, at least not merely as that. The situation reaches far more deeply into the nature of man and prepares for the cosmic close of the poem, which has no direct reference to the growth of factories. The situation of man is a tragic one after the Fall. He was originally destined by God to care for the things of the world: "So the Lord God took the man and put him in his garden of delight, to cultivate and tend it" (Genesis, 2:15). After the Fall man was expelled from the garden, so that he has to tread the world and to sweat: ". . . now, through thy act, the ground is under a curse. All the days of thy life thou shalt win food from it with toil; thorns and thistles it shall yield thee, this ground from which thou dost win thy food. Still thou shalt earn thy bread with the sweat of thy brow . . ." (Genesis, 3:17-19). Man is to blame for the situation, and yet it would seem that, as things stand, he has no choice if he is to live. And of course, Hopkins is well aware of that. Man must now tread the earth, burn and smear creatures, and "rip out rockfire homeforth" like sturdy Dick of "Tom's Garland" (*Poems*, No. 66).

But Hopkins' emphasis is on the "all" of "all is seared with trade." And his complaint is that the soil is not cleared here and there, but it is bare. He is not here condemning man for the Fall, but for what he adds to the Fall from his own personal malice and rebellion against God—"Why do men then *now* not reck his rod?" And, Hopkins states, as man was once destined to serve God by caring for creatures, now he rebels against God by wanton destruction of creatures. We hear the complaint, for example, from those who demand reforestation. We find it poignantly expressed in Hopkins' "Binsey Poplars" (*Poems*, No. 43), where the hacking and racking of "the growing green" is compared to the piercing of the eyeball. We find the moral evil which lies at the heart of such "havoc-pocking" expressed in "On the Portrait of Two Beautiful Young People," (*Poems*, No. 119), where Hopkins cries:

> Enough: corruption was the world's first woe.
> What need I strain my heart beyond my ken?
> O but I bear my burning witness though
> Against the wild and wanton work of men.

In our poem, too, he bears witness against the corruption which stems from man's rebellion. And the very blame which he heaps on man is witness to his vivid realization that man does not need to be destroying nature as he does, that the Fall has been undone by the Second Adam, that, if man would, he could return, in sharing the love of Christ, to the garden of delight, where the sweet ointments of the Bridegroom would be poured out upon him. However, the redemption is not the theme here. The fact of man's rejection of the redemption, as it is evidenced in the wanton destruction of nature, is the present theme. Hopkins is not here expressing an unshod Franciscan love of nature; he is bitterly complaining against the worldly love of money and the oppression which flows from such sinful love. And the poor soil itself is unholy, sharing the curse of man, as the shod foot implies. St. Paul's own burning witness to this fact will claim our attention in a later chapter.

And now Hopkins sweeps into the grandeur of one of the magnificent images of our literature. The image must be huge, because at this point in the poem God Himself enters into the picture, the sole answer to the malice and destruction of man. Hopkins begins with the renewal of the living creatures which have been trampled, the strength of the life which flows into them from the living and eternal Creator. They are never spent because their ultimate source of life is God Himself. That dear freshness flows from the immediate and eternal freshness of God. And the sun to which these creatures owe their renewal, in so far as nourishment and warmth and the protection of daylight are concerned, merges with the symbolic dove to express the deep subject of the poem—the indwelling of the Holy Ghost in creatures and above all in the souls of men.

The world reflecting the sun opened the poem. The sun returns to close the poem. First the flame of the sun itself goes, as in "Winter with the Gulf Stream" (*Poems*, No. 3).

> And slendering to his burning rim
>
> Into the flat blue mist the sun
> Drops out and all our day is done

and blackness springs upon us from the west. Thus the flame of our foil image is swallowed up in the trampling of men. The darkness of John, 1:5, which is the ignoring of God by man, apparently has mastered the light, which in John's terminology is supernatural life in man.

But the sun is only apparently gone. The earliest light of dawn turns the east horizon brown, and from it there springs the source of light, inevitably, since it is the Holy Ghost Who is bringing forth life now as over the barren waters in Genesis. The dove, under the symbol of which the Spirit of God descended upon Jesus after His baptism (cf. Matthew, 3:16-17), is discussed by a theologian in terms illuminating for our image:

> The symbol of the dove descending upon Jesus was doubtless meant to recall to our mind the account in Genesis: 'Darkness was upon the face of the deep, and the Spirit of God brooded over the waters and God said let there be light and there was light' (Gen. i. 2, 3). In Genesis the spirit of God is pictured as brooding like a bird over chaos and darkness, and thus fecundating it through its fostering care and pervading power. . . . It is obvious that all Three Persons sanctified the human nature of Our Lord as something created, though only One Person assumed it as His own. This sanctification, however, is ascribed to the Third Person as the subsistent Holiness of God, thereby revealing to us His special characteristic as Person. For this characteristic the brooding dove was a fit emblem. Should it be asked why not another bird was chosen for this symbol, say, an eagle or a falcon, it is easy to give the reason, that God on this occasion wished no emblem of might or swiftness, but an emblem of that still and tender power of imparting life, which man's imagination joins to the nature of the dove, with which man also associates that of innocence, or sinlessness, which was specially fitting at the baptism of Christ.
>
> (J. P. Arendzen, *The Holy Trinity* [London: Sheed and Ward, 1937], pp. 110-11)

"That still and tender power of imparting life" is indeed the characteristic of the Holy Ghost, and hence the sun in its relation to the growing things of nature is an ideal symbol. And when an artist can do what Hopkins does, merging sun and dove as two perfect symbols for that life-giving and life-protecting function, both of them operating at full potential, he has achieved a height in image-making.

The Holy Ghost is the subject of the poem, the source of the grandeur with which the poem begins. And now the opening images take on a new significance. They too are symbols of the Holy Ghost—the flame and the unction.

The "Veni Creator," the great hymn in the Church to the Holy Ghost, is liturgically perhaps more familiar than any other. It is sung at solemn functions, for example at the ordination of priests, where Hopkins heard it in 1874 and noted it thus: "At the singing of the *Veni Creator* and giving of the Orders I was by God's mercy deeply touched . . ." (*Journals*, p. 260).

The hymn is ascribed to Rabanus Maurus (776-856). A discussion of it can be found in Dom Matthew Britt's *The Hymns of the Breviary and Missal* (New York: Benziger, 1952), pp. 153-57. I use Britt's translation in the note, for the most part.

Veni, Creator Spiritus,
Mentes Tuorum visita,
Imple superna gratia,
Quae tu creasti pectora.

Qui diceris Paraclitus,
Altissimi donum Dei,
Fons vivus, ignis, caritas,
Et spiritalis unctio.

Tu septiformis munere,
Digitus Paternae dexterae,
Tu rite promissum Patris,
Sermone ditans guttura.

Accende lumen sensibus,
Infunde amorem cordibus,

Infirma nostri corporis
Virtute firmans perpeti.

Hostem repellas longius,
Pacemque dones protinus:
Ductore sic te praevio
Vitemus omne noxium.

Per te sciamus da Patrem,
Noscamus atque Filium,
Teque utriusque Spiritum
Credamus omni tempore.

Deo Patri sit gloria,
Et Filio, qui a mortuis
Surrexit, ac Paraclito,
In saeculorum saecula.*

*Come, Creator-Spirit,
Visit the souls of Thy people,
Fill with thy heavenly grace
The breasts which Thou hast made.

Thou art called the Comforter,
The Gift of the most high God,
The living fountain, fire, love,
And anointing of the spirit.

Thou art sevenfold in Thy gifts,
The Finger of God's right hand;
Thou art the solemn promise of the
    Father
Enriching tongues with speech.

Enkindle Thy light in our minds;
Infuse Thy love into our hearts;

The weakness of our bodies
Strengthen with unfailing power.

Drive our enemy afar,
And give peace uninterruptedly;
Thus with You leading the way as guide
We may shun everything harmful.

Through You may we know the Father,
And the Son
And in You, the Spirit of both of Them,
May we ever believe.

Glory be to God the Father,
And to the Son Who rose from the dead,
And to the Comforter,
Forever and ever.

In his notes on "The Contemplation for Obtaining Divine Love," the climax of the Spiritual Exercises which Hopkins performed yearly and prepared a detailed commentary on, Hopkins parallels Ignatius's imagery with that of the "Veni Creator":

The last mystery meditated on in the Spiritual Exercises is our Lord's Ascension. This contemplation is that which comes next in order, namely the sending of the Holy Ghost; it is the contemplation of the Holy Ghost sent to us through creatures. Observe then it is on love and the Holy Ghost is called Love ('Fons vivus, ignis, *caritas*'); shewn 'in operibus,' the works of God's finger ('Digitus paternae dexterae'); consisting 'in communicatione' etc., and the Holy Ghost as he is the bond and mutual love of the Father and Son, so of God and man; that the Holy Ghost is uncreated grace and the sharing by man of the divine nature and the bestowal of himself by God on man ('Altissimi donum Dei'): hence we are to consider 'quantum . . . Dominus desideret dare seipsum mihi in quantum potest'; hence also the repetition in pt. 2 of 'dans.' Remark also how after the benefits of creation and Redemption he does not add, he means *us* to add, that of sanctification. Again in Pt. 2 'templum,' in 3. 'operatur' as above, in 4. 'a, sole . . . radii, a fonte aquae' ('*Fons* vivus, *ignis*') (Dec. 8, 1881). All things therefore are charged with love, are charged with God and if we know how to touch them give off sparks and take fire, yield drops and flow, ring and tell of him.

(*Sermons*, p. 195)

Ignatius, with James in mind, states that all good gifts come from above, "just as the rays descend from the sun, and waters from the spring."[2] That these are life-giving gifts is obviously no accident, as Hopkins stresses in applying the images to the "Veni Creator": "'a sole' . . . radii, a fonte aquae' ('*Fons* vivus, *ignis*')." The rays of the sun "springing" and spreading from the east, as life-giving and as symbolic of the life-giving function of the Holy Spirit, close our poem.

The line, "Et spiritalis unctio," which follows the one quoted above by Hopkins, gives the basis for the oil image. The image of the Holy Spirit as anointing oil poured out is based upon the Old Law, in which anointing with oil signified the consecration and making holy of the object. John gives an immediate statement of the image: "You, however, have been anointed by the Holy One, as you all know" (I John, 2:20). John has been speaking of apostates, and *A Catholic Commentary on Holy Scripture* supplies this note on the text: "In contrast to these apostates are those 'who have the unction from the Holy One,' i.e. from Christ, whose name signifies 'the Anointed One,' and who in baptism anointed them with sanctifying grace and the gifts of the Holy

Spirit, and enlightened them."³ Thus the consecrating oil which should make the earth holy is an admirable symbol for the Holy Spirit Who is giving freshness "deep down things," Who anoints with the sweet-smelling ointments of sanctifying grace, Who came as tongues of flame and even now is the fire of love, warmth, and brightness for every man coming into the world. So the fire and oil, closely associated in the "Veni Creator" and in Christian symbolism for the Holy Ghost, are the small symbols which open the sonnet. And the cosmic fire of the sun, merged with the divine Dove, is the enormous symbol that closes it. There is first the small reflection of God's infinite grandeur, then a huge and growing evil and destruction, and finally a far huger and burgeoning good and rebirth.

Milton's dove, like Hopkins', is drawn from Genesis, and the rhythm and sound of Milton's lines are expressive of the quiet stretching of the dove's wings—an effect similar to Hopkins' but with significant differences of which I shall speak shortly:

> . . . Thou from the first
> Wast present, and with mighty wings outspread
> Dove-like satst brooding on the vast Abyss
> And mad'st it pregnant. . . .
>
> *(Paradise Lost,* I, 19-22)

Another allied image, in Wordsworth's Immortality Ode, a poem which meant much to Hopkins, stresses the light that dispels darkness:

> Mighty prophet! Seer blest!
> On whom those truths do rest,
> Which we are toiling all our lives to find,
> In darkness lost, the darkness of the grave;
> Thou, over whom thy Immortality
> Broods like the Day, a Master o'er a Slave,
> A Presence which is not to be put by. . . .

In discussing Coleridge's criticism of this passage, I. A. Richards makes some remarks which may illuminate Hopkins' image as well as Wordsworth's:

Masters, in general, we agree, do not brood over slaves in any sense of brood. No one will deny the inappropriateness of the image for masters in Rome, South Carolina, the Congo, or Sian fu; but in one instance and that the only relevant instance—the relation of God to his servants in the Christian scheme, the only master-slave relation that Wordsworth is concerned with here—it is perfectly appropriate. And so with *day.* What more natural metaphor for the relation of an immortality to its nursling than that of the day to the young growth of spring which it is drawing up? Moreover that very growth itself, the responsive, eager unfolding is what Wordsworth is pointing to as the child's response. In what way does he *read* 'the eternal deep?' By this very growth.

(*Coleridge on Imagination* [New York: W. W. Norton, 1950], pp. 134-35)

The relation of the sun to life and growth, expressed in "broods," is alike in Wordsworth's and Hopkins' images. Wordsworth, however, is expressing the idea of an insight which will gradually fade; Hopkins, the idea of a continuous resurgence overcoming a continuous trampling.

The rhythm of the Hopkins sonnet is designed to build up to the great smooth flow of the end, expressive of the bursting of the sun over the horizon and the gradual wide-spreading of its rays. The phrases of the octet are short; pauses abound. In the sestet the rhythm picks up speed to the dash after "springs," which I think is expressive of the moment of apparent pause before the rim of the sun bursts over the horizon. And the last two lines, which flow on without pause, build and lengthen in the vowels and alliteration of "world broods," "warm breast," "bright wings," with the last greatly lengthened by being alliteratively reversed and by the long "ah!" which expresses not only the poet's emotion but the physical act of the spreading rays.

While the rhythm and sound emphasize the action of the sun, the meanings of the words themselves, except for "bright," emphasize the action of the mothering dove brooding over its nest. It is a huge nest, from horizon to horizon, west to east, the "round of the world" of which Hopkins speaks in the *Journals*: "From the highroad I saw how the sea, dark blue with violet cloud-shadows, was warped to the round of the world like a coat upon a ball and often later I marked that perspective" (p. 222). Thus we have a metaphor in which three elements,[4] rather than the usual two, converge upon the one verb, "broods": the Holy Spirit Who "forms and warms the life within," like the throstle in "The May Magnificat" (*Poems*, No. 42), the life of each creature in itself, and in man his own life plus Christ's life; the dove which broods over its eggs with warm breast and protecting wings; the sun which broods over all growing things with its warming fire and its penetrating rays.

A chart of "God's Grandeur" may be useful in indicating the total structure of the sonnet:

GOD'S GRANDEUR 43

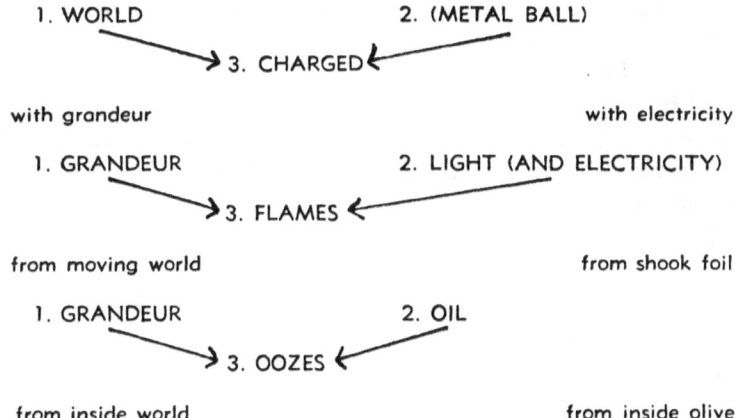

(Then a literal searing and smearing of world in trade and toil that disregard the beauty and the rights of living things, which stem from the brooding Spirit of Genesis. Rebellious man has no care for God's holy ground or for the creatures that reveal the grandeur of the Spirit.

But the Spirit of God still active as in Genesis: nature survives, chaos and darkness do not take over—thus to sun and last great image.)

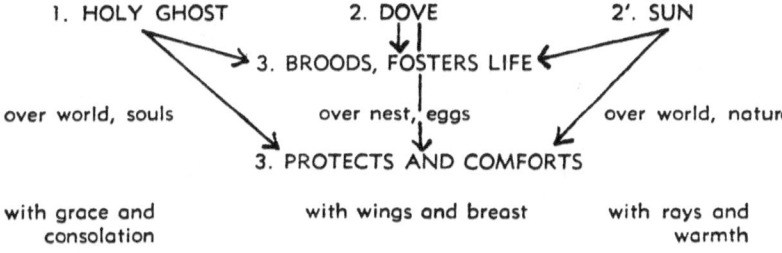

Our own image, then, dwarfed in relation to the final image of the sonnet, has nevertheless an important function to play in the poem. Even its smallness is important, expressing the finitude of the reflection of infinite grandeur and providing a structural contrast to the size of the closing image. Its soft *l*'s and *f*'s and *sh*'s, together with the expressive rhythm of its two short phrases, symbolize well in sound the quiet and loving reaction of the good earth to Love, the proper name of the Holy Ghost, and contribute to the expression of the spiritual reality revealed by the physical. The life-giving glory of

God pouring from eternity into time led the mind of Hopkins to form the image of Christ as sun in the last stanza of *Deutschland* and the image of the Holy Ghost as sun in "God's Grandeur." It is the same spiritual fact, revealed in St. John's gospel from the supernatural side and revealed in the creatures of this world from the natural side, that leads Hopkins to form the image with which we will deal in the following chapter.

CHAPTER 3

The Shekinah

When Moses had gone, the mountain was veiled in cloud; for six days the glory of the Lord abode there on Sinai, wrapping it in cloud. . . .
Exodus, 24:15-16

And behold, thou shalt conceive in thy womb, and shalt bear a son, and shalt call him Jesus. . . . *The Holy Spirit will come upon thee, and the power of the most High will overshadow thee.*
Luke, 1:31, 35

Blessed art thou among women, and blessed is the fruit of thy womb. How have I deserved to be thus visited by the mother of my Lord? Why, as soon as ever the voice of thy greeting sounded in my ears, the child in my womb leaped for joy.
Luke, 1:42-44

And now, in heaven, a great portent appeared; a woman that wore the sun for her mantle. . . . *She had a child in her womb.* . . . *She bore a son, the son who is to herd the nations like sheep with a crook of iron.* . . .
Apocalypse, 12:1-5

Tu regis alti janua
Et aula lucis fulgida:
Vitam datam per Virginem,
Gentes redemptae, plaudite.

"O gloriosa Domina,"
ascribed to Fortunatus

Nel ventre tuo se raccesse l'amore
  per lo cui caldo nell' eterna pace
  cosi e germinato questo Fiore.

Paradiso, XXXIII

Doute is ther noon, thou queen of misericorde,
That thou nart cause of grace and mercy here;
God vouched sauf thurgh thee with us tacorde.
For certes, Christes blissful moder dere,
Were now the bowe bent in swich manere,
As it was first, of Justice and of yre,
The rightful God nolde of no mercy here;
But thurgh thee han we grace, as we desyre.
Chaucer, "An A.B.C."

Rorate Coeli desuper!
   Hevins distill your balmy schouris,
For now is rissin the brycht day-ster,
   Fro the Roiss Mary, flour of flouris:
   The cleir Sone, quhome no clud devouris,
Surmounting Phebus in the est,
   Is cumin of his hevinly touris;
Et nobis Puer natus est.
William Dunbar, "Of the
Nativity of Christ"

THE SHEKINAH

> Mary Immaculate,
> Merely a woman, yet
> Whose presence, power is
> Great as no goddess's
> Was deemèd, dreamèd; who
> This one work has to do—
> Let all God's glory through,
> God's glory which would go
> Through her and from her flow
> Off, and no way but so.
>
> "The Blessed Virgin compared
to the Air we Breathe," *Poems*, No. 60

Humpty Dumpty is a poet and a critic primarily, but I think the theological experiences in the background of his creator were what led to the choice of "glory" for the first striking example of Humpty's mastery over words. There are few words which have been subjected to mastery as absolute, or almost so, as Humpty's.

"And only one for birthday presents, you know. There's glory for you!"

"I don't know what you mean by 'glory'," Alice said.

Humpty Dumpty smiled contemptuously. "Of course you don't—till I tell you. I meant 'there's a nice knock-down argument for you!'"

"But 'glory' doesn't mean 'a nice knock-down argument,'" Alice objected.

"When I use a word," Humpty Dumpty said in rather a scornful tone, "it means just what I choose it to mean—neither more nor less."

(Lewis Carroll, *Through the Looking Glass* [London: Macmillan, 1872], pp. 123-24)

The situation which Alice and Humpty Dumpty face is not as simple as the logic to which their creator reduces it. Alice is, with that Johnsonian common sense which could produce a dictionary and then embrace it with relief as an absolute and sensible norm for tying down wriggly words, asserting the rights of the arbitrary and conventional agreements which make communication by oral sound possible. Humpty, with the arrogance of the artist faced with convention, is asserting the independence of the mind in determining its own meaning. It is the business of the critic, and the serious and vital test of his worth, to safeguard the legitimate claims of both the word and the mind.

The problem which faces us in Hopkins' use of the word "glory" in the passage we treat in this chapter is not the choice of one of two mutually exclusive meanings, as in the case of "breast" in chapter 2. We have here the far more complex problem of discovering what meanings are possible for the word in this context and of determining whether the meanings which do operate here derive from convention alone or whether something individual is added by the mind of Hopkins.

Convention itself here presents a problem. "Glory" in general conventional use will always signify brilliance or splendor of light, or some analogy based on such splendor, such as the effects of praise, of happiness, etc. In a particular religious context the word will, for a Jew, suggest the presence of God over the Ark, the Shekinah. It will further suggest, for a Christian, the presence of God among us in the New Testament Shekinah of John, 1:14.[1] For a Catholic, in a context which includes Mary, it will further suggest the "overshadowing" of Luke, 1:35—through which the glory of which John speaks came into the world—and the "woman clothed with the sun" of Apocalypse, 12:1.

Those are all meanings which can be listed, with many more, in a dictionary as conventional meanings that anyone might use, apart from any individual meanings the word may have in Hopkins' mind. The last noted would perhaps never occur spontaneously to a Protestant, nor the previous one to a Jewish scholar unacquainted with the New Testament, nor the preceding one to a pagan without knowledge of the Bible, nor any of them to a Chinese monk with no knowledge at all of English. "Glory," like every other word, receives its meaning from the mind in which it exists, and being the happily unscientific word which it is, it admits a vast variety of meanings from minds which bring to it a vast variety of experience and education. In dealing with this word the critic must even more than usual follow Joyce's advice: "Wipe your glosses with what you know."[2] If the mind has experienced the word in its uses in English literature and in Catholic theology, as Hopkins' mind had, and, further, if that mind employs the word in a context of imagery never used before in quite the same way, as Hopkins does in this poem, then the possibilities for its meaning are multiplied.

In the individual circumstances of an original and powerful poem, an important word is likely to gather to itself new meanings or shades of meaning which will affect what henceforth happens to it in the minds of those who know and use it. It is an important part of a critic's work to spot and report those new aspects of a word. But it is a fatal abuse of his role to impose meanings upon a word which derive from his own mind rather than from the word as it operates in the poem. Examples of this unfortunate abuse are not hard to find—critics, like other humans, must bring their own backgrounds and opinions to their job, in this case the incredibly difficult task of interpreting the mysteries of human speech—and Richard Ellman provides one in his implied reading of "glory" as involving sexual imagery in stanza 30 of *The Wreck of the Deutschland*: "As might be expected, Yeats had little to tell of beatitude, the immediate apprehension of reality, and his use of sexual imagery is entirely unlike that of a religious poet like Hopkins:

>Jesu, heart's light,
>Jesu, maid's son,
>What was the feast followed the night
>Thou hadst glory of this nun?

With Yeats the reader suspects that the poet may prefer the symbol of beatitude itself" (*Yeats: the Man and the Masks* [New York: Macmillan, 1948], p. 261). The answer to Hopkins' question in the lines which Ellman quotes is "The feast of the Immaculate Conception, December 8," and not, as Ellman evidently supposes, "A Wagnerian beer-session in the Christian Valhalla following a night of nuptial pleasure."

Ellman could defend his reading with arguments based on the context—e.g., the feast as a wedding-feast, the mystical union of bride and bridegroom as in the ordinary application of the Canticle of Canticles, etc.—but they would be arguments to justify a mistake, not to establish a fact. The word "feast" has a specialized meaning here which refers to a fact that cannot rationally call up the picture of Christ and the nun's spirit wassailing at the same board—that is, that the next day was December 8. And while "glory" in a given context could certainly take on the meaning of mystical union, its context here determines a quite different and traditional meaning—the flame of self-sacrifice from a woman who perfectly achieved the Catholic and Jesuit ideal of "Ad Majorem Dei Gloriam." The tone and bias of Ellman's sexual approach, too, while explicable on the basis of Freudian dogma and the critic's immediate concern with the imagery of Yeats, is utterly foreign to Hopkins' habitual approach to the reality under consideration, the union of Christ the Head and one of His members. Hopkins' meaning, as can be demonstrated from Hopkins' contexts, involves the relations between the infinite majesty of the eternal God and one of His creatures, so that the meaning which Ellman finds here is both trivial and contradictory to the reality with which Hopkins deals. Totally grasped, Hopkins' context makes Ellman's notion untenable, that is to say, untenable as a meaning possible in *Hopkins'* poem. Should Ellman prefer his own reading, he could certainly retain it; but as a critic, he should distinguish it from Hopkins' product.

In the passage with which this chapter deals, the background of Catholic theological speculation gives a special aura to the word "glory" that is available to minds that know what that background is. If a reader has no knowledge of it, he will of course miss the special significances of the word. He does not need to study Catholic theology to discover those meanings, though that is one certain and thorough way of doing so. He can also find it by appreciating fully the total imagery of the poem in which this passage appears. But since the imagery of the poem is expressive of a profound mystery of the Catholic religion—expressive and not explanatory—he will find it even more difficult, if not impossible, to appreciate the total imagery without a knowledge of the meaning which Catholic theology gives to these words, as well as the particular meanings which Hopkins gives to them in this poem. For these meanings, then, the reader must turn to Hopkins himself (the best source for his own meanings, since Hopkins was an excellent critic as well as a poet) or to someone who knows what the meanings are from a consideration of Catholic theology as well as of Hopkins' work.

Does this mean that the poem is narrowly "sectarian," written, as Gardner says in his notes on No. 26, "to please Catholics," which, while it makes the Catholic body purr, ignores reality and universality? I suspect that Bridges, to whom any Marianism was exaggerated except the type he himself practiced, in which Mary is treated as a product of the human imagination and not as a reality, might answer "Yes," with perhaps qualifications in the light of the obvious poetic excellences of the poem. Hopkins took Mary with total and complete seriousness, and Bridges, I believe, rightly considered such an attitude as a challenge to his own view of reality. I judge, however, that the universality of the poem may be defended and that the demands which the poem makes upon the minds of its readers may be justified, since those demands are involved in the nature of human language.

The reader who has learned his language in a Protestant or in a pagan culture will almost certainly miss the aura of meaning which Hopkins draws from the word "glory" in this poem. But a critic is bound to accept words as they proceed from the mind of the author, and to accept them, in so far as that is possible, on the author's terms. In order to judge the author's art-product, the critic must see the subject with the author's eyes and judge on the author's premises; at least he must attempt to do so, and the measure of his success will be the adequacy of his judgment of the author's achievement. Here "glory" will yield its basic meaning of light-giving or light-reflective splendor to all, but further meanings must be extracted from the context, which in this case is specifically Catholic.

The glory with which Hopkins is concerned, then, in this passage is God's glory, not Mary's. The ultimate question about the word is whether Hopkins means merely the reflection of God's splendor which can be seen in the creatures of this world, or more than that. He certainly does refer to the reflection of God's splendor, since this glory is spoken of as coming through and flowing off from Mary. It is not God's splendor as God Himself knows it within the Trinity, but His splendor as we see it in this world. This is the usage of St. John: "And the Word became flesh, and dwelt among us; and we have looked upon his glory—such a glory as befits the Father's only-begotten Son—full of grace and truth!" (John, 1:14). In Christ we see the fullest possible revelation of God in this world, and Christ comes to us through Mary.

But an investigation of the poem reveals that by "glory" Hopkins means more than a reflection of God's splendor. In the first of the two main sections of the body of the poem, Hopkins deals with the spiritual life that comes to us through Mary. "Glory" as the life of God is also a Scriptural usage. For example, St. Paul, in a passage which is the stated basis for an image which we shall treat later, speaks of all nature desiring "to share the freedom that comes with the glory of the children of God" (Romans, 8:21). And that it is precisely this glory which causes us to be children of God, sharers in the divine life, Hopkins states in his commentary on a later section of St. Paul's same chapter, where the same mysterious Greek word, της δόξης, appears in its verb form, ἐδόξασεν. The passage, a primary one in any discussion of the Mystical Body, the sharing of the divine life in

Christ, is translated by Knox: "All those who from the first were known to him, he has destined from the first to be moulded into the image of his Son, who is thus to become the eldest-born among many brethren. So predestined, he called them; so called, he justified them; so justified, he glorified them" (Romans, 8:29-30). This being glorified by God, so that the creatures become brothers of Christ, Hopkins speaks of in his commentary on the Greek text as their being "raised to the state when their deeds should be the doing of God in them" (*Sermons,* p. 158). Thus through receiving the glory of God a man shares in the life and activity of God, becomes a child of God and a brother of Christ. Since this glory or divine life flows to us from the person of Jesus Christ as the ultimate source, and since Mary is also a true proximate source, the human channel *through* which that life is brought to us, we are also in a true sense the spiritual children of Mary. That is Hopkins' development of the Pauline text.

St. John, in the opening of his Gospel, links the light shining in the darkness with the revelation of God's glory in Christ. And he speaks, as Hopkins does in the poem, of the Word's taking flesh and thus bringing God's glory among us. Since light in John's Gospel is a constant symbol of the divine life, it is not difficult to see the "glory" of which John speaks in 1:14 as an expression both of the revelation of God to our sight and further of the divine grace which is a sharing of God's life by us and which flows to us from "the Father's only-begotten Son, full of grace and truth." It is this full meaning of glory as a gift of life and as a revelation of God that Hopkins develops in the poem.

Mary's one work, and a work which is possible because of her unique immaculate state, as Hopkins says in stanza 30 of *Deutschland,* is to let this divine life come through into the world, to be the human medium and channel of God's glory. Hopkins' two verbs prepare for the two main sections of the body of the poem: the glory will go through her, as light through air; and the glory will flow off from her. This last verb presents a problem.

The "flow" at first glance suggests liquid and in the context could well recall the life-giving "living waters" of grace which are prominent in John's Gospel and elsewhere. But there is no development of this notion in the poem, and the treatment throughout is of air. A consideration of the text in relation to the rest of the poem leads me to conclude that in an extremely subtle but powerful image Hopkins is referring to the Word of God being brought to us by this air which is

Mary, as the word of another man is carried to our ear by the literal flow of air. Certainly air, or rather Mary, is bringing the Word in this way in the conclusion of the poem:

> Stir in my ears, speak there
> Of God's love, O live air. . . .

Further, this accords with the Johannine text which gives the light-life symbolism, "The Word was made flesh," which is again central in the first section of the body of the poem, which develops the life-giving activity of Mary as bringing forth the Word in us, "Of her flesh he took flesh. . . ." Again, in stanza 30 of *Deutschland,* where Mary Immaculate acts, she is pictured as bringing forth the Word physically, which is the reason why it is now possible for the nun to bring Him forth spiritually. Again, in his exquisite "Ad Matrem Virginem" (*Poems,* No. 138), Hopkins stresses the idea of the Word being "infans," unspeaking, in a profound manner—Mary could speak to her Child in the manger, and although He was mute there, He could answer deep within her soul:

> Quae tu tum dicebas
> Et quae audiebas?
> Etsi fuit mutus
> Tamen est locutus.*

This flow of glory from Mary, further, is developed in the lines that follow our text, in the discussion of the life-giving role of Mary as the source of Christ's human life and the channel of our divine life, so that it is from her that the Word proceeds to us and through her that the Word enters into us. As the Word *was made* flesh, so we *are made* the Word:

> . . . each one
> More makes, when all is done,
> Both God's and Mary's Son.

Hence air, by whose flow any word proceeds to us and through which the word enters into our ears, is a powerful image of the activity of Mary as Hopkins here expresses it. A word from another man flows to us through the air from his vibrating vocal cords and mouth into our ears, and off from the air into the nerves that deliver the word to the brain. So the Word which proceeds from the mouth of the

---

* What were you then saying and what were you hearing? For even though He was mute, yet He spoke.

Father flows to us through Mary, and off from Mary to be one with us in the living unity of the Mystical Body.[3]

That Hopkins finds it necessary or expedient to say explicitly that Mary is merely a woman and no goddess is evidence of pressures which are operating below the surface of the poem—the influence of views which would have Mary a goddess and no woman, or a woman with presence and power no greater than that of any other woman. Hopkins rejects both of those views in his positive statement of Mary's true position as he sees it—views which find their expression in the work of other English poets, like Wordsworth and Yeats, or Milton. I think it may be critically useful in evaluating Hopkins' position in this poem, and the poetic structure which he builds from his material, to glance at what other English poets have done with the same material viewed quite differently. They, too, were expressing theology in their poems, and in their positive positions in regard to Mary they were at least implicitly rejecting the Catholic position. Hopkins is writing in the Catholic tradition, and one way in which the subject-matter of his poem differs from the subject-matter of Marian poems written in the Catholic England of Chaucer and More is that Hopkins reveals the pressures of those opposing views. A consideration of literary expressions of such views, then, while only negatively operative on our passage, may nevertheless illumine it from below.

The deemers and dreamers Hopkins has first in mind are those who, in the pagan (rather, pseudo-pagan) tradition which rooted in the Renaissance, considered the devotion accorded to Mary in the Catholic Church a continuation of the devotion once accorded to female deities, or a revival of such devotion. The Mary of Catholics they considered to be pretty much on the level of the Diana of Ephesus or the Venus of Rome. The Mary who is Queen of Heaven to Catholics became, in their eyes, analogous to the Juno who reigned on Olympus. For them, Mary thus ceased to be a real woman and became instead an ideal, a symbol, a product of the human imagination. Wordsworth illustrates this view, as Hoxie Fairchild, in his excellent discussion of Wordsworth's religious views, points out in a discussion of Wordsworth's "The Virgin": "Wordsworth leans toward certain Catholic doctrines and practices because he feels that, precisely in being superstitious, they contain a precious imaginative element which flouts that 'false secondary power,' the lower reason.... There are times when he would almost be willing to substitute 'I'd rather be a Catholic' for 'I'd rather be a pagan' in *The world is too much with us*" (*Relig-*

ious Trends in English Poetry [New York: Columbia, 1949], 3, p. 230). In Wordsworth's treatment, Mary is not, to use Hopkins' terminology, "taken seriously." Her rights as a real being are discarded in favor of the rights of Wordsworth's poetic imagination. His Virgin is an ideal of womanhood, but she is not real. Wordsworth accepts from Mary what he thinks will fit into the Platonic closet of tranquil recollection; she possesses only that degree of reality which he chooses to bestow. Since Wordsworth is under the impression that he is dealing with reality, he mixes the real with the ideal in a manner which works havoc on his art-product. If, like Yeats, he had seriously attempted to reduce all reality to his imaginative terms, if he had brought Mary and Leda and his daughter into the same imaginative tower and kept them there, then Wordsworth, like Yeats, might have scaled the imaginative heights. Yeats' utter surrender (or perhaps better, dedication) to the imagination as the source of truth is, to my mind, a hideous tragedy for him as a man, but it put him on poetically much solider ground than the hodgepodge mixture of the real and the imaginative with which Wordsworth deals.

In this aspect Hopkins appears to me to be the antithesis of Yeats, surrendering (or dedicating) his powers utterly to reality, so the source of truth for him is the real and the imagination must adapt itself to that. The result is that Hopkins' images and symbols point to something outside himself, ultimately to the infinite and humanly ungraspable; the pagan's images and symbols point to the universe he himself constructs out of the materials at hand. For a pagan, Mary can have no mysteries other than those which the human mind constructs and hence can grasp; for Hopkins, Mary has mysteries bestowed upon her by a sharing in the life and the activity of the real and infinite God and hence available to the mind only in part and analogously. Mary is an easy subject for Wordsworth and for Yeats to deal with, since nothing in her exceeds their control; she is difficult for Hopkins, since the range of her power and presence exceeds the limits of the imagination's reach. Wordsworth and Yeats can say what she is; Hopkins is reduced to saying what she is not—she is not within the limits of human deeming or dreaming, but more than that. From the manageable limits of the circle—or the gyre—the pagan can build structures of poetic wonder. But Hopkins must deal with the infinite.

While he asserts that Mary is no goddess, Hopkins on the other hand denies the view that has developed in the Protestant literary tradition. There Mary, as Herbert well illustrates,[4] tends to disappear altogether. Where she does retain her obvious Scriptural position, as in Milton's poems, there is a striking difference both in tone and in omission between that Mary and the Mary of a Catholic culture—the Mary of the *Paradiso,* of Chaucer, of Hopkins.[5] The warmth of a Catholic's personal love for his own life-giving spiritual Mother, his trust in her unshakable love and her intercessory power for him personally, his need to share in her "fiat" of Nazareth, Bethlehem, Calvary, the present moment, all throughout time—none of these appears in Milton's Mary. And to penetrate to a full grasp of Hopkins' poetic achievement, it is important to understand why that is so.

For the Reformers and especially for their successors, divine grace was no longer a sharing in the divine life as an added principle of human activity. This belief, absolutely central to Catholicism, held by the Church not as something understood but as a mystery revealed by God, is the first thing to disappear when the authority of the Church is rejected. Human reason can neither arrive at the notion unaided nor, without a strong faith, retain the idea. G. H. Joyce, S.J., in discussing sanctifying grace as the vital principle by which we live as sons of God, says:

The doctrine of man's deification is so wonderful that the mind finds it hard to believe it true. Conscious as we are of our baseness, we can scarcely credit that we are to receive—or rather have already received—so amazing a dignity. We ask ourselves if this is not only a metaphor. It needs the repeated and emphatic assertions of the great teachers of the Church to persuade us that it is no metaphor, but the literal truth; that the sanctifying grace with which we are endowed, communicates to us properties which in their essential nature are divine; that through it we are destined to share in the life and the beatitude of the Ever Blessed Trinity.

(*The Catholic Doctrine of Grace* [New York: Benziger, n.d.], p. 39)

It is only in the light of this belief in a real and literal sharing of divine life that the spiritual motherhood of Mary can have validity. She can have a function analogous to that of our own mothers, in giving us spiritual life as truly as our own mothers give us our natural lives, only if a real spiritual life is given to us as a real principle of our activity. Milton can speak of "Life to all who shall believe" (*Paradise Lost,* XII, 406), as the Reformers of course also did, but the words do not mean for the Reformers or for Milton a divinization of human acts and a deification of a human being, as does the life of which Hopkins speaks in his poem.[6]

Mary is, then, in Hopkins' poem, a real source of divine life. Her title of "Mother" is no mere honorary or figurative title when it is applied to her in relation to the members of the Church of Christ. In relation to the rest of mankind, Mary is in a true sense a proximate source of the divine life which she gives, because she, like Christ, though in an infinitely inferior and dependent manner, merited for all human beings all the grace that they receive.

Mary alone among human persons could share in Christ's meriting of divine life for human beings because she alone among humans was in her mother's womb conceived immaculate, with no stain of sin, no tendency toward evil. Hence the importance in Hopkins' poem of the stressed and repeated "wild," the point being that Mary's nature, like the good air, is totally good. "Full of grace" indicates this fact in Catholic traditional interpretation. "Mary Immaculate" stresses the same fact in our text.

Because Mary is totally removed from sin, she can in a unique way share in Christ's redeeming act. In one sense, Mary is redeemed as are all the children of Adam. But she is not, as all others, rescued from the gulf of original sin by being (as it were) pulled out; she is preserved from ever falling in. She would have fallen in had it not been for the redeeming merits of her Son, which operated to preserve her. Hence she is, as Hopkins points out in *Sermons,* "beyond all others redeemed" (p. 197). But in another sense she stands with Christ on the "redeemed" side in His act of redemption, and alone of human persons she so stands. Christ is a divine person, and divine life stems from Him as from its ultimate source. Mary is a human person, a creature, and hence infinitely inferior to her Son, totally unable to be an ultimate source of divine life. But in relation to the rest of mankind she can be and is a real though proximate source of that life for all. Every other human being must come to Calvary as a sinner to receive the gift of divine grace (as the eighth stanza of *Deutschland* dramatically states). And he must receive that gift from the two utterly sinless persons on Calvary, Christ our Saviour and Mary our Mother.[7] All the grace that Christ merited *de condigno* (by nature and by right), Mary also merited *de congruo* (by her good human act, divinized by the grace which she received from her Son, an act of cooperation with His salvific Sacrifice).

As noted above, Hopkins' "Mary Immaculate" and his stress on "wild" at the opening and closing of the poem express the fact that Mary's nature by the predestination of God (beautifully expressed in

Hopkins' Latin "May Lines," *Poems*, No. 139) was preserved from any share in Adam's sin, so that she could be of her own choice a perfect instrument for the Incarnation, physically, but above all spiritually, executing her own natural, "wild" act in cooperation with God's. Mary is a life-giving principle; hence the stress on her womb in the liturgy. But she is not a passive instrument merely. She is a rational creature, and her spiritual assent plays a part in our salvation. This too is a vital point in the determination of Hopkins' imagery in the poem.

In Milton's eyes, Mary acted as a pious Jewish girl accepting God's assignment to be the mother of Jesus and receiving the exalted dignity owing to the office, but certainly not acting spiritually in the name of the whole human race or in any sense giving life to all of the redeemed. In Hopkins' eyes, in freely accepting the proposal of God to the children of Adam (and to Adam, too) who had rejected Him, Mary acted as the delegate chosen by God to receive Him back into our midst, and in a way far more wonderful than the manner in which He walked with Adam and Eve. St. Thomas expresses Catholic tradition on the matter thus: ". . . ut ostenderetur esse quoddam spirituale matrimonium inter Filium Dei et humanam naturam. Et ideo per annuntiationem expetebatur consensus Virginis loco totius humanae naturae"* (*Summa Theologiae,* Third Part, question 30, article 1). The Incarnation, in this view, is a spiritual marriage between God and the human race, and God made His proposal to one member of the race as the delegate for all. In Mary's "fiat" we all speak and are bound; we are each of us joined to God through Mary's act. And through that same act, of course, He comes to us. In giving Christ our human life, Mary brings down the divine life upon herself and upon all who will assent to it. It pours from the human heart of Christ through Mary upon all. Hence Mary's role as spiritual mother of all the redeemed is based ultimately upon her role as physical mother of the Redeemer. This whole question is involved in unattainable mystery, as Hopkins states in the poem. The exquisite exactness and beauty of Hopkins' imaging of this view in his poem, however, can be realized by anyone who perceives what is being imaged. It is not necessary to share Hopkins' belief that the situation he images is a real one; but it is necessary to know what situation he is imaging, to see it as he sees it. His images express it, but they do not explain it; like

---

* . . . that a kind of spiritual marriage between the Son of God and human nature might be shown. And therefore through the annunciation was sought the consent of the Virgin representing the whole of human nature.

mirrors, they reflect, but they do not justify. We must see the real Mary as Hopkins sees her if we are to realize how perfectly his poem reflects her. And if the real Mary is not in reality as Hopkins sees her, then Hopkins is worse off, but the poem is not. He would in that case be deceived about reality, but the poem would remain a perfect reflection of his subjective vision. A poem is the revelation of a mind united with a vision, not a scientific explanation of reality—at least this is true of "The Blessed Virgin compared to the Air We Breathe."

Mary as spokesman for the human race and as both receiver and, in a dependent but real sense, giver of divine life is the Catholic fact in the vision of Hopkins which he exactly and sublimely expresses in the imagery of his poem. These activities of Mary do not appear in the Protestant tradition, as our text implies in speaking of her "presence, power."[8] Note too that the "one work" Mary has to do is to bring forth *Christ*. She conceived Him at Nazareth and brought Him forth at Bethlehem. That is the source and beginning of our salvation and all our spiritual good. She now, Hopkins says in the poem, still brings forth *Christ*, not now in His own human nature, but in ours. The Word is now, in Mary, made, not flesh, but spirit. The Mystical Body grows. Mary by conceiving *Christ* in us makes new Nazareths, by bringing forth *Christ* in us makes new Bethlehems.

Milton, then, would assert, in that position represented in modern times by many Protestant groups, that Mary is merely a woman and that is the end of the matter. Hopkins agrees that she is merely a woman, and can thus join Milton in taking Mary seriously, as he cannot in any way join with the pagan reduction of the real to the terms of the imagination. But Hopkins states that added to Mary's womanly nature is divine grace, a real and physical sharing in the life of God which makes her in reality infinitely more glorious (as it also makes all the redeemed who receive that divine life through her from Christ) than any goddess sprung from the mind of man. The terms Hopkins used, "presence" and "power," are Scriptural terms and immediately suggest the scene of the Annunciation, when Mary learns that the *power* of God will "overshadow" her—a term echoing the Shekinah of the Old Testament which testified to the *presence* of God: "The Holy Spirit will come upon you, and the power of the Most High will overshadow you" (Luke, 1:35).

There remains one phrase of our passage not yet discussed, "and no way but so." This is another statement of the fact that Hopkins asserts in stanza 8 of *Deutschland*, that salvation is from Christ alone. In *Deutschland* Hopkins is immediately concerned with the sacrificed Lamb as the absolute Judge of all human beings (cf. Apocalypse, 5:7 ff.). In this present poem Hopkins is concerned with the life of God which flows from Christ and Mary.[9] Just as there is only one Judge to Whom each man must go whether he wants to or not, simply by virtue of the fact that he is a man, so there is only one ultimate source of divine life to which each who would live must come, Christ; and by God's decree only one human channel of that life, Mary, by whose physical human act the whole race receives its Saviour and by whose spiritual human act the whole race accepts God's proposal and assents to self-sacrifice in union with Christ's Sacrifice. And both those acts result in life—the first, life of which Mary is the principle, human life; the second, life of which Mary is the proximate source or channel, divine life.

Mary as the giver and channel of life for all Christ's members is the subject of the first section of the body of the poem, and in this passage Hopkins achieves, I believe, the most subtle and exact poetic expression of Mary's role in the Mystical Body that the whole vast body of poetry expressing the Catholic view of reality can offer—not excluding Dante. This is, of course, a personal and limited opinion, but one which explains, perhaps, and, if true, justifies, the efforts I am making to present the fullness of Hopkins' view of the matter.

Christ in the Catholic view is one divine Person who "operates" in two natures—i.e., He *is* the divine Nature and He possesses a human nature. Hence He has two "sources" for His life, a divine "source" in the bosom of the Father and a human source in the womb of Mary. Since He comes as the new Adam to give spiritual life to the spiritually lifeless children of Adam and since He is the ultimate source of that life to us because He is the God-Man, it follows that both God and Mary, though in infinitely different ways, exercise a causality on the divine life which we receive. Mary's causality is that of a human instrument, but that does not mean that it is no real causality at all. It does mean that she is no ultimate *source* of divine life, obviously. As a mere woman, from her nature, without any added power, only human life can proceed. But she is a source of human life for the God-Man and hence in a true sense is the new Eve, the mother of all the living. Through her role as mother of the Head of the Mystical Body, she is in a true sense the mother of the members too. And through her spiritual activity in cooperating with God's grace in the

Incarnation, by which activity she consents to accept God to dwell among us, and by her grace-full cooperation with Him in our redemption, she assumes a higher dignity than that possessed by the first Eve before the Fall. Her dignity and her role in redemption are infinitely inferior to those of her Son, since He is God and she is a creature; but they are immeasurably superior to those of other creatures, since she is the one human channel which reunites God to His sinful creation.

Mary's role as spiritual mother of the race and as physical mother of God is shrouded in mystery, because God is intrinsically concerned in both cases. The traditional Catholic view which Hopkins expresses in his poem was expressed by Augustine thus:

Illa una femina, non solum spiritu verum etiam corpore, et mater est et virgo. Et mater quidem spiritu, non capitis nostri, quod est ipse salvator, ex quo magis illa spiritaliter nata est, quia omnes qui in eum crediderint, in quibus et ipsa est, recte *filii sponsi* (Matthew, 9:15) apellantur, sed plane mater membrorum ejus, quod nos sumus, quia cooperata est caritate, ut fideles in ecclesia nascerentur, quae illius capitis membra sunt, corpore vero ipsius capitis mater.*

(*Enchiridion Patristicum*, ed. M. J. Rouet de Journel [Barcelona: Herder, 1951], p. 555)

Mary in a spiritual sense is the child of her Son, as are we all who are His members, but she is, Augustine says, clearly our mother in that spiritual sense; in a true sense we are born out of her love for God and for those whom God wished to join to Himself through her. Hopkins expressed this in his early and relatively trivial verse, Rosa Mystica (*Poems,* No. 27), echoing Dante, when he asked Mary the Rose to "Make me a leaf in thee, Mother of mine." But Mary's sublime role as a channel of the life of God to each man finds the height of its expression in English poetry, I believe, in the development of the image of Mary as air carrying the Word into our souls. "Glory" in its final and fullest sense in our passage means the Word-made-flesh, the Incarnate God, Who comes to us through Mary exercising her divine motherhood, and Who flows off into us from Mary exercising her spiritual motherhood.

* That unique woman is alone truly mother and virgin, in a spiritual as in a bodily sense. For she is spiritually mother, not of our Head, who is the Saviour Himself, from Whom she is most of all spiritually born—since all who believe in Him, among whom she is, are rightly called "children of the spouse"—but clearly spiritually mother of His members, which we are, because she cooperated through love that the faithful in the Church might be born, those who are members of that Head of Which she is corporally the mother.

Since I take "glory" to mean Christ, and since to state, as our passage does, that Christ comes to us through Mary and flows into us from Mary is literally true, it might now seem that our passage is no image at all, but only a literal statement of fact. It *is* a literal statement, except for the difficulties that arise in taking "flow off" in a strictly literal sense, and doubtless taken by itself the passage can be said to be no image. The passage is, however, the second branch of a simile. The poem opens with a description of air (metaphorically treated as mother, mother-bird, nurse, food, literally presented as penetrating everywhere, filling the poet's lungs both to give and preserve life and to give body to these words in praise of air) which is the first branch of the simile, the comparison stated in the title. Then the "minds me" begins the second branch dealing with Mary, where the whole treatment is literal, although the bounds of the literal are put under extreme pressure by the last four lines of our passage, which strain to become metaphor.

The mind of Hopkins, as I hope our eight images will indicate, tends toward metaphor always, for reasons which I intend to touch upon in my concluding chapter. Three of our eight images can be classified as similes, but two of these are preparations for metaphor (i.e., our second image, of the preceding chapter, prepares for the great final metaphor of the poem in which it appears, and the image with which this chapter deals becomes metaphor finally and climactically in the conclusion of this poem), and each element of the other involves metaphor in itself—the seventh image, in which the "groping" of the spirit is carried over into the fruitless search of the blind eyes and of thirst, as we shall see in chapter 7. The mind of Hopkins cannot be satisfied with that detached comparison of beings which produces simile; he is constantly pushing into the identity of an alien nature with a real being, which is metaphor.[10]

Mary in our passage is not air, but is like air. In the following lines, the delicate balance of the comparison is maintained: "*as if* with air" (it is "mercy" that is more properly called, "more by name," Mary); "*like* air's fine flood"; "*like* breath." The air which lets through and diffuses light is like Mary letting through the Light, the sun without air like God without Mary—"*So* God was god of old." But finally, and with the satisfaction of an achieved goal, the comparison disappears and becomes in the conclusion identity—not "Be *like* an atmosphere to me" but "*Be* my atmosphere." The tendency toward metaphor which our passage sets up is justified when, after the prolonged and exquisitely exact comparisons built upon the acts and qualities of air and of Mary, Mary at last becomes the wild and world-mothering air who brings the Word and the Light into our universe.

The words, predications, and images of our passage now lie before us, dissected and inert. To observe their living operation in the poem, we must see in detail their relations to the other parts of the poem. There are four main parts: the introduction, which presents the two aspects of Mary's one work; the two parts of the body of the poem, which develop those two aspects; and the conclusion. Our section is the climax of the introduction, the preparation for the body, and the balance to the conclusion.

The introduction balances the mothering elements of air against the mothering elements of Mary. "Wild" stresses the notion of the natural goodness of air, like the "wildness and wet" of "Inversnaid" (*Poems*, No. 56). "World-mothering" stresses its universality. And then the imagery takes up the tender and penetrating care which air gives. The image of the flix, which is the long, fine hair on the breast of a mother beaver or rabbit and which is used in nestling the young, is a triumph of delicacy—air penetrates between the "flix" of that snowflake which has the most and the frailest fur and disturbs it not at all. The happily climactic verbs, "mixed with, riddles, and is rife" were most unhappily mispunctuated in the first appearance of this poem, in H. C. Beeching's *A Book of Christmas Verse* (New York: Dodd, Mead and Co., 1895), p. 121. There the lines appear,

>   . . . that's fairly mixed
> With riddles, and is rife . . .

—a sad destruction of a vigorous statement and a distracting riddle with no solution, which occasionally reappears, as in the *Oxford Book of Mystical Verse*.

With those verbs, Hopkins approaches the connection of air with life, which is intimate, not as a source of life, but as "This needful, never spent,/and nursing element." Life's law it is that decrees that his lungs must draw in this air, and his drawing it in as a poet to breathe it out in words is a remote preparation for the central image of God breathing out His Word through Mary.

Then follows the application of these considerations to Mary the mother, first in her divine motherhood—"Gave God's infinity,/Dwindled to infancy,/Welcome in womb"—and then in her spiritual motherhood—"But mothers each new grace/That does now reach our race." "Dwindled to infancy" is again a preparation for the image of God sending out His Word, for to be spoken in created air the Infinite had to become small, the Word had to become *"infans."*

All this prepares for our passage, the statement of Mary's role in the universe—the one human person without any stain of sin, in order to be worthily the world-mother, to assume and to raise far higher the seat which Eve had vacated, to be the mother of the Head and in another but equally real sense the mother of His members.

It is this second idea, the spiritual motherhood, that Hopkins first develops. This section has two parts. God's mercy is first conceived as an alms, and Mary as the chief dispenser of that alms. God's mercy, above all His works, which we speak of as overcoming His justice and which is climactically revealed in the Incarnation, is better called Mary, Hopkins states. No doubt he has in mind here the tender intercessory role of Mary unmixed with the role of judge, so that the profound fear which Hopkins very rationally felt toward the One he most deeply loved, as he states in the *Sermons*—"The thought of his gentleness towards children, towards the afflicted, towards sinners, is often dwelt on; that of his courage less. But for my part I like to feel that I should have feared him" (pp. 37-38)—, is here altogether absent. Mary reflects only God's mercy, nothing of His justice.

But principally here Hopkins stresses Mary's intercessory power, a power she has in common with the other saints, but in a higher and unique degree. However, he says, there is much more involved. And here he echoes the development of the introduction. Air is tender and penetrating and secretly serving, but it does more, it feeds life; so Mary dispenses God's graces, but she does more, she feeds life with her own activity.

Now, since Hopkins touches upon the deepest mysteries of the Mystical Body, he begins with an "if" clause, indicating that he is imaging his understanding of the mystery and that, in a matter so profound and so exalted, his own understanding must be presented conditionally. The image he presents is one of protecting and feeding life: as "air's fine flood"—the line is a good example of the operation of *f*'s and *l*'s throughout the poem—pours into the lungs around the heart, the seat of life, in order to lay (i.e., get rid of, as to lay a ghost) the waste matter which the blood delivers to the lungs and to render up to the blood from its own substance the food of life, so Mary surrounds the center of our spirit, where Christ lives in us, and carries off the sinful inclinations which are the wastes of the spirit and renders up her own life to feed us. And yet, as we do not become air when we feed from its substance, so we do not become Mary when we feed from her substance. We are like Christ in Mary's womb. He took flesh from her, and yet He was not Mary but Himself; so now we, in mysterious fashion, take spirit from her, and yet we are not Mary— nor are we ourselves. We are "new self and nobler me"; for the life which Mary gives us is Christ's divine life which pours through her to us, since she conceived Him at Nazareth and bore Him at Bethlehem, giving Him our human life. The Word was made flesh in her, and in her we are made the Word, "Both God's and Mary's Son." This is the core of Hopkins' vision of reality and the center of his thought and action and the power which fuses his profoundest metaphors. This living in literal unity with Christ is the subject of the next image we will consider and of Hopkins' greatest poems—the deepest source of his inspiration: "I am all at once what Christ is, since he was what I am . . ." ("That Nature is a Heraclitean Fire. . . ," *Poems*, No. 72). And as ordinary air brings words into our ears while it brings the food of life into our lungs, so this Air which is Mary brings the Word into our lungs, our hearts, and baffles that principle of the death-dance that Adam left us. In the words of "The Blessed Virgin compared to the Air we Breathe":

> Men here may draw like breath
> More Christ and baffle death. . . .

Thus Hopkins develops the portion of our image dealing with Mary's spiritual motherhood, "God's glory which would . . . from her flow off. . . ."

Mary's divine motherhood is the subject of the next part of the poem. He adapts for this section an image which he had noted for a sermon some four years previously, there to express grace coming through Mary, here to express Christ Himself coming through Mary: "St. Bernard's saying, All grace given through Mary: this is a mystery. Like blue sky, which for all its richness of colour does not stain the sunlight, though smoke and red clouds do, so God's graces come to us unchanged but all through her. Moreover she gladdens the Catholic's heaven and when she is brightest so is the sun her son: he that sees no blue sees no sun either, so with Protestants" (*Sermons*, p. 29). Here Hopkins begins the section with an exhortation to hold the hand against the blue sky and thus to observe better, by contrast, the blueness of it—an artist's trick, I am told. Yet a sky shot through with sapphire, charged with it, steeped in it, will not stain light with its blue. It allows the seven primary hues and the forty-nine or so secondary hues to come through without alteration. Or if some breath of blue does touch a snow-capped mountain peak or a white cloud, it does not obscure the beauty of earth, but enhances it. The *Journals* reveal what he has in mind precisely:

All the length of the valley the skyline of hills was flowingly written all along upon the sky. A blue bloom, a sort of meal, seemed to have spread upon the distant south, enclosed by a basin of hills.

(P. 258)

Cobalt blue was poured on the hills bounding the valley of the Clwyd and far in the south spread a bluish damp. . . .

(P. 261)

. . . long mountains of big happed-up snow-white thundercloud, glossed with silvery shadows, and a gay dazzling invisible blue light playing on them.

(P. 237)

These Welsh scenes are like the "azurous hung hills" of "Hurrahing in Harvest" (*Poems,* No. 38). In the present image, Hopkins employs a delicately rising rhythm which hovers indecisively over the long-vowelled subject and verb:

> Or if there does some soft,
> On things aloof, aloft,
> Bloom breathe. . . .

This, in combination with the expressive *l*'s and *f*'s and the suspension of thought induced by placing the prepositional phrase between the adjective and noun, "soft" and "bloom," reflects not only the visual but the tactile or kinetic effect of the phenomenon described.

Mary's function, Hopkins here suggests, is to let God's glory through without change, so that she is a medium like air, not to be looked at in itself, but to bring the light through and to diffuse it so that "every colour glows,/Each shape and shadow shows." It seems to me that Gardner, in his note and in his other discussions of this matter, thinks that it is Mary who is to be looked at and admired. Actually, Hopkins' image makes it clear that it is Christ who is to be looked at through Mary. We do not see her at all, or only a faint touch of her lovely presence, like the blue bloom of the sky on distant white. But as we need the atmosphere to diffuse the light so that we may see, so we need the secret and loving action of Mary to bring us the Inaccessible Light so that we may see, not her, but Him.

Hopkins' description of what the sun would be like to us if there were no atmosphere to diffuse the light is, like all his mature imagery, painstakingly exact in physical detail, with the vault of the sky, in a line of deliberately unpleasant open vowels, "In grimy vasty vault," described as the black vault of a huge mine, deep in the earth. In this vault the undiffused flame of the sun would burn in one blinding spot and the stars would be like sparks of reflecting crystal in the roof of the mine. A corroboration of this scene, underlining Hopkins' exact knowledge of the physics involved and the vividness of his imaginative construction, can be found in the December 20, 1954, issue of *Life,* on page 46. There, in a painting for an article on "The Starry Universe," the artist reconstructs in the light of present physical knowledge the appearance of the sun in the sky as seen from Mercury. That appearance makes at once evident how happy is Hopkins' "blear" as applied to the sun under such circumstances. In a coal-black sky the stars do not sparkle or glitter, but shoot a cold, stationary spark perfectly described by Hopkins' words as a sharp reflection from flecks of crystal. The description under the picture in *Life* will perhaps give something more of the parallel: "The wastes of Mercury shimmer beneath the baleful eye of the sun, which glares down hot and white, undimmed by atmosphere or fall of night." Such a sun in such a sky, according to Hopkins, is a good image for God as seen before the coming of Christ. Then, as the mothering air coming into that picture would not interfere with the light or alter it, but rather would make it sweeter, bring it to us "sifted to suit our sight," so Mary comes into the harsh picture of the pagan blackness and the Old Law's threatening justice—as she previously (like Milton's snow in the Nativity Ode) "mantles the *guilty* globe," as she will be asked in the conclusion to front his "froward" eye with God's mercy and love—to bring among us the true Light-made-flesh; she shares our human limbs, our nature, with the divine Sun, Whose glory without air and without Mary would blind us, as Moses feared, or at least would not win our love because of our overwhelming fear. The hand of the artist revealing the blue, with which the section opens, becomes at the close the hand of Mary revealing the glory.

This "glory," which is metaphorically the light from the sun and literally here that which is revealed to us by Mary, is again Christ

Himself, the true Light that enlightens every man coming into the world, as John tells us, the Light which is the life of men, and is made flesh and dwells among us so that we can see and share His glory, the glory of God Himself.

This is the development of the other section of our image, "God's glory which would go/Through her. . . ." This image, which is aimed at the eye, is stated first in the introduction, developed second in the body, and again stated first in the conclusion; the other image, aimed at the ear, is second in the introduction, first in the body, and second in the conclusion. And it is this last image, as we have seen, that is tied in closely with the life-giving function of Mary and of air, so that the air carrying the word (and Mary carrying the Word) enters into the lungs about the beating heart. This order of development is psychologically profound, since it is the eye that first sees and is drawn to the beauty of God's glory and draws the will, but it is the ear which brings in and attains the saving "grace and truth" of faith. The eye goes out to the Word, the ear drinks Him in. Two quotations from Isaias in the The Acts of the Apostles and in St. Paul's Letter to the Romans, together with Paul's statement of the ear's role, indicate the Scriptural accord with the poem's development:

Go to this people and say: With all your hearing you will not understand; with all your seeing you will not perceive. For the mind of this people has grown callous, and with their ears they have become dull of hearing. Their eyes they have closed, Lest perhaps they see with their eyes, and hear with their ears, and understand with their heart, And be converted, and I heal them.

(Acts, 28:26-27)

God has given them a spirit of stupor until this present day, Eyes that they may not see, and ears that they may not hear.

(Romans, 11:8)

How, then, are people to call upon him in whom they have not attained faith? And how can they attain faith in him whom they have not heard? . . . Faith, then, depends on hearing. . . .

(Romans, 10:14-17)

And the following passage from St. Paul's solemn words to the Corinthians, which plays so vital a part in *Deutschland* as the background to that "mystery" of the fifth and following stanzas and which Hopkins paraphrases in stanza 26, is profoundly operative also here. The "mystery" is the revelation of the Word (the wisdom of

God) in Christ, and here Paul speaks of this shining forth of the "depths of God" in terms of the glory which God wishes to give us, the glory which streams forth from the crucified Light:

The wisdom we speak is of God, mysterious, hidden, which God foreordained to our glory before the world's beginning, a wisdom which none of this world's rulers knew, because if they had known it, they would never have crucified the Lord to whom belongs all glory. It is the wisdom which, in the words of Scripture, proposes "what no eye has ever seen, what no ear has ever heard, what no human heart has ever thought of, namely, the great blessings God holds ready for those who love Him."

(I Corinthian, 2:7-9)

It is the same wisdom of God, the Word from Whom the Father's glory shines out to our eyes and ears, that Hopkins in his concluding section calls upon Mary to present to his "froward eye" (froward in the sense indicated in the quotations from Acts and Romans above) and to bring into his rebellious ears. There God's love, revealed in the Incarnation, calls forth from him that patience with his own rebelliousness, that penance for his treachery, and that prayer which will bring him home at last. In this section which balances all the tender, mothering elements of the introduction, Hopkins calls upon Mary to shepherd her Son's wandering sheep in the fold of her loving arms, as she once folded the Shepherd.

The rhythms of the poem are quiet ones, the sounds are smooth and subdued, becoming relatively harsh and vigorous only in the second section of the body of the poem, where the world without air is described. The tension between matter and manner is delicate but firmly and perfectly controlled, as the subject demands. There are no striking subtleties of rhythmic expression, since none are called for—though there are appropriate and expressive subtleties, as in the "air's fine flood" and the "soft bloom" passages. But it is, I trust, obvious that this is no didactic poem, in which the rhythms and sounds serve merely to ornament the matter. It is a true poem, in which all the elements combine to make one ultimate whole.

Our passage most deeply indicates, then, that Mary is a real woman who gives real life and that she is greater than any goddess could be judged or dreamed to be because she is the channel of real divine life. She is the instrument of the Holy Ghost in bringing Christ forth in the world and also His instrument in bringing Christ forth in our beating hearts, fronting our eyes with glory of God molded into a human nature like our own, flowing into our ears and spirits with the living and life-giving Word. This divine life, this union with the Word, is the central desire and concern of Hopkins' life, the motive force behind his being a Jesuit and his being a poet, the inspiration of his finest imagery. The human heart of Christ, the vital principle of His own life and of the life of all the members of the Mystical Body, the center of Hopkins' interest, the core of the splendid masterpiece with which the next chapter deals, derives from Mary and through her is united in life-giving unity with our human hearts, as Hopkins' translation of Father Condren's prayer (*Poems*, No. 132) beautifully expresses:

> Jesu that dost in Mary dwell,
> Be in thy servants' hearts as well. . . .

Chapter 4

The Vital Candle

I caught this morning morning's minion, king-
  dom of daylight's dauphin, dapple-dawn-drawn Falcon, in
    his riding
Of the rolling level underneath him steady air, and striding
High there, how he rung upon the rein of a wimpling wing
In his ecstasy! then off, off forth on swing,
  As a skate's heel sweeps smooth on a bow-bend: the hurl
    and gliding
  Rebuffed the big wind. My heart in hiding
Stirred for a bird,—the achieve of, the mastery of the thing!

Brute beauty and valour and act, oh, air, pride, plume, here
  Buckle! AND *the fire that breaks from thee then, a billion*
Times told lovelier, more dangerous, O my chevalier!

  No wonder of it: shéer plód makes plough down sillion
Shine, and blue-bleak embers, ah my dear,
  Fall, gall themselves, and gash gold-vermilion.
        "The Windhover: To Christ our Lord," *Poems*, No. 36

Where, then, death, is thy victory...?
                                I Corinthians, 15:55

Yours is to be the same mind which Christ Jesus shewed. His nature is, from the first, divine, and yet he did not see, in the rank of Godhead, a prize to be coveted; he dispossessed himself, and took the nature of a slave, fashioned in the likeness of men, and presenting himself to us in human form; and then he lowered his own dignity, accepted an obedience which brought him to death, death on a cross.
                                Philippians, 2:5-8

The Spirit himself thus assures our spirit, that we are children of God; and if we are his children, then we are his heirs too; heirs of God, sharing the inheritance of Christ; only we must share his sufferings, if we are to share his glory.

Romans, 8:16-17

THE VITAL CANDLE

> My heart in hiding
> Stirred for a bird,—the achieve of, the mastery of the thing!
>
> "The Windhover: to Christ our Lord," *Poems*, No. 36

The lungs, the ancient Greeks and others thought, drew into the body that world-pneuma which is (or which dwells in) the air and which vitalizes the blood, the seat of life. Inside the body, however, the seat of the vital principle was quite logically held to be the heart. From the heart the vitalized red blood poured out or at least was somehow there contained. The heart supplied the flame by which the body maintained its heat—to this notion Hopkins adverts in his bracketed insertion into Parmenides' discussion of the element *fire* as an "ethery flame of fire, comforting the heart [he is thinking of it perhaps as a vital principle]" (*Journals*, p. 130). For Aristotle and others the heart was the seat of the intelligence, the witness within us not only to life but to truth—as indeed our modern lie-detector still assumes.

Hopkins' attitude toward the heart is so pervasively expressed in his mature imagery that without a good grasp of it much of that imagery will remain obscure. On the other hand, an understanding of Hopkins' thought and feeling toward this central human organ will be the key, not only to the image with which this chapter especially deals, but also to important images in almost every one of Hopkins' major poems. For this reason I wish to be perhaps more thorough than our immediate image requires in my researches into the "heart" of Hopkins' imagery, though the present image, I think, exercises the fullest potential of the real heart as vital principle and of the symbolic heart as vital principle of both the human spiritual activity and the divine life which the Christian shares with Christ.

Hopkins was fully aware of all that the science of his time could tell him about the activity of the heart. We have seen in the previous chapter that he knew that the lungs bring in the fine flood of air about the beating heart, so that the heart can bring to the air-filled lungs the waste matter to be carried away and then dispense through the body the vivifying spirit (the word is exact) brought in by the air. The heart and the lungs are the source of the power of the parts of the mature body, as "Morning Midday and Evening Sacrifice" (*Poems*, No. 48) states:

> Head, heart, hand, heel, and shoulder
> That beat and breathe in power—

and the beat of the heart above all is the vital principle, beginning in the foetus before the act of the lungs, going on without cessation to the end of life. The physical act of the heart, shifting the blood about its chambers, pumping it out with vigor even in an aged body, is the source of Hopkins' exact and powerful characterization of the heart as "Never-eldering revel and river of youth" (*Deutschland*, stanza 18).

The heart is the source of the body's heat, in so far as it pumps the fuel for the body's fire to the cells. Hence the old notion which placed the flame within the heart was not wholly without physical foundation. Hopkins quotes Parmenides as saying "that the corpse which can no longer feel heat, because the fire has left it, feels cold" (*Journals*, p. 130). The fire has left the beating heart, the seat of the vital principle.

In one of his great poems, Hopkins builds his central image on the idea that the flame of life is situated in the heart. In "The Candle Indoors" (*Poems,* No. 50), there are two types of candles and two indoor places involved, one the real candle in someone's house and the other Hopkins' own fire of life, the vital candle set up in his heart, lighted by Christ, the Christian light of Matthew, 5:15, to give light and life in *his* indoors, his heart, and to shine out in a dark world:

> Come you indoors, come home; your fading fire
> Mend first and vital candle in close heart's vault. . . .

In his heart is the fire that he is able to keep aflame and that he is obliged to keep high, though he lets it fade while wondering and worrying about the inner flame of whoever is using that candle whose shining silken ("tram") beams bend to enter his eye. And thus, in danger of judging his neighbor while neglecting his own service of God, he is in danger of becoming the beam-blind (Matthew, 7:3 ff.) hypocrite and cast-out salt (Matthew, 5:13) in Christ's discourse.

This vital flame is the spiritual fire which Christ came to cast on the earth, then, as well as the physical fire of bodily process. It is the flame that results when the heart of the Christian joins with the heart of Christ:

> I whirled out wings that spell
> And fled with a fling of the heart to the
>   heart of the Host.
> My heart, but you were dovewinged, I can tell,
>   Carrier-witted, I am bold to boast,
> To flash from the flame to the flame then. . . .
>   (*Deutschland*, stanza 3)

The fire that breaks from his heart *then*—when the two hearts are united—will be the "heart's light" that bursts from the nun in stanzas 29 and 30, the divine fire of the Word Himself, as stanzas 34 and 35 establish. This vital flame of "The Candle Indoors" is Hopkins' small version of the same flame that is a "blown beacon of light" from the "heart right" of the nun in stanza 29 of the *Deutschland,* of the "beacon, an eternal beam" that flames from the risen body of Christ over the poet's "foundering deck" in "That Nature is a Heraclitean Fire and of the comfort of the Resurrection" (*Poems*, No. 72)—the fire that shines before men as witness to the fire of eternal life that Christ cast upon the earth.

For Hopkins the heart is the symbol of the intelligence and the physical seat for the feelings and love of man, as he states in his sermon on the Sacred Heart: ". . . not the great bloodvessel only but the thoughts of the mind that vessel seems to harbour and the feelings of the soul to which it beats. For the heart is of all the members of the body the one which most strongly and most of its own accord sympathises with and expresses in itself what goes on within the soul. Tears are sometimes forced, smiles may be put on, but the beating of the heart is the truth of nature" (*Sermons*, p. 103). The heart, closer to our nature than the mind (so to speak), guesses at truth that the mind does not grasp and reveals in its intuitive grasp of reality what the mind cannot know. It is the heart, in stanza 7 of *Deutschland,* which "is out with" the great mystery of faith, the presence of God in the universe as part of it, effected by the Incarnation, so that the heart itself may share the divine flame. It is the *a capella* heart, in stanza 18, which by a gleeful, madrigal start reveals the presence of Christ in the storm, a fact available only to faith and thus, for Hopkins, to the heart aiming beyond the limits of mind or brain. The mind must follow the lead of the heart, which knows and reveals the deeper truth. This stanza, in which Hopkins addresses his heart, is worth looking at in some detail:

> Ah, touched in your bower of bone
> Are you! turned for an exquisite smart,
> Have you! make words break from me here all alone,
> Do you!—mother of being in me, heart.
> O unteachably after evil, but uttering truth,
> Why, tears! is it? tears; such a melting, a madrigal start!
> Never-eldering revel and river of youth,
> What can it be, this glee? the good you have there of your own?

The heart, alone (hiding?) and "bowered" in the poet's chest, exercises the authority of its position when, reacting to the terrible situation and to the voice of the nun, turning (stirring) under the finger of God, it makes words break from the poet. It can be authoritative, since not only is it at home in its bower, but it is the mother of the speaker's being. This is the high title of the heart and the source of its superiority over the other parts of the body. It is not merely a Scotistic emphasis on the superiority of the will, ordinarily symbolized by the heart, which explains the heart's position in Hopkins' imagery, but the physical fact that the heart is more than other organs the cornerstone of life and power. The dignity of the heart is illustrated by Hopkins in his sermon on the Sacred Heart by the observation that no matter what illness people have, they prefer, if it is at all possible, to call it heart trouble (*Sermons*, p. 102), so honorable, so interesting is the heart.

The stanza further indicates that the poor heart bears the stigma of Adam's blackguardly rebellion; it is "unteachably after evil." But in spite of the blight of original sin and the consequent concupiscence, the tendency of the will to spiritual non-being, the heart utters truth. Again and again in his poetry Hopkins turns to the revelatory function of the heart. He cannot lie to the truth-knowing heart—

> I'll not play hypocrite
> To own my heart....[1]
>
> ("Peace," *Poems*, No. 46)

The heart of even a young child has heard, from the depths of her nature, of the blight of spiritual death (with its physical echo in the body and in nature in the world) which Adam cast upon her:

> Nor mouth had, no nor mind, expressed
> What heart heard of, ghost guessed....
>
> ("Spring and Fall," *Poems*, No. 55)

The heart delivers the oracle in "Spelt from Sibyl's Leaves" (*Poems*, No. 62), interpreting the message written in the leaves against the sky—"Heart, you round me right with...." The heart goes after the ideal, even at the expense of disregarding the probabilities which follow upon the frail, even foul, natures (since they are human beings, sons of Adam) of soldiers:

> Here it is: the heart,
> Since, proud, it calls the calling manly, gives a guess
> That, hopes that, makesbelieve, the men must be no less;

> It fancies, feigns, deems, dears the artist after his art;
> And fain will find as sterling all as all is smart,
> And scarlet wear the spirit of wár thére express.
>
> ("The Soldier," *Poems*, No. 63)

Our proud hearts do this, too, expressing our honoring of the ideal in monuments like the Tomb of the Unknown Soldier. Hopkins goes on in this poem to state that the heart, while probably wrong in applying the ideal to any given redcoat or tar, is completely right in applying it to the Soldier-Sailor Christ, Who in turn is the only One Who can truly perceive when some given man is repeating in himself that ideal which Christ fulfilled in His life. Again, it is the heart which, in "Carrion Comfort" (*Poems*, No. 64), having become weak from wrestling, laps strength like a weakened soldier (or athlete, perhaps) at a brook or fountain, steals joy, and looks for someone to cheer—and it is deeply significant that the heart does not know whether to cheer Christ or the Christian wretch who had been, in the terrible darkness, wrestling with Christ. This struggle against the union which is so intimate that the heart cannot decide whether to cheer one or both will be treated at more length in a later chapter. Here it is enough to note that it is the heart which carries on the great spiritual struggle and which interprets it when the night is past. It is the heart which must see the horrors and go the terrible ways of this spiritual night:

> ... what sights you, heart, saw; ways you went!
> And more must, in yet longer light's delay.
>
> (*Poems*, No. 69)

Besides knowing truth, the heart has another and even more important spiritual function. It not only knows and reveals the hidden truth, but it desires and loves the good. In his early "The Habit of Perfection" (No. 24), Hopkins was concerned with avoiding mortal good in the interests of immortal spiritual good; he repeats the idea with a more mature grasp on the problem in "To what serves Mortal Beauty" (No. 61), in which his heart is urged to look at heaven's good mortal gifts, to acknowledge the bounty of heaven in mortal beauty, but not to leave home to embrace them:

> What do then? how meet beauty? Merely meet it; own,
> Home at heart, heaven's sweet gift; then leave, let that alone.

The heart, made for immortal beauty and good, is here warned against attaching itself to passing good. When faced with that immortal good, however, as it commonly is in these poems, the heart is not restrained. It breaks out with wings, the mounting spirit doing what it can to go from its dull cage to the eternal good. When the swooning heart of the poet in its terror turns to the heart of Christ in stanza 3 of *Deutschland*, the dove-wings of the psalmist (and of the Holy Spirit) bear it up:

> My heart, but you were dovewinged. . . .

In "Hurrahing in Harvest" (No. 38), when his searching eyes and heart find the response of Christ in His creatures,

> The heart rears wings bold and bolder
> And hurls for him, O half hurls earth for him off under his feet.

In "The Lantern out of Doors" (No. 34), it is Christ's heart that wants His friend, wandering in the darkness. In "Brothers" (No. 54), young John has "no work to hold/His heart up at the strain" which his part demands of him, but his poor brother, who so fears for him, is "heart-forsook" at the crisis. He so desires his brother's success and good, so fears his failure, that his heart sends its flame into his "tear-tricked cheeks," and reveals in passing that blackguardly nature, "bad, base, and blind," yet has good in it, can be unselfishly kind. Hopkins' own heart, his creating thought, in an exquisite and tender image of No. 68, is a bridegroom (or a would-be bridegroom) seeking to be united to the honor of his beloved England in unselfish love, desiring to breed in her wise words:

> England, whose honour O all my heart woos, wife
> To my creating thought, would neither hear
> Me, were I pleading, plead nor do I. . . .

The heart in Hopkins, then, knows and reveals the truth, and loves and seeks the good. It is the principle of life and life-giving, of knowledge, of love—and further, of act.

The heart must keep on pumping if we are to live on the physical level; it must be a *"never-eldering* revel and river of youth." It must also keep on acting on the moral and spiritual level if we are to keep alive spiritually—act with the magnificent courageous "heart-throe" of the nun in *Deutschland,* burn with the fire which is Christ our Lord, "our heart's charity's hearth's fire," or grind on with the pitiful and painful patience of No. 70, where

> We hear our hearts grate on themselves: it kills
> To bruise them dearer. . . .

But act it must, or untwist its strands of man and die in the spiritual death of despair.

This notion of the heart—sluggish to act in the spiritual order because of its inheritance from Adam and its own slackness, yet stirred up both by the beauty of Christ outside and the flame of His Spirit inside—is so vital to our image that I want to consider in detail Hopkins' development of it in a sermon on the coming of the Paraclete (*Sermons,* pp. 68-75). He states that even if there were no sin, the heart of man might need to be *stirred* to activity: "For if there were no sin in the world and yet man as dull in mind and heart as he is now/a Paraclete might well be needed still to stir him up and set him on, to shew him what justice was and how great its beauty, before man would rouse himself to pursue it" (pp. 71-72). A paraclete is one who stirs up, as a spur to a horse, a trumpet to a soldier (as the resurrection is a "heart's clarion" to the overwhelmed heart of No. 72): "A Paraclete is one who comforts, who cheers, who encourages, who persuades, who exhorts, who stirs up, who urges forward, who calls on; what the spur and word of command is to a horse, what clapping of hands is to a speaker, what a trumpet is to the soldier, that a Paraclete is to the soul: *one who calls us on,* that is what it means, a Paraclete is one who calls us on to good"[2] (p. 70). Christ the Soldier and Leader is a Paraclete, crying to the fearful and hiding heart: "If this is to be a Paraclete, one who cries to the heart/ Come on, no wonder Christ is a Paraclete. . . . And did he not cry men on? . . . but best of all by deeds, by his own example: he led the way, went before his troops, was himself the vanguard, was the forlorn hope, bore the brunt of battle alone, died upon the field, on Calvary hill, and bought the victory by his blood" (p. 70). This glorious victory, with "the reins of power on all things drawn into the hand of the crucified victim," is not enough for sluggish hearts, so that Christ sent another Paraclete, His Spirit, who brought the flame of Christ's life and power into the hearts of the Apostles: "First he cheered *them,* but he cheered them on not like Christ by his example from without but by his presence, his power, his breath and fire and inspiration from within not by drawing but by driving; not by shewing them what to do but by himself within them doing it. His mighty breath ran with roaring in their ears, his fire flamed in tongues upon their foreheads, and their hearts and lips were filled with himself, with the Holy Ghost" (pp. 74-75). Here Hopkins expresses himself in imagery familiar to every Jesuit from the *Spiritual Exercises,* based in part on St. Paul's military imagery—Christ the ideal Knight and Leader, masterful, winning all power for Himself and divine life for His followers through the labor and death which He battled and, through complete self-sacrifice, overcame for them; and the sluggish knights, His followers, who will share His glory if they will bestir themselves, who will flame out with His Spirit if they will follow him loyally through labor and suffering. So did the nun in *Deutschland,* so that the triumph of the King was effected in her; so Hopkins prays that the splendid boy of "The Handsome Heart" (*Poems,* No. 51), whose heart knows its true home as a homing pigeon's nature knows, may run and battle to the end of the race and the struggle (note the Pauline images); so the young soldier of "The Bugler's First Communion" (No. 47) will face the "hell-rook ranks," his heart, Christ's darling (the synonym of "minion" in its knightly use), dauntless in the struggle—the knightly imagery continues in Hopkins' armored pleas at the end of the poem, brandling or shaking the adamantine gates of heaven with ride and jar; so does the Jesuit Alphonsus (No. 73), who embodies the Jesuit military ideal in "the war within," whose heroism of armored heart with its beauty and valor and act, with its knightly air and pride and plume hidden except to the eyes of God, follows his King in labor and suffering to the end. These could truly say of Christ that He is

> Pride, rose, prince, hero of us, high-priest,
> Our hearts' charity's hearth's fire, our thoughts'
>   chivalry's throng's Lord.
>
> (*Deutschland,* stanza 35)

In this large context of Hopkins' attitude toward the heart, then, the hiding and unstirring heart of our image offers extensive possibilities of meaning. It is Hopkins' heart which is in question, since the poem is clearly a personal expression and not a dramatization of someone else's insight. And his heart is in hiding. He does not say that his heart is hidden, which might apply to the heart as a mere physical organ inside the chest, but he applies to it the active gerund which expresses the state of deliberate concealment. Hence his heart here is metaphorically treated and is something or someone other than itself—something or someone who will hide and will also stir. "Stir" is an interesting verb. "To stir the ground" is to plow, a meaning unfamiliar to me, but listed in the *OED.* "To stir the fire, or the embers" is an ordinary use. "To stir from sleep, or from hiding" suggests the rousing to action, the being inflamed. "To stir in admiration" suggests a slight movement, a physical accompaniment to the spiritual approval and joy. This last seems the meaning most immediately appropriate to the situation, in which the heart, moved by the mastery and achievement of the bird in controlling the big wind, stirs in admiration.

Since the heart is in hiding, however, it is also possible for it to stir to action. The bird which it admires has done so, drawn up from its own inaction, perhaps its nightly "hiding," by the dapple of the dawn to exercise its magnificent beauty and valor and act, to show to eyes and hearts which could catch sight of it its princely air and pride and plume. The bird is magnificent because it is not in hiding, but in act. The bird is a valorous and dangerous (in the knightly sense of masterful) chevalier and minion and dauphin because it has buckled on all its powers of acting and buckled with its enormous opponent, and with complete success and incredible control. It has acted out its nature.

Hopkins' heart is *his* nature. We have seen that in his eyes the heart is the central and highest organ of the human body and that thus it knows and expresses the deepest movements of the human nature of which it is part. Its acting, Hopkins said in his sermon on the Sacred Heart, is the truth of nature. And hence when Hopkins' heart goes into hiding, it is his nature hiding, and when his heart stirs in admiration, it is his nature stirring at the sight of its own good, at the picture of what it itself should be. When his heart breaks out with a madrigal and gleeful start in *Deutschland,* Hopkins asks it whether it perceives in the nun's act some good of its own (stanza 18). And the answer is that it does see there what it itself could be and should be. The nun's heart acts out fully her own nature and more, the life of faith, the life of Christ within her. The flame that breaks out from her, new-born to the world, is the activity of Christ informing and lifting up her own activity to the divine level. This is the good that Hopkins' heart perceives and that gives it a madrigal start. In our present image his heart stirs in admiration for a lower beauty, not the life of Christ or a mere human life and activity, but a mere brute life and activity. It is a magnificent natural beauty and good, however, and has this advantage over Hopkins' nature—on its lower level it is exercising its full powers to their utmost extent, while Hopkins' nature is in hiding, avoiding the activity for which he was made.

Since Hopkins' heart is here contrasted to the bird and since it stirs in admiration for the bird, evidently motivated by an impulse to emulate it, one might expect that he is treating his heart as a bird, as he does in *Deutschland* and "Hurrahing in Harvest," as he treats the heart of the boy in "The Handsome Heart." Those wings, by the way, which appear on Hopkins' heart from time to time, while unmistakably Scriptural, may have other roots in the pre-Raphaelite atmosphere in which he grew up. This was suggested to me by the reproduction of a casual drawing by Sir Edward Burne-Jones.[3] It represents "The Anatomy of a Good Man" and shows a naked man with upraised left arm, his heart exposed and with powerful wings, flames breaking out in all directions. I have been unable to trace the background for this conception in Burne-Jones' mind, though perhaps Scriptural references and possibly the Catholic representations of the flaming Heart of Christ may have had their influence. But at any rate the drawing is evidence that the winged heart, aspiring to good, is not a conception peculiar to Hopkins.

However, Hopkins' bird is presented not merely as a bird, but as a knight. And what Hopkins' heart admires is the knightly accomplishment of the bird. Hence it appears more likely that Hopkins is considering his heart as a knight in hiding, admiring the achievement of another knight. This likelihood becomes certainty when "my heart in hiding," while being exhorted to come out of hiding and stir into flaming action like the bird's, is addressed as "my chevalier."

My reading, as is evident to anyone who has read some or all of the enormous and ever-swelling critical literature on this poem (a poem which deserves an enormous critical literature), is allied to those readings which hold that in the sestet Hopkins is addressing his own heart. There are, in the main, three positions on our special image (and hence on the poem as a whole) which have been advanced by competent critics. One group holds that Hopkins is merely expressing an admiration for the beauty of natural act and that the "heart in hiding" simply means that his heart is not visible. This group I shall discuss as the *simpliste* critics. Another group holds that Hopkins is hiding from natural act and, while he desires to share the freedom and beauty of the bird, is also desirous of crushing nature in self-sacrifice, labor, and pain—a supposed Christian abnegation. This group I shall discuss as the "pagan" critics, since that view of Christian abnegation seems to me a non-Christian one. And the third group, with which I ally myself, holds that Hopkins is hiding from the natural and supernatural act which he could exercise in sharing labor and pain with Christ. This group I shall designate as the Christian critics.

The principal *simpliste* critics are Jesuits Lahey and Peters, Geoffrey Grigson, Denis Donoghue, and definitely non-Jesuit James Reeves. Father Lahey, in his pioneer biography and critique,[4] states that the poem says that *act* reveals the loveliness of any being, whereas mere potency hides that beauty. Our own special image is merely one of the "added superficial embellishments" which cling to the main statement of the bird as more lovely after its qualities and act are buckled on and it breaks into act, even as a plow and embers are more beautiful when they act.

Father Peters adds a bit to this, taking the "superficial embellishments" somewhat more seriously. His interchange of homophones—"But *rein* is a homophone of *reign*, and this recalls once again that the hawk is a dauphin, is a prince" (!)—seems to me only to confuse the issue, but he makes it fairly clear that he is interpreting the poem as a revelation of the beauty of act and is "very impatient" with critics who "have overlooked what must appear to be the meaning intended by Hopkins himself. . . ."[5]

An admirer of Peters, Geoffrey Grigson, in dealing with the "heart in hiding," suggests that instead of the "hiding *in* the cloister" interpretation of several critics, we should rather perceive that Hopkins once hid from his vocation: "His heart for a while, in fact, was in hiding *from* his vocation, from his proper being, his God, as in a later fragment: 'Once I turned from thee and hid. . . .' "[6] If Grigson seriously held this attitude—that Hopkins' heart is here conceived to be in hiding from the knightly "flame of exploit" which characterizes the windhover and the heart of Christ our Lord—he would belong in my "Christian" category. But he appears to suggest the interpretation merely as a refutation of the "hiding in the cloister" view.

Denis Donoghue, admirer of Winters and Empson, concludes that the real point of the poem, expressed in the first tercet, is that the poet desires a direction of the falcon's thoughtless activity to some definite goal or purpose, presumably the attack upon some prey. In the octet the bird has been flying aimlessly about, and the poet, concerned about the *use* of these undirected powers, addresses the qualities of the bird and, in the imperative, "buckle," he directs them "to join together for purposeful action." Thus used purposefully, they will make a flame more beautiful than the flames the purposeful use of the plow and the use (such as it is) of the embers produce.[7]

Mr. James Reeves gives a "rough paraphrase": ". . . my heart, unseen, responded to his achievement and mastery. At this point (where the falcon turns) your animal beauty, your valour, and your action (Hopkins is now apostrophising both the falcon and Christ) seemed to bend or buckle, O air and pride and plume! and the fiery red dawnlight which then is reflected from you, O my prince, is a billion times lovelier than ever! And no wonder, for the mere plodding of a plough-horse makes a ploughshare gleam as it cuts the furrow; and the cold grey-blue embers of a dying fire, O beloved one, as they fall, split open and reveal a gash of red-hot gold."[8] This interpretation extends to Christ, as symbolized by the bird, and gives some rationale for the "O beloved one" address in the course of the ember image, which Lahey and Peters failed to do. But like them, Reeves stresses merely the beauty of act and gives no hint about why *these* images rather than any others are used. In Hopkins' terms, these *simpliste* critics do well with the over-thought of the sonnet, but fail to touch the under-thought.

As the principal "pagan" critics of the poem, I include Richards, Empson, Phare, Read, Sargent, Leavis, Pick, Kelly, Gardner, Hartman, Heuser, Downes, and Miller. Some of them fit the category only with a little pressure, but I shall state my reasons for placing them in it in each case. Ivor Armstrong Richards set the tone for this whole development in his early *Dial* article,[9] when he asked a number of intelligent questions in dealing with the poem—the poem, he confesses, became "perfectly clear and explicit" only after many readings and several days of reflection. Like the German scientist who reputedly retired to his study to excogitate the true nature of some beast that he had never seen, Richards answered his intelligent questions with the information he found in his own mind, wiping his glosses with what he knew; and since there existed in his mind an almost awesome ignorance of Catholic tradition, of the Jesuit ideal, of the significance of the Incarnation, and of other essentially relevant matters, his answers were considerably less satisfactory than his questions. At any rate, his several days of reflection revealed that Hopkins' heart was in hiding from the freedom of true natural activity, the excitement of fulfilling his nature, since his religious vocation required him to be unlike the bird and like the plow and embers. The misconception of the religious life (as a suppression of nature rather than a fulfillment of nature) which lies behind this reading of the poem is unhappily common enough to have misled others down the same path.

William Empson[10] followed in Richards' steps, clearly aligning the final images of the poems with his impressions of the desolation sonnets of Hopkins' later years as well as with his own conception of Christian self-sacrifice. "*My heart in hiding* would seem to imply that the *more dangerous* life is that of the Windhover, but the last three lines insist it is *no wonder* that the life of renunciation should be the more lovely." This life of renunciation, the life of the Jesuit, is not one of act but of lack of act, of refusal to act. The supposition is that one refuses to act naturally in order to act either supernaturally or according to some concept of what religious act ought to be.

Elsie Elizabeth Phare,[11] like Richards and Empson, thinks that "buckle" means that all those elements buckle or collapse under the bird's dominant impulse. In the sestet, Christ is speaking, either to the poet or to the bird, of the beauty of natural act. Then the poet sorrowfully and resignedly agrees with Christ that the maxim of act giving out beauty is true of plows and embers too. He reproaches Christ with "Ah, my dear," since Christ leaves him in anguish like the embers. However, Miss Phare then rejects her own reading in favor of those of Richards and Empson. In regard to "buckle," by the way, Empson thinks that it means *both* to put on, as a military belt for heroic action, and to crumple, as a bicycle wheel, incapable of natural motion.[12] Hopkins wants both act and non-act and expresses both wants in ambiguous terms. He does it quite crudely, Empson judges.

Herbert Read was taken to task by Miss Phare for his reading.[13] Gardner discusses Read's criticism (*1*, 236-37) and indicates that Read modified his earlier views. In those, however, he found the poem merely a catalog of sensuous delights, and, as Gardner points out, ". . . actually suggests that the dedication 'To Christ our Lord' is a patent deception, added by the poet as a sop to his conscience" (*1*, 237).

Daniel Sargent's generally good essay[14] supposes, too, that Hopkins wants to be like the bird, but chooses to reject that course in order to follow Christ in labor and pain. F. R. Leavis[15] quotes Empson with approval, and thinks that the poem ". . . expresses not religious exaltation, but inner debate." Pick thinks that when the windhover's "flight is crumpled, when 'brute beauty and valour and act, oh, air, pride, plume' in an act of self-sacrifice, of self-destruction, of mystical self-immolation send off a fire far greater than any natural beauty," then the true beauty is revealed (*Pick*, p. 71). Kelly glances briefly at the image of the heart in hiding: "It is perhaps not fanciful to see some signification in the phrase 'my heart in hiding stirred for a bird.' If a bird can display such beauty and power, can excite such admiration by its achievement, what may we not expect from Christ?"[16] When the beauty of Christ buckles or collapses, then His true loveliness shines forth—not through the use of His natural powers, but through their sacrifice. Kelly's argumentation really deals, it seems to me, with Christ the Victim, not at all with the triumphant "caballero" implied in the Kingdom Meditation. As I see the matter, Kelly does not sufficiently stress the influence of the knightly context on the phrase "heart in hiding," on the meaning of the word "buckle," on the heart-fire relationship, and on the contrast (as in the "Alphonsus" sonnet) of inner glorious "flame of exploit" with outward drudgery and bleakness.

Gardner's very rich and rewarding discussion of the poem (*1*, 180-84) is also, to my mind, fatally flawed by his misconception of sacrifice: "For Hopkins, then, the example of Christ's life linked together three relevant and complementary meanings of 'buckle!'—buckle within (discipline), buckle to (labour), buckle under (sacrifice)" (p. 182). He too, like those above, supposes that in sacrifice Hopkins would turn from freedom to act—"Hopkins himself, when free to act, was the curvetting and caracoling knight-errant of poetry" (p. 183)—to non-freedom to act, and this he supposes to be sacrifice. In this he shares the concept of the others listed as pagan critics of the poem. And like so many of the others, he is, it seems to me, drawing his interpretation not only from the text of the poem, but from what other critics have said about it, as if their remarks were more an extension of the text than an investigation into the text. I do not believe that the text itself would lead him to think that "buckle" "strongly suggests the voluntary self-crippling of the Crucifixion."[17] This unchristian notion of Christ's crippling Himself (Gardner goes on to speak of "divine masochism"!) is not Hopkins' thought. Gardner should have noted that the verbs in the quotation he gives from Hopkins' sermon are passive verbs; he should have recalled the words of stanza 22 in the *Deutschland*, "Mark, the mark is of man's make"; he should have remembered what Hopkins said to Dixon: ". . . he would have wished to succeed by success . . ." (*Letters* 2, p. 137). The notion of Christian sacrifice as based on a deliberate and voluntary attack on being and on act is the reason for my term "pagan" for these critics of "The Windhover."

Geoffrey H. Hartman[18] thinks that "buckle" is an optative addressed to the bird and means more than " 'buckle on meeting this heart which, thinking of the ascetic Christ, must refuse its admiration';

it suggests, 'Let yourself like Christ militant for sacrifice be destroyed in submitting to a storm center greater than the power of beauty, valor, or act, and let this example grapple with, become a buckler for, dent my heart.'" That appears to me a meaningless thing to say to a bird, yet all those who suppose that "buckle" can in any sense mean "crumple" are required by the logic of their position, as I see it, to take the crumpled and destroyed bird as a symbol of Christian sacrifice. If the bird let itself be destroyed, as Hartman wants it to, it would be a stupid bird. It could not be a symbol of Christian sacrifice. Hartman goes on to indicate clearly what he thinks Christian sacrifice is:

Thus the flame breaking from windhover or the Christ-assaulted heart indicates self-destruction in the maximum of stress. But why should the AND be in capitals and the resulting flame be described as a billion times lovelier (aesthetically seductive) and more dangerous (morally seductive) than the windhover's previous proud image? The AND expresses the poet's surprise that the splendor of self-destruction should surpass the splendor of equilibrium: the image of the flaming windhover or of the crucified Christ becomes a greater spiritual temptation than could ever have been exerted by the former image of elegant equilibrium.

"Self-destruction" is not sacrifice. It is suicide, and a profoundly unchristian act. That Hartman really means what he says is indicated in his later statement that "'gash' is a transitive verb made intransitive as if to suggest that the coal's wound like that of Christ is self-inflicted."[19] Christ's wound is not self-inflicted. "Mark, the mark is of man's make," Hopkins points out in stanza 22 of *Deutschland*. Christ accepts His wounds from us, not because He loves the wounds, but because He loves us.

Alan Heuser supposes that "The poet's 'heart is hiding' is hid in the holy wounds. . . ." *Then* Christ acts in the heart and "his fire of sacrifice draws wounds that break out in shining soil or gashed coals on the field or hearth of the heart."[20] I do not perceive in Christian tradition or in Hopkins' thought any such opposed distinction between a Christian hiding in Christ's wounds (as in the Ignatian "Anima Christi") and a Christian battling in spiritual warfare. Placing these two notions in opposition to one another seems to me misleading. On the basis, then, of Heuser's apparent supposition that sacrifice is somehow intrinsically destructive, I list him among my "pagan" critics.

David A. Downes will fit here more readily, since he baldly states that "The poem is much more a statement of the value of sacrifice enhanced by what Hopkins' [sic] called 'corrective' grace, the grace of renunciation."[21] When he calls upon beauty to buckle, "The poet wills abnegation of 'mortal beauty.' "[22] The heart then is moved not to act, but to a negation of act. Downes, like Heuser, has wiped his glosses with concepts similar to those used by Richards.

J. Hillis Miller fits in my "pagan" category in a rather special way. As he sees the poem, the poet wants to sacrifice his own being so that it may be "transubstantiated" into Christ's being. The contemplating heart catches the inscape of the bird and then "the self leaps outside of itself and creates a new self by means of a substantial identification with all of perceived nature."[23] Buckling here is the "dive of sacrifice" by which man ceases to be himself. "Only by ceasing to be oneself and becoming Christ can a man avoid an existence which is a continual dizzy falling away in time...."[24] This is not Hopkins' thought. Becoming a "new self and nobler me" does not mean ceasing to be the old self, as Miller himself inconsistently states later: "But even when transubstantiated into Christ a man still remains himself."[25] Miller does a good job in stressing Hopkins' grasp of the incomprehensible "distance" between the being of Being and the being of a creature, the "billion times told" of "The Windhover," but he fails to grasp Hopkins' thought on the open and ascertainable continuity (not "secret," as Miller says) between the Old Man and the New Self, the continuity and the unity profoundly emphasized in the doctrine involved in the devotion to the Sacred Heart. When this union is achieved, when man says "yes" and goes "with a fling of the heart to the heart" of Christ, *then* he can share in divine perceptions and meetings and greetings. The human heart aflame with Christ's divine flame is not less itself than it was, but more. In becoming Him, it in no way "ceases to be itself."

Moreover, Christian sacrifice is essentially a matter of the will, a self-giving. If there were no sin, there would be, in the Catholic view, no labor, suffering, or death, but there would be sacrifice. The positive self-donation which is perfect in the Trinity, in which Each of the Persons gives Himself fully to the Others, is the basis and prototype of all sacrifice, as Hopkins points out in the *Sermons*: "This sacrifice and this outward procession of the Son of God is a consequence and shadow of the procession of the Trinity, from which mystery sacrifice takes its rise ..." (p. 197). After sin and tendencies to evil entered the world and drew the human will away from God to lesser goods, sacrifice involved suffering, pain, and death. But it is still essentially self-donation and self-fulfillment. It is now not *self-*

destruction, as Hartman and most of those listed as pagan critics think, but *sin*-destruction, and that only on its negative side.

If sacrifice were self-destruction, it would be totally evil, diabolical, Manichaean. To suppose that Hopkins in his poem is telling the bird to crumple and thus become a symbol of sacrifice is to impose upon Hopkins an unchristian and pagan notion, as I see the matter. The crumpled bird, in the context of this poem, cannot be a symbol of Christ on the cross. Christ on the cross is beautiful because of the hidden, infinite, and life-giving love which bursts out from His death, freely accepted but *not* self-inflicted, to give life to the world. The plow which prepares for the life which springs from the dying seed, and the embers which send out sparks that can start other fires, can be and, as we shall see, are traditional symbols of Christ's life-giving death. But the crumpled bird, in the context of this poem, would be a symbol of nothing but repression, frustration, death. To ally such a symbol with Christian sacrifice appears to me profoundly pagan, in the full sense of that term.

Others see the matter more or less this way too, a select group who treat the poem in Christian terms, with a Christian attitude toward sacrifice: Ruggles, Doyle, Hill, McLuhan, Schoder, Ward, and Ritz. Eleanor Ruggles has a brief but intelligent critique of the poem, which goes a few steps along the right road. She happily ignores the Freudian tensions which Empson found in his mind as he considered the poem and states that the falcon in its career, reflecting God's immanence, ". . . recalls to the poet his own faulty accomplishment and the degree to which he and his fellow men fail to live up to this ideal."[26] The beauty of selfhood in the bird-chevalier flares brightest when it buckles to its act. So it is, even with a plow and embers. She suggests an identity between Christ and the windhover and suggests further that the final images deal with "a fulfillment effected through trial and distress." What that fulfillment is and how it is effected, however, she does not say. This, it is true, is not a very profound searching into the poem, but it seems to me admirable in sticking to the text of Hopkins.

Francis G. Doyle, S.J., disagrees with Donoghue's opinion that "my heart in hiding" expresses a sense of "inadequacy and weakness" in the poet: "I do not think that Hopkins felt any 'sense of inadequacy,' but rather that the sight of the bird in flight caused him to feel within himself, as he watched, a great admiration, which did not show itself in any external reaction. He stood there and watched and his heart welled up within him, almost without his being able to help it, into an ecstasy of joy."²⁷ Doyle evidently thinks that "in hiding" signifies merely a lack of external reaction. Still, he implies that the heart of the poet, in its admiration for the bird, in its joy in its mastery, desires to be like it.

Archibald A. Hill deals with the word "hiding" more satisfactorily:

> As for "my heart in hiding," I should interpret "the poet's emotional being (heart) has withdrawn seeking safety (hiding)." The notion of safety reappears in "more dangerous," a phrase applied to the sight of the bird which has stirred his heart. It is the bird, then, which is more dangerous as its beauty increases, more dangerous because the beauty breaks through Hopkins' defenses. All this is carried in the poem itself and is not an explanation for which I have gone to metaliterary data. The explanation fits with known metaliterary facts, it is true, since Hopkins had withdrawn from the world and might well fear a sight which could draw him back.²⁸

The "withdrawn" in that last sentence, combined with the assumption that the beauty of the bird could draw Hopkins out of whatever he had withdrawn into, hardly adds up to a "known metaliterary fact" to me. However, Hill's linguistic method, which, in spite of the abuse he gives it by assuming what he purports to prove, nevertheless has the enormous virtue of concentrating attention on the words themselves, aids him to give "hiding" its full value. It is unfortunate that he did not apply the method adequately to "dangerous" also, for he might have discovered that, when a knight is referred to, the word means he is masterful in his own domain. It is not the notion of safety that reappears, but the notion that the *poet's* chevalier is more dangerous, fuller of mastery and lordship, than is the chivalric bird in its domain.

Possibly the most illuminating works written about the poem are by Herbert Marshall McLuhan and Raymond V. Schoder, S.J. McLuhan gets most profoundly into the poem by considering Hopkins as an analogist:

> The bird "literally" mirrors the physical order of sub-rational "valour and act." But, analogously, as "kingdom of daylight's dauphin," it mirrors Christ. As Hopkins transfers his gaze from the first mirror to the second, we see that his own heart is also a hidden mirror (moral obedience) which flashes to God the image not of "brute beauty and valour and act" but a "fire" which is "a billion times told lovelier"—the chevalier image of Christ. We can thus simply, and, I believe for the first time, fully explain the function of "here Buckle!" Rhetorically, fire bursts from Hopkins as he looks at the fiery falcon whose action mirrors the mastery of Christ over

the world. Now, he says, let us take this mirror (St. Paul's "armour") and buckle it here in my hidden heart, raising the image of Christ in the obedience and humility of the heart. Christ's fire will burst on and from the second mirror "a billion times told lovelier" than from the falcon. This is the basic structure of this image.[29]

Excellent and profound as is McLuhan's reading, it has its own fatal flaw, which is that McLuhan does not perceive when analogy ceases and identity takes over. The deepest meaning of the poem (and it has a meaning in order to be) is not that Hopkins' heart is *like* Christ, is a mirror of Christ, but that Hopkins' heart *is* Christ's Heart. It is the difference between simile and metaphor, which is as deep as being itself. The flame which breaks from Hopkins' heart is *Christ*, "our heart's charity's hearth's fire."

Schoder's study[30] seems to me the best of those I have considered. He considers the bird in act as analogous to the radiance of divine grace flaming out from the poet's soul in spiritual combat. He perceives the heart as a crusading knight, the imagery allied to that of St. Ignatius in the *Spiritual Exercises*. The armored heart will set forth to battle more glorious than any the bird can wage, because it will be sharing Christ's labor and pain. My one objection to Schoder's work is that, though it goes far along the right road, it does not reach the ultimate and decisive goal. He lays the groundwork for identifying explicitly Hopkins' reference to the deep union of divine life flowing into human life which has as its result that the beauty, valor, and act proceeding from the human heart proceed also from the Sacred Heart. But he never does make that identification.[31] He does not perceive the final images as life-giving. And his comment that "ah my dear" can hardly have any other object than the poet's own heart indicates that he does not quite see the final goal himself. It is true enough that the object of that cry of sympathy is the poet's own heart, but only secondarily. Primarily, its object is the Heart of the crucified Christ, and Hopkins' cry carries through to that life-giving Heart with which his own heart is (or should be) perfectly one.

Dennis Ward builds on Schoder's interpretation, with somewhat more sensitiveness to movement and sound. He corrects Schoder on "bow" ("an English long-bow held at tension") and on "weary submission" in the final images ("'purposeful' better expresses the spirit and movement of this final phase"). His statement on "in hiding" I endorse wholeheartedly: "What Hopkins is saying in 'My heart in hiding stirred for a bird' is that the Falcon's example has re-animated his failing purpose. But he is saying much more than this. In exciting the poet's emulative desire, the bird has become the instrument of God (here it is worth remembering that a 'minion' is an instrument of the supreme monarch) and has brought the flash of recognition of God's stress."[82] Ward looks for "further support" for holding with Schoder that "thee" and "O my chevalier" are "the re-animated heart." The doctrine and liturgy connected with devotion to the Sacred Heart, whose divine flame bursts from the brute (natural) heart of a valorous, acting Christian, transforming (or better, conforming) the brute beauty to divine beauty, amply furnish such support.

For Jean-George Ritz, "my heart in hiding" means "the poet, hidden in some quiet place";[33] "Dans le secret de sa chambre, mais aussi dans le secret de son coeur. . . ."[34] From here, the poet watches the bird swoop down on its prey as Christ swoops down on His prey, and realizes that, as prey, he himself can humbly imitate the windhover and Christ. It seems to me that Ritz does not give full value to "in hiding" and thus does not arrive at Hopkins' comparison of the two aspects of his own heart—the cold and flameless heart in hiding and the active heart aflame with the fire of the Sacred Heart.

I wish to discuss now my own view about the position of our image in the total poem. We have covered the elements of the image, I believe, except that we should take note that Hopkins' heart admires not "the bird" but "a bird," which seems to me to stress his admiration for the acting *nature* rather than for the individual as such. This is important if one finds, as I do, that there is a comparison in the poem of four natures—the brute nature of the bird, the human nature of Hopkins, and the human and divine natures of Christ our Lord. Since, then, nature is the principle of activity in Hopkins' Aristotelian view and since this poem deals with the nobility and beauty of natural and supernatural act, a focus upon the natures involved is, to my mind, essential.

The octet of the poem deals with the mastery of the windhover as act, its triumph over the wind. Critics who have followed Richards' lead have failed to perceive this, turning the windhover itself into a horse being trained on the end of a rein. The bird is not a horse but a rider; it is not being mastered, but mastering. It is a minion, a dauphin, or properly named, a Falcon—a knightly bird, and since it is riding its mount, the air, it is a mounted knight, a chevalier. The participle (or gerund) "striding" does not necessarily change that image. A knight can be said to be galloping when actually it is the unit of horse and rider which is galloping. The bird and the air together can be doing that striding across the sky, particularly since the moving currents of air are carrying the bird, as the repeated long *i*'s of "striding high" seem to me to suggest. The rising currents are certainly ridden by the hawk as it rings up to an ecstatic height. (What would be the ecstasy of a horse circling at the end of a rein in the manège?) The "rein" here is the wing of the bird controlling the wind, so that the wind remains the horse and the bird the rider. The mastery and achieve of the bird are thus, in Hopkins' text, consistently expressed in terms of the mastery and achieve of a chevalier.

To anyone who observes the significance of the colon in the title (and a colon does indicate a connection between what goes before and what follows it, as we observe, for example, in the title of No. 55, "Spring and Fall: to a young child"), the suggestion of an implied comparison between the Lord (who is a leader of chevaliers—cf. stanza 35 of *Deutschland,* for example) and the princely windhover is at least not unlikely. The comparison seems to me suggested in the opening lines by the address to the bird as the darling of morning, the prince of the kingdom of heaven, and by the utter mastery and control of the powers of the air then observed, which can recall to a lover of Paul's revelation those powers of the air that rule the world of darkness and are opposed to the kingdom of daylight, against whom the Christian knight must stir from darkness and act as a child of the light, buckling on the armor of God:

Once you were all darkness; now, in the Lord, you are all day-light. You must live as men native to the light; where the light has its effect, all is goodness, and holiness, and truth; you have to make it clear, what conduct it is that wins favour with God. . . . Awake, thou that sleepest, and arise from the dead, and Christ shall give thee light. . . . I have no more to say, brethren, except this: draw your strength from the Lord, from that mastery which his power supplies. You must wear ["buckle on" could well translate the Vulgate *induite* and the Greek ἐνδύσασθε] all the weapons in God's armory, if you would find strength to resist the cunning of the devil. It is not against flesh and blood that we enter the lists; we have to do with princedoms and powers, with those who have mastery of the world in these dark days, with malign influences in an order higher than ours. Take up all God's armor, then. . . . Stand fast, your loins girt with truth, the breastplate of justice fitted on, and your feet shod in readiness to publish the gospel of peace. With all this, take up the shield of faith, with which you will be able to quench all the fire-tipped arrows of your wicked enemy;

make the helmet of salvation your own, and the sword of the spirit, God's word.

(Ephesians, 5:8-14, and 6:10-18)

The nature of a child of Adam inclines him to crouch in the dark, refusing to be drawn up by the dapple of the dawn. Thus Hopkins pictures his own heart, hiding from the Light, but yet admiring the glory of Christ the Lord and Master as reflected in this small creature of His, who reveals in brute and analogous miniature the power and control of its Creator's divine nature and symbolizes the knightly valor of its Creator's human nature.

Hopkins' grasp of the effect of sin upon human nature was vivid and profound, as his notes and sermons, and above all his poems, indicate abundantly. One example will serve here to indicate his attitude toward his own nature. Shortly before this poem was written, during the period in which he was preparing himself for his ordination to the priesthood, that inexpressibly intimate joining in the labor and the sacrifice of Christ, he wrote thus to Baillie: "I think I had better also do at once what I might have done at any time and that is to say how very kind you have always been to me, how much kinder than I deserved, and that as I am of a blackguardly nature and behaviour (I believe it from my heart and clearly see it) so as compared with you in particular I appear to myself in the light of a blackguard: it is the word that hits my meaning and I must employ it" (January 6, 1877, *Letters 3*, p. 242). The old meaning of "blackguard," which would well apply to a humble subject in God's kingdom, is probably operative in the background of Hopkins' choice of so violent a word in expressing his relationship to his friend. But he also fully intends the modern meaning. In his letters to Bridges he opposed the word to "gentleman," and indeed in the letter quoted above he begins by reference to his "blackguardly aunts" who have not answered his letters. He means, therefore, one who does not act as he ought, is not "mannerly-hearted" but unmannerly. To be so in relation to a kind friend is blameable, but to be so in relation to Christ is unspeakably unmanly and justly calls forth the full meaning of "blackguard." The knightly founder of the Jesuits could find no stronger condemnation for a man who would not stir to follow such a Leader than that "he would deserve to be blamed by all the world and held as a slothful knight" (the meditation of "The Kingdom of Christ" in *The Spiritual Exercises*). A knight in hiding is a blackguard, and in the quotation above, as in "The Windhover," it is as a blackguard that Hopkins, dedicated by his vows and by his approaching ordination to live the life of his Lord, pictures his heart. In a letter written from the Tertianship some four years later, when he was again probing into his Jesuit ideal, he replied to praise from Dixon in terms which throw light both on the "hiding" of our image and on the plow image which follows in the poem:

This I say: my vocation puts before me a standard so high that a higher can be found nowhere else. The question then for me is not whether I am willing (if I may guess what is in your mind) to make a sacrifice of hopes of fame (let us suppose), but whether I am not to undergo a severe judgment from God for the lothness I have shown in making it, for the reserves I may have in my heart made, for the backward glances I have given with my hand upon the plough. . . . A purpose may look smooth and perfect from without but be frayed and faltering from within. I have never wavered in my vocation, but I have not lived up to it.

(November 2, 1881, *Letters* 2, p. 88)

This is Hopkins' judgment on himself, not Christ's judgment, it should be noted. And this stern judge was to learn to say, in four more years, "My own heart let me more have pity on . . ." (*Poems,* No. 71). But his failure to follow Christ perfectly, his heart as a slothful knight without the armor of its natural beauty and valor and act, without the proud air and waving plume of the mounted chevalier going into battle, without the divine flame of its Lord's Spirit which would join with its natural flame to break out with the beauty of Christ Himself —this finds adequate expression in his picture of the hiding knight crouching in the dark.

In the sestet Hopkins speaks to that hiding heart and exhorts it to stir not only *in* admiration but *to* flaming act, the act for which it was made. "Buckle" must certainly be taken in its knightly meaning, in a context which includes minion, dauphin, bow-bend, valor, plume, dangerous, chevalier, sillion—all of them terms with specific knightly meanings.[35] How could anyone suppose that in telling a chevalier to buckle, one could mean "crumple"? Some have supposed this to be the meaning, led to it by the sacrifice expressed in the final images. But, to my mind, they misunderstand both sacrifice and symbolism in reaching such a reading. Sacrifice sometimes involves destruction, but destruction is definitely *not* identical to Christian voluntary, life-achieving, and life-giving sacrifice. If the bird were crushed, nothing would follow except its destruction. Likewise, if the chevalier were killed in battle, the beauty and pride and plume would lie in the dust, all ruined. Taken merely as such, the bird and chevalier might be symbols of destruction, but not of sacrifice. Sacrifice involves willing self-giving, and it results, in Christ, in life, not in death. To symbolize that life, that divine flame, which comes through labor and suffering, the plow and the embers are adequate, but the bird, which cannot and should not will its own destruction, and the chevalier, who, as such, must will victory, not defeat, cannot symbolize anything of the kind.

Hopkins tells his hiding heart to buckle on the elements that make the bird so magnificent, to put on *its* natural armor as the bird has done. "Brute" should be taken, I think, as meaning "natural," though Hopkins, especially as a Scotist, could possibly have had in mind the qualities of the bird considered as universal qualities, which, when buckled on a rational nature, would be informed by its *haecceitas* (or "thisness") and become rational beauty and valor and act. These in turn, in any case, as his final symbols indicate, become *divine* beauty and valour and act. And the fire breaking from his heart, when that heart leaves its hiding and swings into act, will be immeasurably lovelier and more masterful (the knightly sense of "dangerous") than is the brute bird.

The fire breaking from the heart is a picture vivid to every Jesuit, as to most Catholics, in the representations of the flame bursting from the Sacred Heart of Jesus, the central devotion of the Society of Jesus. That flame is primarily significant of the vivifying warmth and light of His charity, and it is from this flame that the fire of His Spirit is kindled in the hearts of His followers. Thus we pray to the Holy Spirit to enkindle within the hearts of His faithful the fire of divine love. Thus the Church prays in the Mass for the Saturday after Pentecost, linking this fire which the Holy Spirit enkindles in us with the fire which Jesus said He came to cast on the earth, which is the final image of the poem; "Illo nos igne, quaesumus, Domine, Spiritus Sanctus inflammet: quem Dominus noster Jesus Christus misit in terram, et voluit vehementer accendi."* It is this same vital flame which Hopkins treats in "The Candle Indoors" (*Poems*, No. 50), as I have noted above. In that sonnet, not only does the structure parallel the structure of "The Windhover" (the octet dealing with an outer flame and activity, the sestet turning to the inner flame and activity), but the fire of the vital candle, as of the chevalier, is the fire of Christ. In the dramatic liturgy for Easter Saturday, the paschal candle, which represents the Risen Christ, is first of all lighted from the flame struck

---

* May the Holy Spirit, we beg, Lord, inflame us with that fire which our Lord Jesus Christ cast on the earth and desired vehemently to be kindled.

outside the church. Then from this flame all other candles in the church are lighted, and each person holds one. Thus is symbolized the spreading of the life of Christ, the springing up of innumerable fires from the coals which He cast upon the ground in His passion. It is this symbol which, together with the symbol of the yoke pulling the plow, forms an important part of the intensely moving liturgy dealing with the Sacred Heart, to which Hopkins turns as the explanation of the immeasurable superiority of his own chivalric act to that of the bird.

The bird in its act speaks and spells only its own chivalric nature, like the creatures of No. 57:

> Each mortal thing does one thing and the same:
> Deals out that being indoors each one dwells;
> Selves—goes itself; *myself* it speaks and spells;
> Crying *Whát I dó is me: for that I came.*

But the Christian in his one act speaks both his own chivalric act and Christ's. He says more than the bird (cf. "*I say more,*" *Poems*, No. 57), and a billion times more. As "brute" acts, acts considered only in themselves as flowing from their own natures, the act of the bird and the act of the man are pretty much on a par. Both are finite reflections of infinite Beauty and Act. Hence to say that the act of the human heart in its spiritual domain is a billion times told lovelier than the act of the bird in its domain of air might well give rise to wonder.

But there is no wonder that it is so, the poem states, because the heart of the Christian can be one with the Heart of Christ, and that is not true of the bird. This fact is expressed in symbol—which is the only way it can be brought to its most adequate human expression—pointing to intimate union between Christ and the Christian, the Head of the Mystical Body and His members, the Vine and His branches. Hopkins, like every Christian, shares with God the human nature that God assumed, a thing that is true neither of angels (Hebrews, 2:11 ff.) nor of lower creatures like the bird. Because the eternal God became temporal man, man can through Him and with Him and in Him become a true child of God, sharing the divine life, as Hopkins points out in *Poems*, No. 72:

> In a flash, at a trumpet crash,
> I am all at once what Christ is, since he was what I am, and
> This Jack, joke, poor potsherd, patch, matchwood, immortal
>   diamond,
>   Is immortal diamond.

Like a diamond drinking in and intensifying and becoming the flame of the sun, so the sons of Earthy (the literal translation of the Hebrew for "Adam") can become Christ, since the true immortal diamond Who is "the radiant reflection of God's glory" (Hebrews, 1:3) Himself became a son of Earthy. The bird of our poem, in so far as it is a symbol, reflects primarily the divine nature of the Word in its power and mastery, and secondarily the human nature of Christ in its knightly victory over the powers of the air. But to explain why his own human nature in act will exceed the loveliness and mastery of the bird's nature in act, and that "a billion times," Hopkins needs symbols which will reflect primarily the human nature of Christ, and further that human nature not in Its victory over sin and God's curse of labor and death, but in Its earthly activity which preceded and brought about that victory, in the labor and death of His heroic battle. These are the acts that Hopkins, the man, can in this terrestrial campaign share with God-made-man, and while to the natural eye they are still the toil and death with which God cursed Adam and his seed, to the eye of faith they have become through and in Christ divine acts preparatory to the divine life and eternal victory that we see effected in our divine Head. They are no longer the sterile acts to be passively accepted as punishment as in the Old Law, but the life-giving acts of willing self-sacrifice which Christ has made of them. The life of man, even in his labor and his painful death, has in Christ become a divine life and is thus infinitely superior in its intrinsic loveliness and in its mastery of opposing powers to any merely natural life and activity.

The first of the two final images is that of a plow executing its humble natural act (preparing the earth for the seed) and in the process showing forth a reflected flame itself. It is the plow that shines, not the sillion. Hopkins does not say "ploughed-down," nor is the sillion a furrow, as some notes mistakenly indicate. The English "selion" now and in its earlier form "sillion," which came to us, with "minion" and "dauphin," with the knightly Normans, means a field for plowing. Hence the picture cannot be of a gleaming furrow, like the "With-a-fountain's shining-shot furls" at the end of "Harry Ploughman" (*Poems,* No. 67). The "plod" is the act of the yoked oxen or horses, and the slow-starting rhythm, gathering speed in the paired and shortening vowels of "pl*ou*gh d*ow*n" and "si*lli*on," breaking out in the long and lengthened vowel of "Shine," expresses the act and the beauty of the plow and of the plodding animals and, perhaps, of the plowman (as in No. 67)—or so it seems to me. The plow is the perfect and traditional symbol of Christ's and a Christian's labor, too, because it represents the humble and necessary work which prepares for life. It makes ready for the sower (cf. Matthew, 13). It prepares for the harvest, Christ's great image of the results of His works, an image familiar in Hopkins' poems (e.g., *Deutschland,* stanza 31; No. 32; No. 64; No. 74). It prepares for the seed of life, which is Christ's teaching, and far more, in an image deeply significant for the tie-up with the concluding symbol of the poem, for the Seed of divine life which is Christ Himself in His life-giving death: "Come at last is the hour for the Son of Man to be glorified! I tell you the plain truth: unless the grain of wheat falls into the earth and dies, it remains just one grain; but once it has died, it bears abundant fruit" (John, 12:23-25). Christ is here speaking of His passion and death, and from His death will spread the divine life which He came to bring, and the waving fields of grain for the barns of heaven will all be sharing the life of the divine Seed Whose heart was opened on the cross to pour out blood and water, symbols of the life-giving sacraments of Eucharist and baptism. We have seen above Hopkins' reference to his own religious life as a plowing, a reference to Christ's words in Luke, 9:62: "Still another said: 'I would like to follow you, Lord: but first allow me to say farewell to my folks at home.' But Jesus replied: 'No one who puts his hand to the plow and then looks back is fit for the kingdom of God.'" These references are all operative in the Christian symbols of the plow and plowing, which reflect the work which Christ and the Christian (and in a special sense the Jesuit and the priest) share.[36] But there is another element of the image which is contained in the so-called Great Appeal: "Come to me, all you that labour and are burdened; I will give you rest. Take my yoke upon yourselves, and learn from me; I am gentle and humble of heart; and you shall find rest for your souls. For my yoke is easy, and my burden is light" (Matthew, 11:28-30). The yoke of Christ, some spiritual writers point out, is a double yoke and easy because He is pulling along with His follower. This text plays a central role in the liturgy for the Sacred Heart and is chosen for special honor by Jesuits, for example, in the Gospel read on the feast of Claude de la Colombiere, the modern apostle of the Sacred Heart. It is the basis of the prayer which the Church prescribes for every priest vesting for the Sacrifice of the Mass as he puts on the chasuble, the outer vestment bearing the outline of the cross: "Domine, qui dixisti: Jugum meum suave est et onus meum leve: fac, ut istud portare sic valeam, quod consequar tuam gratiam."* As he

---

* Lord, who has said: My yoke is sweet and My burden light: grant that I may so carry it that I acquire your grace.

wrote his poem, Hopkins was preparing for the greatest event of his life, when he would as a priest take upon himself that yoke with Christ. As a Jesuit priest, he was most naturally considering the role of his "inward-steeled" chivalric heart in taking up the plodding, humble labor of His King and Lord. The work of the plow, which looks forward to future life, but which can nevertheless in preparing for that life of the harvest also reflect in its humble self something of the glory of the kingdom of daylight, is a pregnant symbol for the Jesuit priest's work in preparing for the spreading of Christ's life; and the symbol of the yoke, which is the means by which the Christian joins with Christ in doing His plowing, is the perfect symbol to indicate the union of Christ and Christian in labor.

The plow is humble, but the embers are, at first sight, far inferior to the plow. They are apparently useless, representative of dying and of death, like the "glowing of such fire" of Shakespeare's Sonnet 73 or the "fading fire" of Hopkins' "The Candle Indoors." But they also excellently represent the scourged, despised, and dying Christ, and He Himself so used them: "It is fire that I have come to spread over the earth, and what better wish can I have than that it should be kindled?" (Luke, 12:49). Christ is here speaking of His passion to come and of the fire which will spread from the ember thrown on the ground as the life spreads from the seed dying within the earth. The Jews did throw coals into the dry stubble to start the fires that would spread through the stalks and weeds, converting them to flame (cf. Wisdom, 3:7), and Christ's image is taken to refer to the fire of the Holy Spirit. That image is used in the Mass for the feast of the founder of the Jesuits, so powerfully does it express the triumphant Jesuit ideal of complete self-giving in union with the King Who offers His heart to be opened so that the embers of His life may fall upon the earth and spread out to the hearts of His followers, lighting there the divine flame that will break at last into life everlasting.

The immediate source of these two final symbols, I believe, is the Office for the Feast of the Sacred Heart, where they are found in the order in which Hopkins uses them:

V. Tollite jugum meum super vos, et discite a me.
R. Quia mitis sum et humilis Corde.
Ad Magnif. Ant. Ignem veni mittere in terram, et quid volo nisi ut accendatur?*

* Versicle: Take my yoke upon you, and learn of me. Response: Because I am meek and humble of heart. Antiphon for the Magnificat: I have come to cast fire upon the earth, and what do I wish but that it be kindled?

THE VITAL CANDLE

Here the symbols used by Christ Himself are employed to express the labor and the sacrificial death of Christ, the Sacred Heart. Since Hopkins wishes to express his own inner and outer sharing in the life and activity of Christ and that in terms of the intimate union which the theology of the Sacred Heart vividly states, these two symbols are perfect for his purpose.

The image of the plow is not only the traditional symbol for apostolic Christian labor, but it is also readily integrated with the images of sowing, of watering, of removing weeds, of harvesting, and so forth, which abound in the Gospel as images of the spreading of the divine life. The liturgy of the Sacred Heart stresses the relation in Matthew, 11:28-30, between the meek and humble heart of Christ and His yoke; the image of the heart of Christ and the heart of the Christian as yoked oxen, laboring as a single principle in pulling the plow, expresses vividly the physical union between the Head and His member. In Hopkins' image it is the plow that shines, but the plodding is proper rather to the oxen and the plowman than to the plow. Thus plowman, plow, and oxen can be considered as a unit in the image, working together to plow the ground and producing together the unexpected beauty that appears from the plow.

The image of the ember, the still-live coal which can start many fires, ties up in Christian tradition and liturgy with the spreading of the flames of Pentecost throughout the world. When the founder of the Jesuits, for example, sent his men out with the words "Incendite omnia," he was thinking of the flame of divine life. And when, in the Mass for his feast, Christ's words are repeated, "I have come to cast fire upon the earth...," that flame which is "our hearts' charity's hearth's fire" is meant. It is significant too, I believe, that from Hopkins' ember "vermilion" emerges. The etymology of the word certainly recalls, in its context here, that the fire of divine charity burst from the heart of One Who, in the words of the psalm He quoted as He hung on the cross, was "a worm and no man." Again, the combination of gold with the red fire recalls the fire and gold of stanza 23 of *Deutschland*:

> ... Are sisterly sealed in wild waters,
> To bathe in his fall-gold mercies, to breathe in his all-fire glances.

The ember as a symbol of the Sacred Heart, as it is used in the liturgy, joins with the plow as humble symbol of the "meek and humble" Heart and by its bursting fire recalls the chivalric, flaming heart of the Christian emerging from hiding; and further it gives full point to the "ah my dear" exclamation which is wrung from Hopkins in his vision of Christ's heart gashed open to pour forth its divine fire upon the earth.

Hopkins is attempting to express a union which does not lend itself to expression by simile or even by metaphor, since there is nothing else within our experience like it. It may be useful to consider what A. Theissen well says about this union in analyzing St. Paul's discussion of it in his great eighth chapter of his letter to the Romans: "The value of this argument from the resurrection of Christ to the resurrection of every Christian must be judged not by the rules of logic but by the specific Christian and Pauline doctrine of every Christian's mystical-sacramental union with Christ, the living head of the living Church. Unless this union is believed and understood St. Paul's argument has neither force nor meaning" (*A Catholic Commentary*, p. 1064). And in commenting on St. Paul's teaching that we share the life of God in union with Christ, so that we too become heirs to the kingdom of daylight, minions and dauphins (Hopkins' words, not Paul's, of course), Theissen on the same page goes on to say: "This conclusion, or better application, again defies all logical explanations. As in the question of the resurrection of the body the whole argument presupposes a union between every Christian and Christ which is above and different from any even spiritual union known to us in time and space. Its existence and character must simply be accepted as one of the mysteries of God revealed in the Gospel. But however incomprehensible this mystery may be, without a firm hold on its meaning, no reader can follow St. Paul's argument." What Theissen says of Paul is, to my mind, equally true here of Hopkins. We have seen how Hopkins employs Paul's position on the resurrection of the body of Christ as an intrinsic revelation and sure proof of the resurrection of the Christian in his "That Nature is a Heraclitean Fire and of the comfort of the Resurrection" (*Poems*, No. 72). Paul's position on the Mystical Body, in which Christ's life flows into ours in a unique and mysterious union, is also a central source of Hopkins' thought and imagery. As a unique mystery, it is literally and even metaphorically inexpressible. Thus, to express in his poem the nature of that union, Hopkins employs the symbols chosen by Christ Himself to point to His life-giving activity. Hopkins' choice is guided further by the Church's application of those symbols to the devotion closest to Hopkins' own heart, the liturgy dealing with Christ's Heart.

Hopkins has expressed this mysterious and unique union between Christ and Christian elsewhere and in clearer if less comprehensive terms. Speaking of the life of grace in the *Sermons*, Hopkins says that it is activity both on God's part and on the creature's part: on the part of God, it is Christ's spirit acting; on the part of the creature, it is the natural act raised to a new plane; looked at in its totality ("in esse quieto") it is made up, this one act, of an inextricably intimate oneness of Christ and His member:

For grace is any action, activity, on God's part by which, in creating or after creating, he carries the creature to or towards the end of its being which is its selfsacrifice to God and its salvation. It is, I say, any such activity on God's part; so that so far as this action or activity is God's it is divine stress, holy spirit, and, as all is done through Christ, Christ's spirit; so far as it is action, correspondence, on the creature's it is *actio salutaris;* so far as it is looked at *in esse quieto* it is Christ in his member on the one side, his member in Christ on the other. It is as if a man said: That is Christ playing at me and me playing at Christ, only that it is no play but truth; That is Christ *being me* and me being Christ.

(*Sermons,* p. 154)

In his commentary on Ignatius's "Contemplation for Obtaining Love," Hopkins says that "God rests in man as in a place, a *locus,* bed, vessel, expressly made to receive him as a jewel in a case hollowed to fit it, as the hand in the glove or the milk in the breast. . . . And God *in forma servi* rests *in servo*, that is, Christ as a solid in his member as a hollow or shell, both things being the image of God; which can only be perfectly when the member is in all things conformed to Christ. This too best brings out the nature of the man himself, as the lettering on a sail or device upon a flag are best seen when it fills" (*Sermons*, p. 195). Thus the self becomes more the self when it becomes Christ, as the sail becomes more fully and evidently itself when it fills with wind. Its own being is not disturbed, but is filled out, fulfilled, completed, neither destroyed nor diminished. When the heart in "The Windhover" becomes both God's and Mary's Son (i.e., Christ our Lord), then it becomes fully itself too, so that labor and suffering and death are no longer merely negations, no longer merely curses, but are also occasions for the revelation of a divine and fertile fire within the plodding or gashing heart. Note the significance of Father LaFarge's remark on Ignatius's thought: "Hence his own spiritual philosophy conclusively completes the circle of God descending to man by sharing man's humiliations; man's ascending to God, by sharing God's humiliations when on earth" ("Ignatius Loyola and Our Times," *Thought*, 31 [Summer, 1956], 185). Hopkins' final three lines in "The Windhover" are expressive of the sharing of the humiliations of the Lord of the universe, the "war without" which becomes the "war within" in Jesuits like St. Alphonsus Rodriguez.

In two other great poems Hopkins has expressed the idea of union with Christ in structure almost identical with that of "The Windhover," as I read the poem. He is like a painter with a fascinating composition, who paints it again and again with varying figures. In No. 57, Hopkins in the octet describes various creatures acting out fully their natural acts, the full expression of their being. *They* speak themselves; but *I* (i.e., the just man, as in St. Paul's "I live now, not I, but Christ lives in me") speak more than myself—I say, in my just act, both myself and Christ, "new self and nobler me." In the sestet Hopkins states that the just man ("just" in the Scriptural sense) exercises the very act of justice and literally (not analogously) is Christ, for the divine life of Christ is acting in him, flowing into his heart (the seat of his life and activity) from the Heart of Christ:

> Í say móre: the just man justices;
> Kéeps gráce: thát keeps all his goings graces;
> Acts in God's eye what in God's eye he is—
> Chríst—for Christ plays in ten thousand places,
> Lovely in limbs, and lovely in eyes not his
> To the Father through the features of men's faces.

Here poetry attempts what would seem to exceed the power of human language—to express the incomprehensible mystery of which Theissen speaks above and to reveal and make vivid to human minds and imaginations the activity of grace as divine life. And with its own mysterious power, gleaming with the beauty of the poet's vision, the poem does express, not with scientific clarity but with metaphoric obscurity, the profound and intensely exciting and vivifying mystery that was real enough to Hopkins to bring him to dedicate his life and every act to living it out and to make words break from him in an effort to express the inexpressible.

In *Poems*, No. 63, Hopkins deals with modern knights, redcoats and tars. These differ from the creatures of No. 57 or from the sea and the skylark of No. 35, which have no choice in acting out their pure natural act. Those are "brute things that only think of food or think of nothing. . . . Nevertheless what they can *they always do*" (*Sermons*, p. 239). But men must choose to give God glory if they are to do it. By nature they will, in their fallen state, tend the other way, "frail clay, nay but foul clay." But these soldiers and sailors wear the outer trappings, the "air, pride, plume," of a high ideal, of the beauty and valor and act of the courageous warrior, and the heart honors them because it wants to find them as manly as the ideal which their uniforms proclaim. However, Hopkins states in the sestet, only one King ever fulfilled that ideal completely in truth, in His Heart. He did not wear the uniform, but He perfectly fulfilled the ideal of manliness. He was a warrior, the one perfect chevalier, the ideal in the concrete. And now, in His victory, He sees His other soldiers in that same battle against the powers of evil, burdened too with labor and pain and death, yet doing what they can to fulfill that same ideal of manliness, and He can truly judge—not like the heart of the octet, which had to make a guess (Hopkins uses eight verbs to express the effort of the heart to manipulate the facts to its desires) based on the uniform. Christ can see the heart, and when He sees a man doing the best that he can do, using his human nature as well as he can, then Christ leans forth to give that man the Scriptural embrace and kiss[37] and states the true identity of that act with the activity of Christ Himself:

> There he bides in bliss
> Now, and séeing somewhére some mán do all that man can do,
> For love he leans forth, needs his neck must fall on, kiss,
> And cry 'O Christ-done deed! So God-made-flesh does too:
> Were I come o'er again' cries Christ 'it should be this.'

As in these two poems, so in "The Windhover" Hopkins begins with the ideal as concretized in the knightly bird. He combines the natural act of the creatures in No. 57 and the chivalric ideal of the soldiers and sailors of No. 63 in the one creature, who is doing all that a valiant bird can do in mastering the elements which oppose it and is thus a perfect symbol for Christ the Lord as He is and for Hopkins the Christian as he ought to be. In the sestet Hopkins urges his cowardly heart to be like the lion Heart of the true Chevalier, for then his heart will flame with a fire lovelier than any in the natural universe because it will share the Christ-done deeds of God-made-flesh, the labor of the yoke and the plow, the utter self-sacrifice of the flame-spreading embers.

Read thus, the poem expresses the profoundest depths of the Jesuit ideal, which is an utter and complete giving of self in love and loyalty to Christ our Lord, a living and acting in such union with Him that humble labor and suffering and death are if possible chosen, because He chose them. The brand the Jesuit wields is unseen, the heroic breast not outward-steeled, but God sees the proud heart's fierce battle and He crowds career with conquest because this is a Christ-done battle and victory. The triumph belongs both to the Christian and to Christ, Who triumphs all over again in the Christian; it is His deed, too. Thus the proud heart of the nun, which (in stanza 28 of *Deutschland*) unfalteringly faced danger and death for and with and in Christ, triumphed not only for herself, but Christ also triumphed in her, since He was acting in her act:

> . . . there then! the Master,
> *Ipse,* the only one, Christ, King, Head:
> He was to cure the extremity where he had cast her;
> Do, deal, lord it with living and dead;
> Let him ride, her pride, in his triumph, despatch and have
>   done with his doom there.

The battle of the Christian chevalier is with the powers of evil, as was Christ's battle, and with the human weakness and sweat and pain and death which result from evil, but which Christ overcame and which He calls upon His followers to face, buckling on the armor of God and fighting to the end. And this Jesuit poet, who so loved his King that the very symbol of the King's greatest battle, which He won through voluntary acceptance of suffering and death, wrings from his heart a cry of sympathy, "ah my dear," could nevertheless count it his own greatest glory that he shared in the labor and pain of the same battle, because from his battling heart there shone forth to God's eyes not only his own human flame but, inextricably mingled with it, the divine flame of God's own Heart, of Christ our Lord.

The meaning of a symbolic poem and, further, one which symbolizes the ineffable mystery which is at the center of Christianity is not easily come by. But even when it is established, one has only laid the foundations for considering the poetic excellencies of the poem. The poem is magnificent in its meaning, but not because of it. As a poem, its beauty must be found in the physical and imaginative elements which embody that meaning and make it incarnate in a structure. These are so complex here, where Hopkins calls upon every technical resource he has to make the rhythms and the sounds expressive of the acts, of the sounds and sights and feel of the bird and the chevalier and the plow and the embers, and the whole is such an expressive unit, that I will not attempt to repeat in full what has been in part well done by Gardner, Schoder, McLuhan, and Miller, and especially by Hartman, to uncover the physical beauties of the poem. I will examine briefly my own special image and one or two points which seem to me to have been misinterpreted or ignored.

In a poem so perfectly welded, or rather so organically one, as this one is, any one part involves all the others completely. The hiding chevalier is intelligible here only in the light of the chevalier at the beginning who is mastering the big wind and the Chevalier at the end Who is mastering labor and death. In a similar way, the rhythm of our passage is part of the rhythm which precedes and preparation for the rhythm which follows. The sweep of rhythm, imitative primarily of the action of the bird in the wind, runs on from the first word of the poem to the end of our passage with scarcely a pause. The first and only slight pause in the whole eight lines occurs with the beginning of our passage and constitutes a preparation for the slow-up which our passage effects. Then the rhythm picks up again, with growing vigor and power and a heavier beat, expressive, I think, of the rhythm of a greater chevalier bursting from hiding into full activity, for the first three lines of the sestet. The slower and broken beat of the final three lines is exquisitely expressive both of the act concerned and of the reaction of the poet's heart. The gathering speed of the plow we have already considered. The even, soft, broken rhythm, balanced in b's, and l's, m's and r's, of line 13 describes the state of the embers, the "fall, gall themselves, and" expressing their insignificant (but deeply meaningful) tumble and the "gash gold-vermilion" their impact, the effect of the spreading and soft-dying-away shower of sparks coming through in the repeated short final vowels drawn out by the l and the n.

The "movement" of the bird in our passage is, at the outset, its hovering in one spot, in spite of the big wind which bounces it slightly, but cannot sweep it away. In the repeated vowels, in the alliteration, and in other ways, Hopkins expresses the control of the bird over the great flow of rhythm expressive of the big wind. The "rolling level underneath him steady air" is a triumph of sound and kinetic expressiveness, giving the mind the bump in the psychological order (when the contradictory adjectives "rolling" and "level" run into each other) that the wing of the bird feels when the burl of air hits it and is ironed out level and steady as it flows out from under that masterful wing. The "rung upon the rein" is by no means, to my mind, "a term from the manège," as Richards says it is. Both the situation and the rhythm seem to me to deny this. The falcon is doing the riding, so that if there is a horse, it is the rolling air. And it is the falcon that is doing the ringing. Richards wants us to picture someone holding the rein while the horse circles on the end of it. If the wing is the rein, then the rest of the falcon would have to be considered to be the horse, and an invisible hand would be holding the end of the wing. But since the control comes from the falcon and since the falcon is riding the wind and since "ring" is a falconry term for spiraling upward (a fact that Richards might have ascertained by introducing a dictionary into his few days of reflection), one should take the word "rein" in its general sense of "a curb, a check, a means of controlling or holding back," as when Hopkins says in his sermon on the Paraclete that "the reins of power on all things were drawn into the hand of the crucified victim" (*Sermons*, p. 74). The wing of the bird is a rein on the wind in the sense that it controls it completely, and to that extent the wind is a bucking horse and the falcon the masterful chevalier. However, in regard to the ringing, it is not the wind that is circling but the falcon that is spiraling up, so that the literal statement, so far as I can grasp the situation, does not permit any horse-and-rider image to operate in regard to the spiraling, though it can operate in regard to the control the falcon exercises upon the wind. The rising and shortening of the four feet, "how he rung/upon the rein/of a wimp/ling wing," with the growing smallness of the turns emphasized by the roundness of the alliterative *r*'s compressing into the labial puckering of the alliterative *w*'s, express in sound and rhythm the rise and lessening of the spiraling motion of the bird. Then follows its great sweep from the height in a shallow curve like that of a longbow, with the sound brought close in the long vowels of "sweeps smooth" and dying away again. On page 109 I have attempted to reproduce something of what the voice gives these lines.

The final two lines of the octet seem to me rhythmically and phonetically expressive of the bird's bouncing in one spot while the wind sweeps beneath him—at least the accented syllables "-buffed" and "big," with the syncopation in the accented "wind," and the "heart" and "hid-" and "stirred" and "bird" keep the one point of reference bouncing in the ear. Then the movement irons out and flows through

THE VITAL CANDLE

the two surges of "the achieve of, the mastery of" to a close in "the thing!" Note that "achieve" leaves the motion open, whereas "achievement" would close it.

A chart of my picture of the poem's total structure may be helpful:

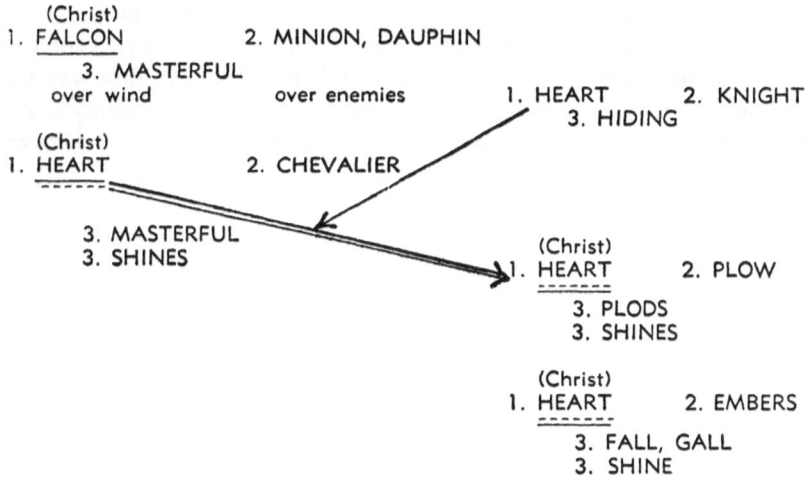

The solid line under the nouns of the chart indicates *natural* beauty and mastery. The broken line indicates *supernatural* beauty and mastery.

In the bird, the reflection of Christ is purely natural. In the acting heart, it is, in the first instance, natural and supernatural, with the emphasis on the natural; in the second instance, supernatural and natural, with the emphasis on the supernatural. That is, the first comparison of the poet's heart with the bird's nature leads to the picture of the poet's heart glorified by its union with Christ; the last images are not a comparison of heart and bird, but a symbolizing of the identity of heart and Christ, in which the accent falls not on the heart (as it did in the comparison with the bird) but on Christ. And the labor and sufferings of Christ are filled up in His members, as St. Paul has so gloriously written: "Even as I write, I am glad of my sufferings on your behalf, as, in this mortal frame of mine, I help to pay off the debt which the afflictions of Christ leave still to be paid, for the sake of his body, the Church" (Colossians, 1:24).

"The Windhover" does not yield its riches easily. Its vivifying depths sink into that infinite mystery which is, in the Catholic view, the center of interest and of life. The "ah my dear" which expresses Hopkins' emotion at the piercing of Christ's heart carries the sympathetic hearer close to the greatest revelation of God's love. One can thus understand why Hopkins considered, in 1879, that this was the best thing he had written. He was not speaking as a literary critic when he said that—at least not only so. He was speaking as a lover.

CHAPTER 5

Peace

When will you ever, Peace, wild wooddove, shy wings shut,
Your round me roaming end, and under be my boughs?
When, when, Peace, will you, Peace? I'll not play hypocrite
To own my heart: I yield you do come sometimes; but
That piecemeal peace is poor peace. What pure peace allows
Alarms of wars, the daunting wars, the death of it?

O surely, reaving Peace, my Lord should leave in lieu
Some good! And so he does leave Patience exquisite,
That plumes to Peace thereafter. And when Peace here does
   house
He comes with work to do, he does not come to coo,
   He comes to brood and sit.
"Peace," *Poems*, No. 46

My name is Jave, and there is no other to rival me; I, the fashioner of darkness, the creator of light, I, the maker of peace, the author of calamity. I, the Lord, am the doer of all this.
Isaias, 45:6-7

I have forewarned you of this event, that you may find peace of soul in union with me. In the world, afflictions are in store for you. But have courage; I have overcome the world.
John, 16:33

Of patience, indeed, you have need, that, having done the will of God, you may receive the promised reward.
Hebrews, 10:36

> And so he does leave Patience exquisite,
> That plumes to Peace thereafter.
>
> "Peace," *Poems*, No. 46

Christ our Lord, the "he" of our image, is here a robber and a plunderer, a bird-snatcher, a nest-rifler. Hopkins tells Bridges, in a letter of August 21, 1884, that by the "reaving" of the line which precedes our image he means "rob, plunder, carry off" (*Letters 1*, p. 196). It is Christ Who has robbed and plundered Hopkins' boughs of the wild wooddove, Peace, and carried it off. Hopkins, looking after that so much longed for and now departed Peace, reflects that his Lord *should* have left him some good, having taken that precious life-giving dove. Thus Hopkins reveals his faith in the good will of his Lord, even after this harsh robbery.

As a good Lord, Christ should leave something to His plundered knight, and indeed He does do what He should—He leaves little Patience, plumeless in the nest, yet exquisite as a newborn baby in the cradle, perfect in smallness and full of promise for the future. That this fledgling is the offspring of the dove is neither stated nor certain, and it may be that the Robber who took away the sweet dove may have brought this small and plumeless substitute with Him. Yet, given time, the fledgling grows into that longed-for dove.

In his sensitive and careful discussion of the poem, Gardner happily refers to Patience as "the changeling-virtue" and as "the dubious nestling" (*Gardner 2*, p. 287). However, I do not find in Gardner's delineation the whole picture which reveals why Patience becomes Peace—that dove and fledgling are both aspects of the Holy Ghost's work in us, that they are the effects of the growth and operation of Christ's divine life in our hearts. Peace is the act of divine charity in us, the effect of our union with Christ, the tranquillity of order which follows upon the aiming of our "heart right" and "single eye" at Christ alone. Patience is the reaction of the Spirit in our hearts to the forces which tend to separate us from Christ, to the attacks aimed at bending our wills to disloyalty and rebellion. Yet both peace and patience are the acts of the Spirit within us:

> Let me say this; learn to live and move in the spirit; then there is no danger of your giving way to the impulses of corrupt nature. The impulses of nature and the impulses of the spirit are at war with one another; either is clean contrary to the other, and that is why you cannot do all that your will approves. It is by letting the spirit lead you that you free yourselves from the yoke of the law. It is easy to see what effects proceed from

corrupt nature; they are such things as adultery, impurity, incontinence, luxury, idolatry, witchcraft, feuds, quarrels, jealousies, outbursts of anger, rivalries, dissensions, factions, spite, murder, drunkenness, and debauchery. I warn you, as I have warned you before, that those who live in such a way will not inherit God's kingdom. Whereas the spirit yields a harvest of love, joy, peace, patience, kindness. . . . Since we live by the spirit, let the spirit be our rule of life. . . .

(Galatians, 5:16-25)

Peace and patience are central to the living out of the life of the Holy Ghost within us. Through peace and patience we live to inherit God's kingdom.

Peace, then, the gift that the Risen Christ wanted first for all those to whom He appeared, the condition of spiritual growth, is aptly a dove, the symbol of the Holy Ghost Who brings about the development of the divine life in our hearts. But it is, in the opening lines of the poem, a dove whose shy wings keep it from settling down to "form and warm the life within" the nest. Since it is a dove and a dove settles for its life-giving and warming work on a nest and a nest is found in the boughs of a tree and Hopkins wants this dove inside him, Hopkins is a tree with boughs. It is true that a dove might settle on a bough whether a nest were there or not, if that dove wished only to rest and coo. But, as the poem reveals, this dove has work to do under these boughs, to brood and to sit. A nest is essential. Further, the plumeless Patience would be hard put to it, one imagines, to cling to a bare bough. The nest is Hopkins' heart, the seat of his own life and of the life of the Spirit. It is the heart that is longing for the dove of peace in the opening lines. Hopkins admits to his questioning and pleading heart that the dove does come sometimes with its warmth and protection for the living nest. But his complaint, and the heart's, is that the dove does not stay. It lets itself be driven away, or, as we shortly discover, snatched away by a nest-robber. It allows its own life to die in the daunting wars, and then what will become of the dove's life in the bereaved nest?

The existence of those wars indicates the deficiency of the Peace treated in this poem. It is a poor peace if it does not stay; if it were peace wholly it would not *allow* the wars that kill it. These wars and their nature are discussed fully in Hopkins' later great sonnet on Patience, *Poems*, No. 70. I turn now to examine this poem, which, since it expands the statement of our image and discloses what happens as Patience plumes to Peace, is worth careful consideration.

Patience is up at auction as the poem opens, as in No. 32 there is also an auction for the pure peace of Christ and patience is there money to bid and buy with. Here patience is the prize up for auction, and it has a hard price: war, wounds, weary times and tasks, "To do without, take tosses, and obey." The religious vows of poverty, chastity, and obedience are well described, and their faithful observance by a chevalier of Christ brings forth rare patience ("exquisite" it is called in "Peace"), which roots in this soil of self-denial and no place else. From these roots the rich ivy covers the heart. This is itself an exquisite image to express the work of patience, which does not rise and fly to union, as Peace does. Patience has no plumes for flying. It is rooted in pain and endurance, it stays with the suffering heart, wrecked so often in its past high endeavors, and masks the scars. Or, as in our special image, it simply stays in the besieged nest, keeping the divine life growing there until once more the plumed bird can rise on the wings of peace or brood and sit on the nest.

The sestet of No. 70 indicates that the wars are within the heart, that the heart grates on itself because its rebellious will rejects the good which is God and goes after a good which is not God. In this struggle, peace dies. But by patience, we bear the war and wounds, we bid God to make war on our malice and by His power bend our rebellious wills back to Him in spite of further war and wounds. Patience cannot fight, but it can willingly bear as much war and as many wounds, as much jading and jar of the cart, as is necessary to achieve once more that union with God which the heart right, the single eye, the will aimed solely "ad majorem Dei gloriam," will bring. In a few words, patience hangs on until it becomes peace.

In the final lines of No. 70, Hopkins develops further Paul's thought in Galatians, 5:22-23, as quoted above. Peace is followed by patience in Paul's list, and patience is followed by kindness. This kindness, which is the honey of charity in action, is distilled from patience. The patient man bears all things from others, and is yet kind. It is patience that works to fill up the honeycombs of the kind man's heart, so that at the end of this poem patience, too, has work to do, as does peace at the end of our No. 46.

These spiritual wars, then, are within the heart. "Thoughts against thoughts in groans grind" in the heart of "Spelt from Sibyl's Leaves" (*Poems*, No. 62), as we shall have occasion to consider carefully in the following chapter. And they are to be expected in Adam's children, whose hearts tend so naturally, it seems, toward malice and rebellion.

The result of this struggle of the divided heart, wrested toward God by the indomitable will to serve Him, twisting away from God by the self-centered will to serve self, is the death of peace. How can Hopkins justly go on to say, as he does in our poem, that *Christ* plunders him of peace?

The answer is that it is Christ in him and the Spirit sent by Christ Who are fighting along with his God-centered will against his self-centered will. "The impulses of nature" of which Paul speaks in the quotation above are those desires and aims which lead the heart from God, "the impulses of the spirit" are those which lead to God. These last are the divine life which Christ gives, which the Holy Ghost fosters and broods over. And Christ throws Hopkins into extremities, as He did the nun in *Deutschland*, so that those evil tendencies may be brought out of hiding and into war with the Spirit and conquered. Thus in *Poems*, No. 64, "Carrion Comfort," all through the dreadful night of his spirit Hopkins wrestled with a terrible beast Who turns out to be Christ when the light of morning dawns. It was Christ there, reaving peace so that through war "my chaff might fly; my grain lie, sheer and clear." And Hopkins finds that though he fought against Christ in the night, he also fought alongside Him. The war was in Hopkins' heart, which was grinding against itself. Hopkins comes to know that he fought on both sides, but Christ on only one.

But Christ provokes the war. He will not let the heart be, but, as in *Deutschland*, drives it to bay and forces it to fight. And here in our poem Hopkins considers one aspect of the fight only—the loss of lovely Peace. Christ has taken it from him, but He leaves him a lesser good, the Patience which does not share in the fight but does what it can to fill up the place of vanished Peace. Its apparent uselessness is only apparent, for though it does not, like the dove Peace, foster and increase the growth of divine life in the heart, it sustains that life in itself and throughout the struggle grows and develops until, the struggle past, it is itself Peace and happily at home in the heart in which it has grown. And, housing there, it broods and sits, bringing with its warm breast and bright wings an increase of divine life. It is the Holy Spirit Who, during the night of struggle, operates as Patience within the battling heart and, during the quiet of the brooding daylight, operates as Peace.

Hopkins' ambiguous attitude toward the "wild wooddove" is thus explained. He indicates at first that the dove is too shy to settle under his boughs. There is no question of war there. The bird simply hovers about, finally out of shyness refusing to shut its wings. It sometimes settles, but those wings open again and it roams once more in tantalizing nearness. And yet Hopkins asks the dove why it *allows* the wars which kill it. The question is similar to the ones addressed to the great beast of No. 64:

> ... why wouldst thou rude on me
> Thy wring-world right foot rock? lay a lionlimb
>   against me? scan
> With darksome devouring eyes my bruisèd bones? and fan,
> O in turns of tempest, me heaped there; me frantic to
>   avoid thee and flee?

And the answers are similar. In No. 64, the reason is to prepare Hopkins for the heavenly barns: "Why? That my chaff might fly; my grain lie, sheer and clear." In our poem, the reason is so that another good, Patience, will operate and develop, and implied in that other good is a flying of chaff, for Christ takes away our peace only to make war on our malice, to bend our rebellious wills to Himself, to prepare us for the further and deeper development in divine life under the renewed Peace. In both cases, the living out of divine life in this world is the subject, and our poem concerns itself with the diverse operations of the Spirit in our hearts in times of quiet and in times of struggle.

Patience, St. Thomas tells us, is most of all an effect of the Holy Spirit's activity, for it preserves the soul in times of struggle from being overwhelmed and crushed with sadness.[1] It preserves the soul from presumption, from rashly leaping into wars and expecting God to sustain and strengthen it, on the one hand; and on the other, it preserves the soul from despair, the giving up of hope and activity, the horrible death of the spirit. From presumption Hopkins apparently had little to fear; but from despair he was more than once in serious danger, as we shall have further occasion to see. When his sad self urged him to give up hanging from the cliffs of fall, to give up bruising his poor heart yet dearer, then patience was the virtue that he needed. As early in his religious life as 1874, when he was a hard-working scholastic teacher, he could write: "Our schools at Roehampton ended with two days of examination before St. Ignatius' feast the 31st. I was very tired and seemed deeply cast down till I had some kind words from the Provincial. Altogether perhaps my heart has never been so burdened and cast down as this year. The tax on my strength has been greater than I have felt before: at least now at Teignmouth I feel myself weak and can do little. But in all this our Lord goes His own way" (*Journals*, pp. 249-50). It is his Lord Who thus tries him, Who gives him much to do and little strength with which to do it, and he has need of patience to bear up, especially if the "delicious kindness" which on this occasion refreshed him is not forthcoming. That he had the "patience exquisite" to write that final sentence in his time of weakness, of trial, of loss of peace, is illustration of his Lord's leaving that good in lieu of the plundered peace. It was a virtue that Hopkins needed often and that was a large factor in his living out his aim of perfect union with Christ his Lord:

> Buy then! bid then!—What?—Prayer, patience, alms, vows.
> (*Poems*, No. 32)

> Stir in my ears, speak there
> Of God's love, O live air,
> Of patience, penance, prayer....
> (*Poems*, No. 60)

> Yet God...
> Could crowd career with conquest while there went
> Those years and years by of world without event
> That in Majorca Alfonso watched the door.
> (*Poems*, No. 73)

Felix Randal was almost lost for lack of it:

> Sickness broke him. Impatient he cursed at first, but mended
> Being anointed and all....
> (*Poems*, No. 53)

The Church, Time's Andromeda, must have long and growing patience in the wars she endures while waiting for the return of her Perseus:

> ... forsaken that she seems,
> All while her patience, morselled into pangs,
> Mounts....
> (*Poems*, No. 49)[2]

In *Poems*, No. 68, Hopkins dramatically delineates his tremendous need for patience. That great poem can, in fact, be grasped as a unit only in the light of the nature of patience as the virtue of endurance in the war which results from the union of our fallen nature with Christ, the struggle of nature and of spirit of which Paul speaks. The poem describes that union with Christ, Who is Hopkins' peace, the Christian's peace, as involving war, "parting, sword, and strife," and war, moreover, with those most dearly loved, family, countrymen, even the soil of Hopkins' passionately loved country. Hopkins here follows Christ's prediction to His followers: "Do not suppose that it is my mission to shed peace upon the earth; it is not my mission to shed peace but to unsheath the sword. For example, it is my mission to set a man at variance with his father, a daughter with her mother, and a daughter-in-law with her mother-in-law. In fact, a man's enemies will be the members of his own household. He who is fonder of father or mother than of me is not worthy of me; he who is fonder of son or daughter than of me is not worthy of me. Again, he who will not shoulder his cross and follow me is not worthy of me" (Matthew, 10:34-38). That parting which Christ brings is not easy, nor is it intended to be easy. Christ compares it to carrying a cross to crucifixion, and goes on to say that His followers must be ready to lose their lives for Him. He knew what He was asking, and He demanded it and Himself fulfilled the request in "the dense and the driven Passion, and frightful sweat." Hopkins' No. 68, "To seem the stranger. . . ," is a complaint against this pain, an echo of Christ's "Father, if it be possible . . ." (Matthew, 26:39). It is a patient complaint, because Hopkins accepts the war and wounds, but his lonely state as stranger in the world, unheard and unheeded when his heart speaks its intimate and wisest word, is deeply poignant.

Since the poem, No. 68, carries on a development of the process with which our image deals (the metamorphosis of patience into peace), I shall consider it also in some detail. It begins with the protagonist as Time's Stranger, as in a later poem and a development of the same situation he is Time's Eunuch. He stands, like Ruth amid the alien corn, cut off from family and country because of his nearness to Christ his peace. His lot is to seem a stranger every place; his life is lived out, in this world, among strangers. He left his home to become a Catholic, to join thus with Christ, and his most dearly loved father and mother and brothers and sisters are not near him in Christ. Those last two words are most vital to the meaning of the poem. He was near his family and visited them from time to time, but in Christ they were parted and at war. And Christ is Hopkins' peace because they two are one, are perfectly and literally united, so that to be at war with his loved family in Christ is to be parted from them in the dearest and deepest part of his being, to be a stranger in what counts.

The same thing is true of his relations to England, which he pictures as a beloved woman, as a wife. Here again, in the things that count, he is at war with his countrymen. This he has brought about not only by becoming a Catholic, but much more so, and specifically so in relation to England, by becoming a Jesuit, his most intimate union with Christ. He wants England near him *in Christ,* and the deepest urging of his heart is to plead with her to join him (which means that she will join him in Christ, since he will not leave Christ his peace even for England his beloved). But he knows that she would not listen to him if he did plead, so he stifles that urge. When he pleads, it means only war, "sword and strife," the hatred of which Christ spoke in the passage quoted above and in other passages. For example, Christ knew what it was to be rejected by his own Galilean countrymen and there is a deep sadness in his words, ". . . believe me, no prophet finds acceptance in his own country" (Luke, 4:24). And in the torrent of overwhelming love that Christ poured out for His followers in His Last Discourse, He tried to prepare them for exactly this situation: "If the world hates you, be sure that it hated me before it learned to hate you. If you belonged to the world, the world would know you for its own and love you; it is because you do not belong to the world, because I have singled you out from the midst of the world, that the world hates you" (John, 15:18-19). Christ had singled Hopkins out in a special sense, leaving him isolated from his England, his wife. And Hopkins practices the "doing without" which gives ground for the roots of patience. The "weary his times" of No. 70 is found here in "I weary of idle a being but by where wars are rife." "Weary" here (No. 68) is strongly emphasized and lengthened by acting as a bridge between the last two lines of the octet, and the whole statement expresses that painfully exasperated weariness with which a husband might say, "Why should I plead with her? I'm tired of doing nothing but fighting." This is, I think, Hopkins' meaning—"I am weary of being idle in regard to England, whose honor I long to serve, in whose ears and soul I long to bring forth my wisest and most intimate word (the Word, my peace), everywhere except at those places where the 'sword and strife' over Christ is going on." England will listen and react to Hopkins the Jesuit on only one point, and on that point only to war with him. There is no peace in

Christ between Hopkins the Jesuit and England, but only war—and this wearies him, since he does not want to fight England, his most dearly loved, his wife.

He wants to build ("Birds build, but not I build," *Poems*, No. 74), to construct for life, to find room in the world for the children of the Christed heart. But he is wholly occupied with only one job, the attempt to save something from the terrible and continuing wreckage, with no time to think of success in any building at all:

> And I not help. Nor word now of success:
> All is from wreck, here, there, to rescue one—
> Work which to see scarce so much as begun
> Makes welcome death, does dear forgetfulness.
>
> (*Poems*, No. 112)

And apart from such rescue work in his war-wracked times, he must be idle, for no one will form a home-in-Christ with him in this world, not family, not countrymen. The children of his loving heart find no nourishment or shelter, even no birth, since he knows they will not live in the ears and hearts of his family and countrymen.

Mother and father were parted from him in his first remove into the Catholic Church. England was parted from him more fully in his second remove into the Society of Jesus. And now, the sestet goes on, he is even physically removed from both. Not only his family and the soul of his England, but now even the soil of England—all are strangers to him. In each remove there is kind love, that delicious kindness which flows from patience. He and his family love each other with kindness; he and his countrymen too give and get kind love. For example, Bridges could stand for England here as a countryman of Hopkins, and the evidence of kind love between the two men is open at least in the patient pen of Hopkins (Bridges destroyed his own letters). But the wisest word his heart breeds is not heard or heeded because of the separation in Christ. That wisest word is not merely his poems. It is every word that deals with "he my peace," the life and bridegroom of his heart—his poems, his sermons, his poor unborn books, all his words which could express the one great love of his heart, Christ our Lord, the one important subject. Hopkins states this to Bridges, in a letter which goes on to try to plead with Bridges (with England) to join him in Christ: "When we met in London we never but once, and then only for a few minutes before parting, spoke on any important subject, but always on literature" (January 19, 1879, *Letters 1*, p. 60).

Bridges' reaction, as it is reflected in Hopkins' painfully careful attempt to refine his meaning and to "take the bad taste away" (Jan. 29, 1879, *Letters 1*, p. 62-65), gives a sample of the activity Hopkins the Jesuit was compelled to engage in when he tried to plead with England. And a few years later he speaks to Bridges (and in a sense to England) about his deafness to Hopkins' wisest word and the bitterness that brought to the soul of Hopkins: "And indeed how many many times must you have misunderstood me not in my sonnets only but in moral, social, personal matters! It must be so, I see now. But it would embitter life if we knew of the misunderstandings put upon us; it would mine at least" (March 26, 1883, *Letters 1*, p. 177). His wisest word, Hopkins says in his poem, is barred from life by God's baffling decree, or it is thwarted, in its attempts to live, by the spell of evil. The "ban" would imply God's ordering the barring, for some good purpose, either to give His servant opportunity for spiritual growth (as in our No. 46, in No. 62, in No. 70) or for other reasons; the "spell" would imply the paralyzing effect of hell in the heart of Hopkins, the death-dealing power of evil. Hopkins doesn't know which is the *ultimate* cause for the lack of survival of the dearest children of his heart. He only knows the fact. Either they are never born, or being born, they are ignored. He wants to speak his (and Christ's) words to his beloved family, to his beloved countrymen, but they will not hear. And thus his words lie lifeless in his heart, or lifeless in their ears, for he is a stranger to them, far from them in Christ. And he has no home, no parents, no wife, no children of his body or of his heart. He is a stranger, and all he has left is, not even a mere beginning, but a began. Thus I read that last hopeless but patient word.[3] Bridges is puzzled and suggests in his note that Hopkins means "leave me a lonely (one who only) began." That is possible, obviously, but less powerful and significant than the simpler approach that "began" is here a noun, not a verb—the same noun as "beginning" except for tense. The subject of the poem's last sentence, as I read it, is the infinitive phrase, "to hoard this"; the verb is "leave"; and the object is "a began." *Not* to hoard it, to give birth to the wisest word, would leave Hopkins with a beginning or with an achievement. But, with the frustration put upon him by some power (heaven or hell), he stands in time with nothing at all except within his heart the record of a past effort to begin something, a "began." It is for such a heart that the patience of No. 70 is needed:

> Natural heart's ivy, Patience masks
> Our ruins of wrecked past purpose.

In No. 68, as in No. 46, Hopkins is dealing with peace and with war—the peace of Christ in union with the heart, the sword and strife which flow in part from the pain of separation from those who will not share that union. It is a profoundly expressive poem based upon Christ's words and upon Hopkins' experience—which in its essence is the experience of every Christian, more so of every Jesuit (of all who live under the yoke of the vows). Mr. Gardner does the poem no service when he introduces into the poem, in his note (*Poems*, p. 250) and in his long discussion of the poem (*Gardner* 2, pp. 341-45) the political differences between Ireland and England under Gladstone. He is led to this, if I am not mistaken, not by anything in the text, but by his own knowledge from Hopkins' letters that the political difficulties between Ireland and England bothered Hopkins considerably. Hence when Gardner sees that wars are mentioned in connection with England and that Ireland appears immediately thereafter, he concludes that the wars in question are between England and Ireland.

The text of the poem does not say that. The speaker in the poem says that *Christ* is strife, wars, for him, that England won't hear him, and that he is weary of doing nothing except where there are wars. The only wars mentioned so far in the poem are those concerning Christ, and the enemies for the poem's speaker are, as Christ foretold, those of his own household and country.

Then Ireland appears, and nothing is said about wars in respect to Ireland, but the speaker merely points out that his being in Ireland is another step in the "*parting*, sword, and strife" (I add italics for emphasis) which Christ is to him. Ireland constitutes for him the third remove from family and country, and his physical separation from them makes it impossible or even more unlikely that they will hear his wisest word, i.e., his Christed word. The first remove to separate him from them in Christ was his entering the Catholic Church, the second was his entering the Society of Jesus, and now the third is his living in Ireland, his being sent there on the work of Christ, his "parting."

The wars in question, the text seems to me to make very clear, are those about Christ, between Hopkins on the one hand and his family and country on the other. To bring in the wars between England and Ireland is to do violence to the text, as I see the matter, and to make a grasp of the real issues in the poem impossible. The political differences between the countries do contribute to the difficulty of Hopkins' position in so far as they make more complete and unpleasant his separation from his beloved England, but they are not the "wars" of line 8, which separate Hopkins from family and country.

Christ's position in our image from No. 46, then, is that of the Lord Who, while He gives the deepest and most basic peace to the heart united to His, yet can truly say that he comes to bring not peace but war. But, though His follower has no true and lasting peace with others in this world, yet in enduring the pain, separation, and loss, in being a stranger in this world out of love and loyalty to Christ, he grows in the beauty of patience. In No. 46 Hopkins is considering the divine activity in his heart as the work of the Holy Ghost. That divine activity is objectively the work of the Second Person of the Trinity as well as of the Third Person (and of the First Person too, for that matter). Here Hopkins is considering the divine life within him as stemming from the human nature of Christ (for it is the Word-made-flesh Who brings no peace but war to His followers—it is this Lord Whom Hopkins follows, Who reaves Hopkins' peace in the poem) and as developing in his heart through the activity of the Holy Ghost, the brooding dove, and as enduring in his bereaved heart while the war rages, through the activity of the Holy Ghost, the fledgling Patience.

The sonnet is a shortened one, a curtal sonnet, in the proportions of six to four and one-half rather than of eight to six. The more exquisite structure fits the delicate treatment of the subject. Throughout, the quiet repetitions and the re-echoing vowels imitate the cooing of doves in the woods. Hopkins justifies the transposition of "to my own heart" to "to own my heart" on the grounds that it is "for rhythm's sake" (*Letters 1*, p. 196). The opening rhythm, imitative of the dove's roaming and shifting, itself shifts from falling to rising, but could not support "to my own heart" at the beginning of the line, with the two slacks building up to the abrupt juxtaposition of the two stresses; the stresses and slacks must alternate to give the soft, continued beat of the dove's wings. Bridges evidently objected to what he considered the weakness of the verb "come" in the fourth line,[4] but in doing so he ignored at least one striking effect of the sound there, in suggesting a momentary settling on the part of the dove (as do "piecemeal peace" and "poor peace" and "pure peace")—and then the dove rises in the lifting "allows alarms," receiving blows perhaps in the hard *d*'s of "daunting" and "death," these being almost the only tongue-point stops in the poem. The dying away into the two insignificant syllables which end the octet and are therefore spotlighted, "of it," is expressive of the ignominious disappearance of Peace.

The play on the soft opening *p*'s and on *l*'s and *r*'s throughout the poem gives the quiet and smooth lilt that expresses both the subject and the mood. The vowels in a line like "O surely, reaving Peace, my Lord should leave in lieu . . ." are rather rounded or rolled than stopped. The curve of the rhythmic line rises and falls in smooth and quiet arcs, as it does throughout except in line 6, where it roughens, and in the final half-line, where it levels off and stops.

The sweetness and quiet loveliness of this poem express one of the moods with which Hopkins approaches the activity of the divine life within him. The development of all life involves some pain, some struggle, some war. The child's first breath is terribly painful, evidently, to the folded lungs. The growth of Christ's life in our hearts involves the destruction of much that is close to us and most dear, as well as that malice within us which is perhaps closest of all to our blackguardly hearts. Most of Hopkins' later poems deal with the growth of that life within him and most powerfully with the pain which his poor heart so deeply feels. In this poem, Hopkins is still able to accept that pain and that grinding struggle under the symbolic activity of the dove and of the fledgling. He has not yet felt the ultimate and keen blasts which will make him cry like Lear,

> . . . the tempest in my mind
> Doth from my senses take all feeling else
> Save what beats there.

CHAPTER 6

That Small Commonweal

*Earnest, earthless, equal, attuneable, vaulty, voluminous, . .
   stupendous
Evening strains to be time's vást, womb-of-all, home-of-all,
   hearse-of-all night.
Her fond yellow hornlight wound to the west, her wild hollow
   hoarlight hung to the height
Waste; her earliest stars, earl-stars, stárs principal, overbend
   us,
Fire-féaturing heaven. For earth her being has unbound, her
   dapple is at an end, as-
tray or aswarm, all throughther, in throngs; self in self steepèd
   and páshed—qúite
Disremembering, dísmémbering áll now. Heart, you round me
   right
With: Óur évening is over us; óur night whélms, whélms, ánd
   will end us.*

*Only the beak-leaved boughs dragonish damask the tool-smooth
   bleak light; black,
Ever so black on it. Óur tale, O óur oracle! Lét life, wáned,
   ah lét life wind
Off hér once skéined stained véined variety upon, áll on twó
   spools; párt, pen, páck
Now her áll in twó flocks, twó folds—black, white; right,
   wrong; reckon but, reck but, mind
But thése two; wáre of a wórld where bút these twó tell, each
   off the óther; of a rack
Where, selfwrung, selfstrung, sheathe- and shelterless, thóughts
   against thoughts ín groans grínd.*
      "Spelt from Sibyl's Leaves," *Poems*, No. 62

The times are nightfall, look, their light grows less;
The times are winter, watch, a world undone:
They waste, they wither worse; they as they run
Or bring more or more blazon man's distress.
And I not help. Nor word now of success:
All is from wreck, here, there, to rescue one—
Work which to see scarce so much as begun
Makes welcome death, does dear forgetfulness.

Or what is else? There is your world within.
There rid the dragons, root out there the sin.
Your will is law in that small commonweal . . .

Poems, No. 112

Óur tale, O óur oracle! Lét life, wáned, ah lét
   life wind

Off hér once skéined stained véined varíety upon, áll on twó
   spools. . . .

      "Spelt from Sibyl's Leaves," *Poems*, No. 62

  The leaves of the ancient sibyls revealed, for the most part, sombre truths about life and fearful, if cryptic, warnings. The cosmic view of the ancient Greeks was a realistic one, concerned with suffering and pain and death as well as with pleasure and joy and life. They did not practice that power of Positive Thinking which is built on the notion of God as a cosmic Tinker Bell to be kept in existence by the grinning trust of determined believers—a notion which Brooks Atkinson, John Mason Brown, and others consider to be the essence of Christianity, to judge from their reviews a few years ago when Graham Greene's *The Living Room* played so briefly on Broadway. The religious myths of the Greeks concerned themselves as much with the gods of Night as with the gods of Day, perhaps more. And this was proper. In the opening of his Gospel, St. John speaks of that darkness which struggles against the true Light; and St. Paul tells all Christians that they will share Christ's glory only if they share His sufferings. The sufferings of Christians are no less real than those of Pagans and may perhaps be more intense for being better understood.

  The Christian is as such not only a stranger in this world, but since he is a child of Adam with his roots firmly in the earth, the struggle to reach beyond the universe to the infinite life of God (so to speak—the analogy is lame) will tear him in two directions, so that he will be tempted to give up the struggle, to make himself as much at home as possible in this world and to give up the hope of sharing in Christ's Sonship. Mr. J. Robert Oppenheimer, in his moving radio address on the Columbia University Series, "Man's Right to Knowledge," over the Columbia Broadcasting System, spoke of the loneliness of the man of science in our civilization, and it is this loneliness which the man of God feels in far greater intensity. Both find that the world has assigned them the role of stranger, and both find life a struggle. *The New Yorker*, discussing Mr. Oppenheimer's words in its "The Talk of the Town," remarked, "Like all men of science, though, he is torn two ways: by the urge to add something to the store of knowledge (no matter what it is, no matter what the cost) and by the desire to make the world a better place. The conflict is evident when he speaks"

(January 15, 1955, p. 19). When he speaks sincerely from his heart of the reality and the pain of the struggle involved in his attempting to follow a noble ideal in a world which seems bent on smashing that ideal, the man of science is a tragic and a moving figure. And so in a higher sense is the man of God when he speaks from his heart of being torn two ways in his attempt to follow a divine ideal which not only the world but his own inmost nature seem bent on crucifying all over again.

The poem from which our image comes is founded upon and saturated with the ancient Greek attitude toward nature and the lot of man. As in "The Windhover" Hopkins builds his poem in the air of medieval chivalry, with its vigorous and colorful ideal of manly activity, so in "Spelt from Sibyl's Leaves" he constructs his dense and complex structure in the somber and solemn atmosphere of that culture in which the destiny of man was lost in the dark and threatening unknown and the Stoic was a noble figure. Not, of course, that Hopkins stops there. Nor is he being pedantic. He finds that world verified in the world he sees outside him, the world he lives inside him, and knows that while the pagan vision is not the whole truth, it contains truth.

But already I have falsified the position of the poem, and I do not know how to avoid doing so. There has been much excellent writing about this poem (notably Fr. Raymond Schoder's brilliant article, "Spelt from Sibyl's Leaves," in *Thought*, 19 [December, 1944], pp. 633-48, and Mr. Gardner's remarks in his two volumes), but all of it falsifies, to my mind. The difficulty lies in the excellence of the poem, I believe, in its profoundly subtle statement of a difficult point. Father Schoder's reading and critical presentation of his reading are far superior, in my judgment, to anything else that has been said about the poem, and yet I find that in one vital matter he goes badly astray. I am painfully aware that, in attempting to correct what I take to be his error, I am more likely than not to waver off into some other one. This delicate business of interpreting and transposing into prose the complex and miraculously exact poetic statement of a rich and profound mind can be put to a few sterner tests than the one presented by this poem.

This is not a pagan poem, as what I previously said would surely lead an unwary reader to conclude. But it includes the atmosphere of the pagan attitude. The Christian view is not set off in opposition to the pagan and other views, in so far as those latter are true records of human experience and true conclusions from those experiences. Christianity claims to include much more, because it claims to have truth from other sources than human experience. But it does not therefore exclude what human nature, pagan or Jewish or Christian, truly reveals. And Hopkins here sees the world outside him as Sophocles might also see it and the world inside him as Hesiod might see it. But he also sees those worlds as Christ saw them and as a Jesuit can see them. They are all men, they all see the day fade and night grow, they all suffer. And if Hesiod interprets what he sees and feels in terms of natural powers which he deifies, and Christ in terms of the infinite God Which He sees and is, and Hopkins in terms of the infinite God known by faith but not seen, that does not alter the fact that their eyes record the same events and their hearts beat with like thoughts and emotions. It is in this large and inclusive sense that Hopkins' poem is Greek—it deals with a man in reality without blinking at the truth. But at its core moves the Christian virtue of patience, at which the Greeks could barely guess in their most exalted moments. The poem deals with the Christian response to evil and to suffering, ultimately with that ideal which Plato guessed at but did not see fulfilled: "Plato the heathen, the greatest of the Greek philosophers, foretold of him [Christ]: he drew by his wisdom a picture of the just man in his justice crucified and it was fulfilled in Christ" (*Sermons*, p. 37).

The influence of the Greek meters, echoed again and again in this solemn verse, is thoroughly covered by Gardner in his several references to the poem. The length and incantatory quality of the eight-stress lines recalls the cryptic hexameters of the sibylline utterances. And Hopkins has a noble forerunner in Catholic poetry for the appeal to the evidence of natural religion in the witness of the Sibyl. One of the greatest of Catholic hymns, the *Dies Irae*, familiar in Catholic liturgy, cites the Sibyl as witness to the terror of the day of judgment (part of the substance of the sibylline oracle of our poem, too):

>Dies irae, dies illa,
>Solvet saeclum in favilla:
>Teste David cum Sibylla.

David the Jew is an inspired witness, the Sibyl a natural witness to the impending doom. And when Hopkins' heart, which speaks truth, repeats in echoing rounds the terrible threat that closes the octet and delivers the oracle read from the leaves in the sestet, Hopkins the

Christian reacts to it, not with relief, as Schoder thinks, nor with weak terror or regret, as others think, but with the grim and supernatural patience that lay within those blood-soaked words, "My Father, if it is possible, let this chalice pass me by; only not my will, but thine, be done" (Matthew, 36:39).

In our special image, Hopkins is speaking of life. The emphasis here is not, as in "The Windhover," on supernatural life. There Hopkins was speaking of both his own natural life and the divine life which he shared with Christ, with the emphasis on the divine life. Here Hopkins is also speaking of his full life, natural and divine, but the emphasis, as one can expect in an oracle with a sibylline root, is on the natural life. The emphasis at the beginning of the poem, with its solemn, vowel-opening stress on night as the source of life, rather than on the brooding Spirit of Light, and on night as the end of life, prepares for attention to the natural life we live out between birth and death. And the terrified whisper of the heart at the end of the octet also speaks of the end of nature, the dissolution that follows upon the waning of life. In the sestet, it is true, the will overcomes the terror of the heart and voluntarily accepts the situation. It determines to act, to do what it can even under these terrible conditions. But there is no looking forward to the end of the racking and the wringing.

It would be stupid indeed to conclude that Hopkins is despairing of the eventual relief, that his faith in God's mercy is giving way; if he did not hold hope and faith strongly, the positive assent of his will would have no roots at all. If he were weakening, the obvious course would be to let go, which he does not intend to do. His grasp is no weaker, but the attack upon him is much stronger. And in the suffering which that strain brings him, his unshaking resolve is to keep on saying "Yes" to God, to say and to mean those words his Master dictated for all His followers: "Thy will be done on earth as it is in heaven."

I interpret Hopkins' statement to mean: "Let life reduce itself to these two acts of 'Yes' to right and 'No' to wrong, since I have strength for no other acts." I do not find there the relief that Father Schoder finds. Father Schoder, I believe, really interprets Hopkins' words in our image as, "Let life reduce itself to these two acts, since this is the law of the spiritual life as the coming of night is the law of the natural order around us," and he finds that Hopkins is accepting the night and realizing with relief that a dawn will follow. As I have said before, I believe that Father Schoder's criticism of the poem is magnificently revealing, but I also judge that it is at this point erroneous. What he says about the spiritual life and its laws is certainly true, and Hopkins also knew that it was true. But that it is true does not warrant the conclusion that Hopkins is here saying it, and the imagery reveals, if I am not mistaken, another truth that does not include relief.

Life wanes when the power to act begins to go. We have seen in the previous chapter Hopkins' complaint that he could not bring to birth and to life the children he conceived in his heart, not there because of lack of power on his part, but because of lack of listening and heeding in those who would not be at peace with him in Christ. A deeper complaint is that his very power to act is going or gone. He writes to Bridges concerning the encouragement someone has given his music: ". . . if I were otherwise than I am it would brisk me up and set me to work, but in that coffin of weakness and dejection in which I live, without even the hope of change, I do not know that I can make or, making, could keep up the exertion of learning better" (April 1, 1885, *Letters 1*, pp. 214-15). Later he could make an even stronger statement:

It is now years that I have had no inspiration of longer jet than makes a sonnet, except only in that fortnight in Wales: it is what, far more than direct want of time, I find most against poetry and production in the life I lead. Unhappily I cannot produce anything at all, not only the luxuries like poetry, but the duties almost of my position, its natural outcome—like scientific works. I am now writing a quasi-philosophical paper on the Greek Negatives; but when shall I finish it? or if finished will it pass the censors? or if it does will the *Classical Review* or any magazine take it? All impulse fails me: I can give myself no sufficient reason for going on. Nothing comes: I am a eunuch—but it is for the kingdom of heaven's sake.

(January 12, 1888, *Letters 1*, p. 270)

The quotation reveals some of the outside pressures that were crushing the creative impulse, but as Hopkins states often in his intimate statements to his friend, it was the lack of power that crushed him most, or rather the feeling of the lack of power:

For it is widely true, the fine pleasure is not to do a thing but to feel that you could and the mortification that goes to the heart is to feel it is the power that fails you: *qui occidere nolunt Posse volunt*; it is the refusal of a thing that we like to have. So with me, if I could but get on, if I could but produce work I should not mind its being buried, silenced, and going no further; but it kills me to be time's eunuch and never to beget. After all, I do not despair, things might change, anything may be; only there is no great appearance of it. . . . soon I am afraid I shall be ground down to a state like this last spring's and summer's, when my spirits were so crushed that madness seemed to be making approaches. . . .

(September 1, 1885, *Letters 1*, pp. 221-22)

That quotation gives an insight into the psychological background from which our poem and its imagery sprang—it was conceived and composed during that period. And the poem itself, this living and magnificent expression of a Christian's Gethsemane, proves that Hopkins was wrong in feeling himself a eunuch.

This complaint of "life waned" echoes through Hopkins' last sonnets in his desire for the food of life, for the light and warmth of day, for water for his roots, for power to breed. He tells Bridges that "There is a point with me in matters of any size when I must absolutely have encouragement as much as crops rain; afterwards I am independent" (May 17, 1885, *Letters 1*, pp. 218-19). The "eunuch" image comes from our Lord's words to his followers: "There are some eunuchs, who were so born from the mother's womb, some were made so by men, and some have made themselves so for love of the kingdom of heaven; take this in, you whose hearts are large enough for it" (Matthew, 19:12). Hopkins concludes his complaint to God his Friend, *Poems*, No. 74, with these images:

> . . . birds build—but not I build; no, but strain,
> Time's eunuch, and not breed one work that wakes.
> Mine, O thou lord of life, send my roots rain.

In that splendid poem relegated by his editors to the "Fragments" section because they consider it cynical, No. 122, Hopkins finds unprofitable and self-centered man a contemptible animal, which, in one view of him, and apart from his special relationship to God, he certainly is. The lightning of nature is glorious, even if fearful and death-dealing; angels are magnificent natures, even in their rebellion and fall —the glory of both lightning and fallen angels is short-lived and destructive; but man! When this creature rebels against God, as he does, when he strikes out like lightning or like angels, the effect is only ridiculous and petty. The imagery is homely, vivid, and powerful. Let the man's name be blazoned in brilliant neons, yet he, not ashamed of spiritual crime, locks the bathroom door when he must act as a mere animal:

> What bass is *our* viol for tragic tones?
> He! Hand to mouth he lives, and voids with shame;
> And, blazoned in however bold the name,
> Man Jack the man is, just. . . .

That passing from the implied tragic viol of the fallen angels to the trivial bathroom shame of proud man was too strong for Bridges, I suspect, and plays a bigger part in effecting the banishment of the poem than does the alleged cynicism. The poem is not cynical at all. It states a truth, however, that the conventional and complacent Bridges was not likely to want to face. Hopkins faced it fully, and his vivid statement here of man's essential limitations throws light on our special image and its sequel.

In the final lines of No. 122, Hopkins adverts to his "life waned" in this special light of disgust with the rebellious animal that man is. "Dogged in den" was God's rebel in *Deutschland*, with the reflected dignity that the presence of God gives even to the rebel. But here man is considered in the light of his own tiny, flickering fire, not with the blasts of the Holy Spirit bursting about him, but only his own tameable tempests. Life's masque, even, he sees only in the spoons which require so much of his attention, since they bring him the food he must eat (and void) to feed his little flame and winds:

> And I that die these deaths, that feed this flame,
> That . . . in smooth spoons spy life's masque mirrored:
>   tame
> My tempests there, my fire and fever fussy.

I fear that in dismissing this poem, Bridges was attempting to form Hopkins in his own image—not consciously, but in fact. This uncompromising acceptance of reality in all its aspects was as distasteful to Bridges, I suspect, as the exaggerated Marianism of which he speaks. But without it, the vigor and the uncompromising sternness of Hopkins' devotion to the real, his full grasp of man's situation, is at least less obvious. To Hopkins, even the privy held its place in reality, as indeed it did to Christ his Lord (cf. Matthew, 15:17).

The waning of life and vigor receives quite different treatment in a sonnet Bridges admired more and which is addressed to him, *Poems*, No. 75, "To. R. B." Here once more God is in the picture, that flame which is the flame of natural life and the symbol of the Holy Ghost and His divine life here being treated as the male principle of "immortal song":

> Sweet fire the sire of muse, my soul needs this;
> I want the one rapture of an inspiration.
> O then if in my lagging lines you miss
> The roll, the rise, the carol, the creation,
> My winter world, that scarcely breathes that bliss
> Now, yields you, with some sighs, our explanation.

Those broken, final lines are patient. They were written only a few weeks after the "fire and fever fussy" disgust of No. 122, only a few weeks before Hopkins' early death. They are good lines for a follower of Christ to end with, since they suggest that the patience he wanted to share with his Master had endured the rack and overcome the disgust at last.[1] But they also poignantly express in other terms the pain of "life waned" of our special image, the "winter world" when life is frozen and apparently (but patience knows, not really) dead.

In our image, Hopkins' heart is, probably, stating the oracle. Recovered somewhat from its terror at the end of the octet, enough at least to receive from the eyes the vision of the stark black leaves against the "wild hollow hoarlight" of the evening sky (the same sky that Prufrock sees as the bleak sheets covering "a patient etherised upon a table"), the heart interprets the grim message of that vision. It is the telltale heart that reveals to the poet the meaning of his experience, his life, his "tale." And it says, "Allow life to wind off the once rich and colorful skein onto two spools." That imperative "let" does not indicate that Hopkins wants it that way. It means, as I see the meaning in the imagery, that since there is absolutely nothing that can be done to prevent life from fading and winding off on those two spools of right acts and wrong acts, one to be willed and one to be resisted and rejected, then, the oracle advises, let it be so. In a fatalist, such an act would be the end of the matter. In a Christian, such an act is the exercise of patience, or endurance of "dark heaven's baffling ban" or of "hell's spell" (*Poems*, No. 68). The verb, "let," is the echo of what Hopkins told Bridges at this time: "The long delay was due to work, worry, and languishment of body and mind—which must be and will be" (May 17, 1885, *Letters I*, p. 216).[2] It must and will be, so let it be. The fatalistic echoes of the statement are expressed in the image, since life is a thread, in the Greek mind, from the skein of the Fates, the daughters of night and the determiners of good and evil. Hesiod so describes them, expressing the common notion, in his *Theogony*: "Also she [Night] bare the Destinies and ruthless avenging

Fates, Clotho and Lachesis and Atropos, who give men at their birth both evil and good to have, and they pursue the transgressions of men and of gods: and these goddesses never cease from their dread anger until they punish the sinner with a sore penalty." (in *Hesiod, the Homeric Hymns and Homerica,* trans. Hugh G. Evelyn-White [London: W. Heinemann, 1936], pp. 217-22). The mother of these ladies is the threatening evil of the poem, and it is Milton's blind Fury with the abhorred shears who presides at the end of the octet. The Spinner Clotho is usually pictured with the skein of life piled on her spindle, and the lot-giver Lachesis (cf: "To seem the stranger lies my lot" of *Poems,* No. 68) winds it off, in this case on two spools. The once richly stained and veined skein has faded, waned, Hopkins states. The word "waned," note, comes as an interruption in the sentence: "Let life [which has waned, faded], ah let life wind. . . ." The "ah" is the emotional response to the contemplation of the fact of that dying down, that fading.

The skein of life is wound off on two separate spools. Since this image is part of the long final sentence and since the *two* opposites are the central concern of the whole sentence, the spools should be considered in relation to the white and black sheep which follow in the next image. The black and white sheep in separate pens are like the black and white, or at least light and dark, threads on separate spools. The color and vigor of life are reduced to these, and since it *must* be by command of God or by the spell of hell or by both, let it be so. The two spools give a remote but not a direct preparation for the final image of the torturing rack, on which two opposed drums will wind the stretching and rending ropes.

Hopkins used the image of thread winding off one skein to another in "The Sea and the Skylark" (*Poems,* No. 35) to totally different effect:

> Left hand, off land, I hear the lark ascend,
>   His rash-fresh re-winded new-skeinèd score
>   In crisps of curl off wild winch whirl, and pour
> And pelt music, till none's to spill nor spend.

In discussing with Bridges the original version of these lines, Hopkins explains his image thus:

The *skein* and *coil* are the lark's song, which from his height gives the impression of something falling to the earth and not vertically quite but tricklingly or wavingly, something as a skein of silk ribbed by having been tightly wound on a narrow card or a notched holder or as twine or fishing-tackle unwinding from a *reel* or *winch* or as pearls strung on a horsehair: the laps or folds are the notes or short measures and bars of them. . . . The lark in wild glee *races the reel round*, paying or dealing out and down the turns of the skein or *coil* right to the earth *floor*, the ground, where it lies in a heap, as it were, or rather is all round off on to another winch, reel, bobbin or spool in Fancy's eye, by the moment the bird touches earth and so is ready for a fresh unwinding at the next flight.

(November 26, 1882, *Letters 1*, p. 164)[3]

In our image, one skein is wound off onto two distinct spools, where life then lies divided. The spools, we discover at the end of the following companion image, are right and wrong (day and night). They represent the terrible struggle between the light and darkness of which the poem treats, of which St. John speaks at the opening of his Gospel. And now neither light nor darkness is in full force. It is the balanced and stretched ("equal, attuneable") hour of evening, in the soul that hour when vigor is gone and the soul is stretched between the will to serve God and the tendency to drop into the abyss of evil, when the light has waned and the darkness threatens but has not swallowed up the light.

The physical act of the winding is admirably expressed by the sound and rhythms of the passage. The first interruption occurs when "waned" breaks the rhythm in imitation of the hesitant beginning of the winding off—and perhaps the two directions of the winding can be found in the shift from "waned" to "wind." At any rate, after the interruption the rhythm speeds and whirls through the repeated vowel-plus-*n* combinations. The speed grows, it seems to me, from the vowel of "her" followed at a distance by the *n* of "once" through the repeated vowels of "skeined stained veined," with a slight fall-off in the first vowel of "variety" and a catch after "upon," where the second interruption in rhythm occurs. The thought expressed after "upon" is that not part but all of life is transferred to those spools. Hopkins' will no longer rides on the wings it wore in his earlier life, his heart no longer feels the warmth and the protection of the divine Sun and the Dove. All that color and beauty has waned, and now the brilliant skein of his life lies reduced to these two bleak colors, contrasted like the black boughs of the tree etched against the bleak white evening sky.

The companion image which follows is not pagan but Scriptural. Here, too, Sibyl the Greek rubs shoulders with David the Shepherd.

The image, treated also in the *Dies Irae*,[4] is very properly one of judgment day and its terror and is given by Christ: "When the Son of Man returns in his glory, and escorted by all the angels, he will seat himself on a throne befitting his glory. All the nations will assemble in his presence, and he will part mankind into two groups just as a shepherd parts the sheep from the goats. The sheep he will range at his right, and the goats at his left" (Matthew, 25:31-33). So now Hopkins exhorts himself to divide the whole of life into two flocks. Note that in this Christian image Hopkins is *acting*. In the image of the thread of life, with its fatalistic overtones, he is acted upon, and he cries, "Let it be so!" In this image, in which the mind proceeds from the woolen thread spun by the Fates back to the sheep from which the wool originates, his will is active. He is no longer acted upon merely, but is an extremely busy shepherd, parting the black sheep from the white, getting each group into pens, pushing and packing them in—the verbs suggest the fullness of the folds. This image must be added to the first to express the full notion of the separation involved. In part it is an activity from outside to which Hopkins' will assents, "Let it be!" That much a Greek could understand. But it is also a voluntary act on Hopkins' part, for he himself busily acts and sweats to effect this same separation. This is an aspect of Christian sacrifice which Hopkins expresses so perfectly in the "wants" (i.e., desires) of these lines from *Poems*, No. 70:

> Patience who asks
> Wants war, wants wounds; weary his times, his tasks;
> To do without, take tosses, and obey.

Whoever asks for patience also asks to suffer, to obey with Christ, even, it may be, to death on a cross. *That* a Greek could not understand: ". . . to the Jews, a discouragement, to the Gentiles, mere folly . . ." (I Corinthians, 1:23).

The verbs that follow in "Spelt from Sibyl's Leaves," calling upon the mind to concern itself with the right and wrong of its faded and sterile acts and not to bother longing for productivity, beauty, variety, could be spoken in both a purely Greek and Christian sense. To "reckon only these two," with a subtle connection to the "tell" of the following line, exhorts the mind to count up the amount of black and the amount of white, to resist the growth of one and the loss of the other. To "reck but these two" means, as in "God's Grandeur," to acknowledge the importance and authority of these two acts, of no others. "To mind but these two" orders the mind to give its faded powers to this task and to no other. Both Greek and Christian could do this, though from different motives. The Greek would proudly bear the sufferings inflicted by fate and face them without flinching; the Christian faces them and even seeks and embraces them. With Christ he chooses and wants wounds, he wills the right and rejects the wrong though every cell of his being revolts even to the point of producing a sweat of blood.

This deliberate willing of suffering and (in a sense) of defeat is not easy or even possible without the grace of God. Ignatius taught his men to say, "Passion of Christ, strengthen me." Hopkins, like Christ in Gethsemane, had to regret the crushing and stifling of his powers, which he knew to be great ones (and that made it all the harder to will their destruction), and his bitter complaints over their loss reveals how much and how deeply he did regret it. Yet even when he could do no more than will to do a good act, not a great or a noble but only a good act, and reject any wrong act, even then he could and did patiently exhort himself to accept that situation and to do what could be done, to reject despair.

In Caradoc, the villain of "St. Winefred's Well" (*Poems*, No. 105), Hopkins draws a vivid picture of a rebel against God, a man who sees his knightly heart exercising the valor of virtue and the resolution of right in carrying out his own law, not God's. And he embraces despair:

> Now be my pride then perfect, áll one piece. Henceforth
> In a wide world of defiance, Caradoc lives alone,
> Loyal to his own soul, laying his ówn law down, no law nor
> Lord now curb him for ever. O daring! O deep insight!
> What is virtue? Valour; only the heart valiant.
> And right? Only resolution; will, his will unwavering
> Who, like me, knowing his nature to the heart home,
>   nature's business,
> Despatches with no flinching. But wíll flesh, O can flésh
> Second this fiery strain?
> . . . .
>   What do nów then? Do? Nay,
> Déed-bound I am; one deed tréads all dówn here, cramps
>   all doing. What do? Not yield,
> Not hope, not pray; despair; ay, that: brazen despair out,
> Brave all, and take what comes. . . .

There are many, no doubt, who would (or perhaps do) admire Caradoc while they feel contempt for the submission of the protagonist of "Carrion Comfort" (*Poems*, No. 64), who kisses the rod which threatens him. That would be a reaction, it seems to me, not unlike the reaction of those who admire Milton's Satan for his "heroism" and condemn Adam's (unhappily not successful) attempt to submit to God's law, and Caradoc is a character somewhat like Milton's Satan. To those for whom God is an "Idea" or a "Force," the vigor of rebellion will hardly suggest treachery or self-deception. But, as I see the matter, that vigor appeared both to Milton and to Hopkins in a perspective large enough for its progressively self-destructive and basically infantile fury to appear in its true pathetic minuteness. Perhaps the most revealing words Hopkins spoke to lay open his mind on the nature of the Christian spirit of complete self-sacrifice were those he spoke to Canon Dixon in regretting the loss of a great opportunity for Dixon to use his great gifts:

> I could wish you had been elected to that Chair. But 'life is a short blanket'—profoundest of homely sayings: great gifts and great opportunities are more than life spares to one man. It is much if we get something, a spell, an innings at all. See how the great conquerors were cut short, Alexander, Caesar just seen. Above all Christ our Lord: his career was cut short and, whereas he would have wished to succeed by success—for it is insane to lay yourself out for failure, prudence is the first of the cardinal virtues, and he was the most prudent of men—nevertheless he was doomed to succeed by failure; his plans were baffled, his hopes dashed, and his work was done by being broken off undone. However much he understood all this he found it an intolerable grief to submit to it. He left the example; it is very strengthening, but except in that sense it is not consoling.
>
> (July 3, 1886[?], *Letters* 2, pp. 137-38)

And in his personal notes at this period, when he was considering that selfless willingness to choose whatever will *best* serve God which Ignatius demands of the Jesuit, whatever is "Ad *Majorem* Dei Gloriam," Hopkins repeats for himself the words of Christ about His own self-sacrifice: "And the other things on earth—take it that weakness, ill health, every cross is a help. Calix quem Pater meus dedit mihi non bibam illud?" (*Sermons*, p. 256). Christ told James and John, and through them all His followers, that they would indeed drink the cup that He would drink (cf. Mark, 10:39), and He knew that what cost Him a sweat of blood would not be easier for the weaker and the guilty. Yet He demands it, and here Hopkins, in the midst of terror and loneliness and pain, responds. And the love within that act, the love in which it is rooted, is not exteriorly in evidence, but it is evident to the eyes of the poet in the conclusion of No. 63, who sees here, too, the poor faded act of a man doing all that this man can do.

The last two lines depend from the imperative "ware." I take it that the primary meaning of that verb is, as in "mind," "be aware" of such a world and such a rack. Keep your eye on it, so that you will be ready to perform the necessary acts that you can still perform. Don't give up, don't feed on the carrion comfort, despair. The notions of "be cautious" and "avoid if possible" are not absent and may in fact be primary. But I think the main exhortation is to keep as alert as is possible and not to give up watching.

The first of the two things that the mind must be aware of harks back to the opening of the poem, where the day is balanced against the night, so that they "tell" or count off one another—as one grows the other decreases. This recalls the Greek view of the matter as reflected in Hesiod's *Theogony*:

> There Night
> And Day, near passing, mutual greeting still
> Exchange, alternate as they glide athwart
> The brazen threshold vast. This enters, that
> Forth issues; nor the two can one abode
> At once constrain.
>
> (In *The Greek Poets,* trans. Moses Hadas [New York: The Modern Library, 1953], p. 113)

Hopkins is concerned, or the oracle which his heart delivers is concerned, with maintaining that balance. He wants to be day if he can, but since he can't, he wills to be evening and hang on to as much day as possible. Evening is over him, as his heart informs him at the end of the octet. And though the heart then says that night will whelm and end him, it has not done so and will not do so as long as he can hang on to some of evening. So, in opposition to Schoder, do I interpret this exhortation to himself. Schoder takes the blackness to be that of the dark night of the senses or of the soul, as spoken of by the mystics. Schoder's picture of the sonnet, in brief, is this: Evening grows into night, the sky expands. Before darkness triumphs, yellow light, like candlelight glowing through a horn lantern, clings fondly at the horizon, while the hollow, gray monotone of evening sky climbs to the zenith. The stars appear (and Schoder, a distinguished Greek scholar himself, points out the echo of Hopkins' favorite Greek poet, Aeschylus, in "earl-stars" and "fire-featuring heaven"). Earth's color goes, giving an analogue to his spiritual state. His oracle reveals the truth to him, that his drab, undappled spiritual state is a natural phenomenon of the spiritual life, as irresistible as the advance of night, not abnormal. Hence he must no longer fear or struggle. "With a sigh of relief and resignation (not of discouraged defeat!), he counsels his heart to let life too, in her evening hours, yield up in patience her 'once skeined stained veined variety' and submit to have all her conscious affairs carded, parted among just two starkly opposed extremes—'black, white; right, wrong'" ("'Spelt from Sibyl's Leaves,'" *Thought*, 19 [December, 1944], p. 645). He is willing, now, to bear the trial, since he understands its nature and necessity.

But the imagery which closes the poem has no ring whatever of relief, patience, or resignation to my ear. It sounds with strain, fear, and dreadful self-inflicted suffering, the self's attack on non-beings. Further, Hopkins states that the "black" he is talking about is "wrong" (or moral non-being). The mystic's "darkness" is not and cannot be a submission to "wrong." My own picture is that Hopkins is telling himself *not* to do what earth has done. She has unbound her being and given way to night. Hopkins is, at the very core of his being, tempted to untwist the last strands of man in him and give way to despair, to wrong, to desertion of Christ. He is unflinchingly resolved not to do so, even though the advance of that vast blackness seems to bear down upon him as resistlessly as does night upon the world. He can't stop it from coming, so he says, "Let it come; in fact, do more, *act* to separate these things into these two basic categories. The black is there, but so is the white, and I will hang onto the white even while the black drags and pulls and stretches me in torture." Original sin and personal sin, for Hopkins, were not abstract ideas. He found them operating, as did St. Paul, at the center of his being, attempting once more to crucify Christ in him. And it is this struggle between right and wrong in himself that Hopkins expresses in the final imagery of the poem as I read it.

Hopkins here indicates, then, that the black is "wrong," like the "darkness" of John's Gospel, and that if it overwhelms him it will end him. If the "white" is the symbol of the now bleak "right" and the "black" the symbol of dismembering "wrong," then the situation is not as it was in "God's Grandeur." There the last lights off the black west go and night descends, but one can look forward to the dawn. Thus in "Carrion Comfort" (*Poems*, No. 64), the wrestling and desolation take place in a year of night which ends in a consoling dawn. But here there is no suggestion that a dawn will come if the night overwhelms. There is in fact a definite statement that if and when night does whelm, that will be the end. This is rather the situation of *Poems*, No. 65, in which the speaker desperately clings to the face of a bottomless cliff, and to drop into that darkness would certainly be the end. So here.

And as a companion to that Greek passivity, that determination to maintain the *status quo* if possible, follows the tremendously active Christian image of the torturing rack.[5] These two opposites of right and wrong form the rollers between which Hopkins' heart is stretched, a rack on which he wills to be stretched—which again opposes the idea that he is with relief accepting a dark night of the soul. On this rack he is wrung, as in *Deutschland*, stanza 9, his heart was wrung by God the Master, Who was nevertheless also the Father and Fondler. There God was Master and the malicious rebel was the slave, and there God was doing the wringing of the heart in order to kill the malice and bring to life the son and heir; He was being Master in order to become Father. Here, however, God is not doing the wringing. The heart itself is crushing itself, stringing itself, not to duty as in *Poems*, No. 41, line 78, but to torture and to endurance, actively resisting the advance of self-induced darkness, hanging on to what is left of day. And this struggle proceeds from inside the heart—hence the sheath of armor cannot protect, there is no shelter from self in the very center of the being—not from outside as in *Deutschland*. The heart does not have to be on this rack; it could give way and let night engulf it. But it will not. And the threatening moral night proceeds from that same heart, from the malice and the weakness which tempt it to rebel or to despair.

There is a careful correspondence between this image and the situation of earth in the octet. There earth has done what Hopkins' heart will not do—she has unbound her being, unstrung herself and given way to night. Hopkins here, as in No. 64, refuses to

> ... untwist—slack they may be—these last strands of man
> In me ór, most weary, cry *I can no more.*

He strings himself to resist that torture, that wringing, which he himself inflicts on himself. He will cry later in No. 71,

> ... let
> Me ... not live this tormented mind
> With this tormented mind tormenting yet.

But here he wills to remain on this rack of torment. And as the colors of earth were destroyed by her loosening their tension so that they turned in on themselves,

> ... as-
> tray or aswarm, all throughther, in throngs; self ín self
> steepèd and páshed, ...

so Hopkins' thoughts would not grind on each other in his heart if he would loosen the tension, if he would consent to give up trying to maintain his divine ideal, if he would relax into being a rebellious or disloyal man (there is no other choice, since every man by nature is a subject of Christ the King—cf. *Deutschland,* stanza 8) and give up reaching for a share in God's life. And as the colors of day were forgotten and broken up,

> ... qúite
> Disremembering, dísmémbering áll now, ...

so the all of his life and his thoughts would be disremembered if he allowed himself to untwist his last strands of man, if he himself performed that dismembering which the rack strives to do but cannot. And it cannot because the Christian will is free and powerful and not subject to the Fates under absolute rule, as the Greeks would hold. His Christian will *can* act and *will* act, in spite of echoing groans, in spite of a racking that produces a sweat of blood.

The rack in this classical atmosphere brings in the notion of a slave, for only slaves could normally be racked in classical times. Christ exhorted his followers, when they looked at themselves, to see slaves whose services are not needed by Him Whose state is kingly: "Apply this to yourselves: when you have carried out all the orders given you, just say: 'We are good-for-nothing slaves; we have merely done our duty'" (Luke, 17:10). St. Paul, as he builds up to the magnificent chapter 8 of his Letter to the Romans, with its treatment of the divine life within us, has much to say of slavery: "You know well enough that wherever you give a slave's consent, you prove yourselves the slaves of that master; slaves of sin, marked out for death, or slaves of obedience, marked out for justification. ... I am speaking in the language of common life, because nature is still strong in you.

Just as once you made over your natural powers as slaves to impurity and wickedness, till all was wickedness, you must now make over your natural powers as slaves to right-doing, till all is sanctified" (6:16-19). And the racking of the struggle of self against self Paul expresses in this way: "Inwardly, I applaud God's disposition, but I observe another disposition in my lower self, which raises war against the disposition of my conscience, and so I am handed over as a captive to that disposition towards sin which my lower self contains. Pitiable creature that I am, who is to set me free from a nature thus doomed to death?" (Romans, 7:22-24). Hopkins' answer to that question is the same as Paul's, but in this poem he is not concerned with the answer, but with enduring the terrible, pressing problem. In stanza 27 of *Deutschland,* Hopkins states that in time of stress the heart does not ask for ease, nor is it concerned with desire to share the passion of its Lord. Its whole attention is taken up with the present stress, with maintaining itself in being, with acting to preserve its good. And here the good for Hopkins is almost but not quite the good which was all St. Alphonsus had left in the terrible stress of diabolical attack. Speaking of himself in the third person, having been ordered to set down his experiences, Alphonsus wrote that diabolic apparitions so bitterly assailed him that they left him "nothing but a refusal of his consent" (August Poulain, S.J., *The Graces of Interior Prayer,* trans. Leonora Smith [London: Kegan Paul, 1910]). Hopkins has here more than that. He can still positively will to continue the struggle, to "brace sterner that strain" (*Poems,* No. 51). It was well, perhaps, that his oracle could not reveal to him the yet more terrible demands that the growth of divine life would place upon him, experiences which he would be compelled to write in blood.

Chapter 7

The Valley of the Shadow

My own heart let me more have pity on; let
Me live to my sad self hereafter kind,
Charitable; not live this tormented mind
With this tormented mind tormenting yet.
   I cast for comfort I can no more get
By groping round my comfortless, than blind
Eyes in their dark can day or thirst can find
Thirst's all-in-all in all a world of wet.

Soul, self; come, poor Jackself, I do advise
You, jaded, let be; call off thoughts awhile
Elsewhere; leave comfort root-room; let joy size
At God knows when to God knows what; whose smile
's not wrung, see you; unforeseen times rather—as skies
Betweenpie mountains—lights a lovely mile.
Poems, No. 71

Vegna ver noi la Pace del tuo Regno,
   che noi ad essa non potem da noi,
   s'ella non vien, con tutto nostro ingegno!
Purgatorio, XI

I wake and feel the fell of dark, not day.
What hours, O what black hoürs we have spent
This night! what sights you, heart, saw; ways you went!
And more must, in yet longer light's delay.
   With witness I speak this. But where I say
Hours I mean years, mean life. And my lament
Is cries countless, cries like dead letters sent
To dearest him that lives alas! away.

*I am gall, I am heartburn. God's most deep decree
Bitter would have me taste: my taste was me;
Bones built in me, flesh filled, blood brimmed the curse.
    Selfyeast of spirit a dull dough sours. I see
The lost are like this, and their scourge to be
As I am mine, their sweating selves; but worse.*

Poems, No. 69

THE VALLEY OF THE SHADOW

> I cast for comfort I can no more get
> By groping round my comfortless, than blind
> Eyes in their dark can day or thirst can find
> Thirst's all-in-all in all a world of wet.
>
> *Poems,* No. 71

"To cast" in the mind is the application of a hunting term which refers to having the dogs spread out and search in different directions for a lost scent. That Hopkins is fully aware of the potentialities of his term is adequately evidenced by his later development of the implied image, when his thoughts are dogs to be called off from their busy search for the escaped prey, comfort. In our image he indicates that he is out hunting at least for the scent of comfort, so that he can track it down, since there is no trace of comfort to be found within him. The "groping" indicates the darkness in which he searches, vainly. And there is no comfort in his soul, his "comfortless." The substantive raises to a state the quality of being without comfort.

The words of the two similes which follow should be read with as much care as Hopkins used in choosing them. "Blind eyes" does not denote "a blind man," and "thirst" does not denote "a thirsty man." Bridges has this note for the passages: "Line 6, I have added the comma after *comfortless*; that word has the same grammatical value as *dark* in the following line. 'I cast for comfort, (which) I can no more find in my comfortless (world) than a blind man in his dark world . . .'" (*Poems,* p. 250). Hopkins, however, does not compare himself to a blind man. He compares himself to blind eyes. And he does not compare himself to a thirsty man, as Gardner unfortunately thinks, nor even to a thirsty stomach (which would parallel "blind eyes"), but to thirst itself. And Hopkins' image, if one grants its words their rights, with its precise and profound gradation, adequately expresses the Christian's longing for Christ, the human soul's utter need for its God.

I presume that Bridges is correct about the grammar of the passage, though it would be possible to read "day" as a verb meaning "to produce daylight." However, I think the most natural reading is, "I can no more find comfort in my comfortless self than blind eyes can find light in their dark selves or than thirst can find relief in its yearning self."

Hopkins' point about the blind eyes is that their light does not come from themselves but from outside themselves. They can be blind either because they have bandages over them or the curtains are pulled down, so that there is no light for them, or because through some internal defect they do not receive the light effectually. In any case, they can't get light by groping in themselves, and they can't manufacture it. They have to wait until it comes to them.

A thirsty stomach is of course in the same situation in regard to water. It can't find in itself the water to relieve its thirst, but must wait for it to come from the outside. And much more is this true of thirst itself, which is the sheer longing for water or for something wet. Thirst is completely helpless to do away with itself, to dissolve itself in water; it can only yearn for the wet that will swallow it up. This is true even though the whole world is full of thirst-quenching wet. Thirst can't get at it, but must wait for it to be brought. Likewise, though the world is full of light, blind eyes of themselves can't get at it, but must wait for it to be brought. And though the whole world is full of God's comfort, Hopkins can't get at it, but must wait for it to be given to him.

Gardner's treatment of the thirst image seems to me a good example of what can happen even to a sensitive and competent critic when he fails to read the words of the text. He states:

> The last image in the octave:
> "or thirst can find
> Thirst's all-in-all in all a world of wet,"
> is, of course, a reminiscence of the Ancient Mariner's
> "Water, water, everywhere,
> Nor any drop to drink."
>
> The "world of wet" suggests Glendower's "world of water" (I *Hen. IV.,* III. i. 94)—i.e. copious brackish tears; it also suggests endless devotions which do not bring the expected spiritual comfort, as in No. 41, lines 3 and 4:
>
> "Mary, mother of us, where is your relief?"
>
> (*Gardner* 2, p. 347 n.)

That "of course" is here, as it seems normally to be in the writing of critics, including my own, a clear signal that the writer is somehow aware that he doesn't know what he is talking about. It appears in many cases to reflect that act of the will by which the intellect is carried over a hiatus in the evidence or an uneasy suspicion that something is wrong, to an especially strong statement of a conclusion—"*Of course* it is this way!" Such emphasis often indicates that someone (or some small inner voice) has said, "Are you sure?"

Coleridge's Mariner is surrounded by undrinkable salt water which will harm him. He doesn't drink it because it isn't good water. The "world of wet" which surrounds Hopkins' thirst is paralleled to the light which surrounds blind eyes and to the comfort of God which surrounds Hopkins' comfortless soul. Not only is there no implication that that "world of wet" is harmful as salt water is to a thirsty man, but to posit such a suggestion threatens destruction to the entire image.

The Mariner is a man with power to drink good water if he can find it. Thirst is not a man and has no power to drink anything. It can only long for some of the wet all around it, but has no way to get it, like the eyes and the soul in regard to light and to comfort. To parallel Hopkins with a blind man and with a thirsty man is indeed possible, but it is by no means what Hopkins does. He speaks of "blind eyes" and of "thirst."

Gardner, having through his misreading of Hopkins' text introduced the idea of salt water, went on to find other ideas connected with salt water, and the picture becomes one of the thirsty poet with only tears to drink, copious and brackish. This picture operates delightfully in *Alice in Wonderland*, where Alice draws a moral as she is threatened with drowning in her own tears, but it finds its place here only as a result of original failure to give the word in the text its rights. Gardner seldom makes such an error, and when he does, it is a slip and does not result from an erroneous critical principle. In this case, Gardner noted in Hopkins' text the notions of thirst and a great deal of water (really of "wet"), recalled that Coleridge had the same notions, and then allowed himself to confound the real meaning of Hopkins' text by smothering it in the familiar context of Coleridge's poem. If he could be convinced that Hopkins had nothing of the same situation or none of the meanings in mind that Coleridge had, Gardner would, I think, withdraw his statement as an error. He would not, like Geoffrey H. Hartman, argue that Hopkins was not concerned with precise meanings and structures.

Hopkins' repetition of the word "all" in the final line of our passage is perhaps behind Hartman's perception of a "rhythmic stuttering" in this passage. Before quoting our image, Hartman states: "In some of his later poems everything tends to become subordinate to a method of rhythmic stuttering, as it were, that would make the word a point, the strongest and non-referential intention of speech, inseparable from the nervous effort which precedes it. . ." (Geoffrey H. Hartman, *The Unmediated Vision, an Interpretation of Wordsworth, Hopkins,*

Rilke, and Valéry [New Haven: Yale, 1954], p. 187). I have attempted to indicate throughout my study how deeply I hold, like Hartman, that the sounds and the rhythms of the language, with the nervous efforts and the physical movements of lips, tongue, throat, the flow of air, etc., all enter into the imagery and the poetry of Hopkins as a part of it, and an essential part. But I must also hold and have also attempted to show that Hopkins in no sense shared the opinion that meaning is not essential to a word or to speech in or out of poetry.[1] Hartman misinterprets Hopkins' statement of a commonplace scholastic distinction between the image and the concept, both of which enter into a word (p. 187). He then concludes that Hopkins at times "cares little about grammatical precision" (p. 188). This is unfortunate critical procedure, proceeding from a misunderstood statement of the author to a conclusion which is in radical contradiction to the evidence offered by the poems and by Hopkins' own critical pronouncements and defenses. If my study does not indicate that Hopkins cares for grammatical precision as much as anyone who ever used language, then it has failed in at least one of its aims.

The repetition of the word "all" is not stuttering in any sense. "All-in-all" is an ordinary emphatic statement of the whole or of the ultimate desire. "In all a world" emphasizes the extent of the whole vast expanse. The echoing of *all* stresses the meaning of the image, the yearning for the one thing desired, which for thirst is wet, for eyes is light, for Hopkins is that comfort which springs from union with the one Beloved. The word sounds here the cry and the yearning that exist throughout Hopkins' work:

> Love, O my God, to call Thee Love and Love
>
> (*Poems*, No. 16)[2]

> ... but she that weather sees one thing, one;
> Has one fetch in her. ...
>
> (*The Wreck of the Deutschland*, No. 28, stanza 19)

> Ah well! it is all a purchase, all is a prize.
>
> ("The Starlight Night," No. 32)

> I walk, I lift up, I lift up heart, eyes,
> Down all that glory in the heavens to gleam our
>   Saviour. ...
>
> ("Hurrahing in Harvest," No. 38)

THE VALLEY OF THE SHADOW

> ... And my lament
> Is cries countless, cries like dead letters sent
> To dearest him that lives alas! away.
>
> (No. 69)

The word expresses elsewhere, too, the whole of life or of activity:

> ... áll on twó spools; párt, pen, páck
> Now her áll in twó flocks. ...
>
> ("Spelt from Sibyl's Leaves," No. 62)

> And fain will find as sterling all as all is smart. ...
>
> (["The Soldier"], No. 63)

> ... all
> Life death does end. ...
>
> (No. 65)

> Undenizened, beyond bound
> Of earth's glory, earth's ease, all. ...
>
> ("Tom's Garland: upon the Unemployed," No. 66)

> ... all is in an enormous dark
> Drowned.
>
> ("That Nature is a Heraclitean Fire...," No. 72)

> ... and why must
> Disappointment all I endeavour end?
>
> (No. 74)

Thirst's all-in-all is wet, and even in a whole world of wet thirst is helpless to reach its desire. This is Hopkins' situation in regard to God, Who is his All-in-all, Whom he is utterly helpless to reach of himself, Whose comfort (though Hopkins knows he is surrounded by it) must be given by Him.

The physical repetition of "all" is expressive, too, of the physical movements and sounds of worlds of water, the sway and the lilt, stressed also in the *r*'s and *w*'s of the other words.

The following chart may be useful in presenting the relationships involved in the image as I see it, though it fails to stress the splendid gradation from the person (I) through the organs (eyes) to the very yearning itself (thirst):

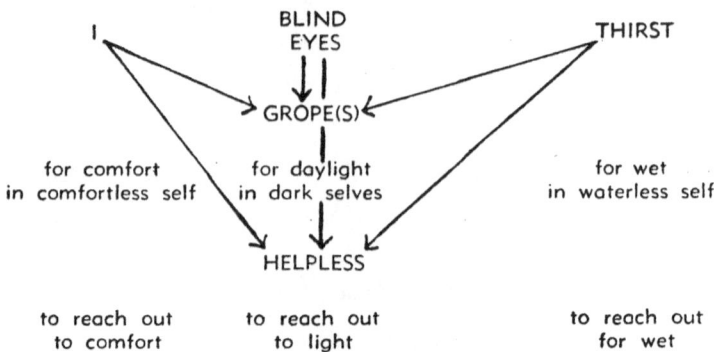

Our image operates in the poem as the second of its three parts. Most briefly, the thought development of each part may be suggested in this outline of Hopkins' conversation with himself:

Part I: Take it easy.
Part II: But I can't find comfort.
Part III: Then wait for God to give it.

The heart for which Hopkins urges more pity is the racked heart in which "thoughts against thoughts in groans grind" and more. It is the heart of *Poems*, No. 65. My personal conviction is that No. 65 is the poem "written in blood" to which Hopkins refers in his letter to Bridges, quoted in the note to No. 64 (*Poems*, p. 245). Bridges thinks that No. 64 is the poem, and certainly the octet of No. 64 deals with ultimate spiritual desolation and trial, when Hopkins, like St. Alphonsus, is left with nothing but the refusal of his consent. Or rather, Hopkins gropes in his soul for some positive act of hope, of wishing the terrible night to pass, of rejecting the second element in Hamlet's dichotomy. But in the sestet of No. 64, the light breaks, and the relief, the joy, the overwhelming wonder and awe shine out from the weary struggler. There is no such relief in No. 65. Here the whole poem deals with the horror of the storm and the struggle, and the only comfort that appears is that the pain can't last forever because the weak wretch who suffers must both sleep and die.

We see the torment of "this tormented mind" at its ghastly depths in No. 65, as the opening line makes clear. Hopkins' heart is strung up past the pitch of grief, and beyond grief what is there? The pangs which wring him here, as in *Poems*, No. 62, are educated in their work on him by the pangs which went before, so that they can do their job more thoroughly:

> No worst, there is none. Pitched past pitch of grief,
> More pangs will, schooled at forepangs, wilder wring.

The Comforter, the Holy Ghost of warm breast and bright wings, the Paraclete, brings him no comfort, and Mary, who is no Judge but only a Mother, yet brings him no relief. His cries, like sheep in a storm, huddle in that one great woe which is, I think, sin, "the blight man was born for," with its horror of crucifixion and havoc in the poor racked heart of redeemed but sinful man. As in stanza 10 of *Deutschland* God forges His will on His rebel, bending the rebellious will to Him as again in *Poems,* No. 70, so here Hopkins' cries are the nerve-grinding wince and sing of the sharp grinding of iron on iron—a most vivid poetic expression of the metallic quality of those pains which accompany severe nervous headaches. The "Then lull, then leave off" suggests, at least to me, the quiet period between such pains, with the tense waiting for the next pang to wring and twist. And in the poem the shriek of Fury and the tension poetically achieved by splitting and lengthening the metallic center of "lingering" suggest the advent of the next pang. Fury must be brief because the victim can't stand prolonged torture of such intensity.

In *Deutschland* the heart of Hopkins swooned with a horror of height, the frightening action of God from above. Here in the sestet of No. 65 the poor mountain-climbing heart fears not only the sheer height but the black and bottomless depths, and its only comfort, since it sees in the whirlwind which buffets it no hope, up or down, is to creep out of the blast under the poor shelter, the shelf of rock perhaps, of the thought that it can't last forever.

In Sister Mary Humiliata's reading of this poem—"Hopkins and the Prometheus Myth," *PMLA,* 70 (March, 1955), pp. 58-68—the protagonist cannot creep under a shelter, since she has him, like Prometheus, nailed to the rock. She carries the parallel too far, though her discussion is both intelligent and illuminating. She does not follow Gardner in his shallow view of the triviality of human guilt (as when he says of Hopkins that "It is hard to believe that his sins amounted to very much more than a failure to perform the impossible . . ." [2, p. 339]), but she does conclude that Hopkins must be thinking of himself as a voluntary co-victim with Christ in expiating the sins of the world. There is no doubt whatever that Hopkins did so think of himself, since that is a central point in the devotion to the Sacred Heart and in "The Windhover," but I do not believe that the notion of co-victim is operative in this poem. Hopkins' view of human guilt, and most intimately of his own, was as vivid and as profound as one would expect it to be in a passionately intense student of St. Paul, who knew as few others what sin is and what it has accomplished in crucifying the Lord of life. As I indicate elsewhere, I hold that in No. 65 Hopkins is expressing his struggle *against* Christ, like the wrestler in "Carrion Comfort," not his struggle alongside Christ against the sins of the world.

It is this poor struggling and tortured mind, with those cliffs of fall and those storms and efforts, that Hopkins exhorts himself in *Poems*, No. 71, to go easy on. "Let it be so," he said in *Poems*, No. 62, of his mind racked by his mind. But now in No. 71 he says, "Let that not be so; let me not live tormenting this tormented mind with this tormented mind. Let me be pitiful to myself, patient and kind to my wretched self too, not driving myself on up the sheer cliffs or racking myself with opposed thoughts."

In the second half of the octet, our special image in No. 71, Hopkins deals with that feeling of being separated from God and being trapped in self (the very definition of hell), the profoundest nature of all spiritual desolation. He had treated this experience in *Poems*, No. 69, a most poignant poetic expression of desolation. There he wakes to find the night not over and the longed-for light delaying. He feels not the soft skin of rosy-fingered dawn but the hairy hide of the bestial dark. And his poor heart, which has walked through so many black ways (as it must do, too, at the conclusion of our No. 71), must go on that way, since the light will not arrive.

"With witness I speak this," cries Hopkins, and it is his life that he is lamenting, the seeming separation from the One he loves, so far away that he must send Him letters—and they are dead letters, since they seem never to reach Him:

> I wake and feel the fell of dark, not day.
> What hoùrs, O what black hoürs we have spent
> This night! what sights you, heart, saw; ways you went!
> And more must, in yet longer light's delay.
>   With witness I speak this. But where I say
> Hours I mean years, mean life. And my lament
> Is cries countless, cries like dead letters sent
> To dearest him that lives alas! away.
>
> (*Poems*, No. 69)

In the sestet he pictures his bitter and sour interior, bearing the lonely curse of God on sinful man, without the honey-sweet presence of Christ and the sweet odor of His ointments, without the yeast which is the life of Christ, the Spirit of the Kingdom. He does not taste gall or feel heartburn—he is those. And it is God's most deep decree that orders this poisonous draught. Yet God brings nothing in from the outside for this. He simply leaves Hopkins to himself. The bitterness he tastes is not brought in from outside or inflicted on him by God. It is simply his sinful self alone with himself. He himself is the curse, built up with bones, filled out with flesh, brimmed to the full with cursed blood. The curse is as intimate to him as he is to himself, as are his bones and flesh and blood to him.

The reason why this is so is expressed in his adaptation of Christ's image of the yeast, the hidden working of the Spirit which gives health and life and sweetness to the whole mass of dough: "He told them yet another parable: 'The kingdom of heaven reminds me of a handful of yeast which a housewife mixes with three measures of flour, to work there till the whole mass has risen'" (Matthew, 13:33). The action of the Spirit is toward God, and lifts the whole mass, bones, flesh, and blood, to a sweet and vivified loaf. But when the activity of the spirit in a man is toward self and not toward God, then there is no rising, no working through the mass, and that yeast which should be the principle of life and sweetness rots and becomes the principle of sourness and corruption. Nothing is added to the self to work this corruption. It is simply the self turning in on self instead of out toward God. And this, Hopkins sees, is the very essence of damnation, to be left to self, to be trapped in self, cut off from God. The "sweating selves" here recall "man's smell" of "God's Grandeur" (*Poems*, No. 31). And the scourge of the condemned and cursed wretch is not wielded by God, but by self on self, by self rejecting God and turning in upon and rotting with self.

One difference between the experience of true spiritual desolation and the condition of the damned in hell is that for them there is no hope. This difference is enormous, but it doesn't seem so while one is suffering the spiritual desolation, and it is expressed by those two small words which seem to be almost a *sotto voce* afterthought following upon the statement of the horror. Yet those two small words, "but worse," express the act with which the poet resists the horror which fills his very being. They indicate the apparent smallness of his determined "Yes" in the face of overwhelming darkness, the apparent weakness of his grasp upon the cliffs of fall during the violent whirlwind. They measure the size and violence of the attack upon him against the resistance he is able to make. And they indicate too, in their solemn and measured finality, in their quiet, positive assertion, and in their position of ultimate emphasis in the last foot of the poem, the quality of this human will that opposes the worst that "the hellrook ranks" (cf. *Poems*, No. 47) can pour upon him. These two small words, in my judgment, comprise the most expressive, poignant, and significant measure in all of Hopkins' work.

In our special image, too, Hopkins expresses the situation of being trapped in self. His thoughts range restlessly in search of the scent of comfort, set on it by him, since he knows that comfort has left him and that there is within him only the dark longing for the true Light and an ever growing thirst for the Living Water. We have seen before the Johannine and life-giving light-and-water imagery, strikingly combined in Hopkins' description of the blind pilgrims coming to Winefred's Well to be cured:

> While blind men's eyes shall thirst after daylight,
> draughts of daylight. . . .
>
> (*Poems*, No. 105)

And the Person Who is the source of the Light the poet yearns for and the Living Water to quench his thirst is named in Hopkins' translation of St. Thomas' familiar hymn to the Blessed Sacrament:

> Jesu whom I look at shrouded here below,
> I beseech thee send me what I thirst for so,
> Some day to gaze on thee face to face in light
> And be blest for ever with thy glory's sight.
>
> (*Poems*, No. 131)

In the octet, Hopkins begins with an attempt to pull his divided forces together, it seems to me. He addresses his soul, the commander of all his forces, of his sinew-service, of his tortured heart and opposing thoughts,[3] and reminds it that it is a poor self. He urges it, the poor jaded Jackself, to give up its frantic activity in searching for the way to union with the Light and the Living Water. The soul, like Jack, is not an elegant figure, but a workaday, ordinary human soul, made for human activity yet destined for divine life and activity if it will act "in Christ," like the "Jessy or Jack" of *Poems*, No. 50, who in their humble task by the small candle can, if they will, aggrandize and glorify God. A Jack is a male representative of the nature of something, and it signifies the individual *supposit* or person with reference to his nature merely, without speaking of his individual good or bad qualities. The "jack" of a jackrabbit or a jackass merely points to the kind and sex (or merely the kind) without reference to individual size, strength, stubbornness, or weakness.

Hopkins' use of the term is illuminating of his attitude toward himself, as expressed in his poems. When, in No. 122, he wants to take man just as the kind of thing he is, rather than as the naturally dangerous or majestic rebel against God that he imagines himself to be, he reduces man to his natural size with the term Jack—and the corresponding female term Jane (or Jenny or Jessy) slips into a related but perhaps more contemptuous term: "Man Jack the man is, just; his mate a hussy." At the resounding close of No. 72, Hopkins wants to contrast the "mortal trash" in his nature to that part of him which will survive death. The mortal trash is described in five nouns, "Jack, joke, poor potsherd, patch, matchwood," each of them expressive of that in human nature which is cheap and laughable (objectively considered, that is); and the lasting things in man, which naturally considered are his soul and its activities independent of the body, are described as "immortal diamond." All of this, natural trash and natural diamond, is transformed and transfigured by a share in the risen life of Christ and becomes that final glorious and supernatural "immortal diamond":

> Flesh fade, and mortal trash
> Fall to the residuary worm; world's wildfire, leave but ash:
> In a flash, at a trumpet crash,
> I am all at once what Christ is, since he was what I am, and
> This Jack, joke, poor potsherd, patch, matchwood,
>   immortal diamond,
>   Is immortal diamond.[4]
> ("That Nature is a Heraclitean Fire...," *Poems*, No. 72)

The soul of "Jackself," then, is the human soul considered just as it is, without reference to the divine life that can and does raise it to a divine level. It is the common human self, and here it is "jaded," which suggests that it is a weary plow horse, or, better, a "jackass"—like the "Brother Ass" which was St. Francis' favorite name for his body. Hopkins is giving this weary but dogged soul advice. He doesn't command it, since it evidently goes its own way. But he seriously advises it. Come now, he says, let the activity stop for a pace and rest. He makes clear in the following imagery that the activity to which he refers is the tormenting, the casting for comfort, of the octet. The hunting signified by "cast" is developed when thoughts are called off as hunters call off panting dogs that cannot find the scent. Call them off elsewhere, not on the trail of comfort any more. Then the image changes, and the over-zealous hunter-soul becomes the over-zealous gardening-soul, so intent on rooting out sin and fault and planting virtues that it leaves no root-room for comfort to grow in its garden. Let joy get bigger, the adviser continues, not at the time chosen by you and because of the event or object chosen by you, but at the time and because of the event chosen by God, "At God knows when to God knows what." Hopkins' word "size," which Gardner finds "a personal twist which makes for obscurity" (*Gardner 1*, p. 116), is precisely used in the same sense by Keats in *Endymion*:

> The gulphing whale was like a dot in the spell,
> Yet look upon it, and 'twould size and swell
> To its huge self. . . .
>
> (III, 205-7)

This advice to wait for God's time and event is followed by the kind lesson, "whose smile/'s not wrung, see you." That is the vital lesson that the soul must now learn and has not so far learned. It is still trying to master God, instead of saying "Yes" to Him as Master. It won't yet say, with full sincerity, "Thy will be done." It will at least try to fix the time and occasion on which His will should be done. And the deepest significance is that the soul, which was wrung on the rack of its own tormented mind at the opening of the poem, is actually trying to rack God, to wring from Him that smile which is light and water, which is life. Learn this, soul, Hopkins says, that you cannot rack God; but if you will quietly wait, his smile will shine upon you.

St. Ignatius, in the eighth of his Rules for the Discernment of Spirits for the First Week, has this to say: "Let him who is in desolation strive to remain in patience, a virtue contrary to the troubles which harass him; and let him think that he will shortly be consoled . . ." (*The Spiritual Exercises*). Hopkins is repeating to his soul, with the same "let it be" advisory tone, the lesson he learned from his own spiritual father. And to his pilgrim soul, walking in the darkness of faith and not in the light of vision,[5] and walking now through the valley of the shadow of death, the bright sky will replace the overhanging cliff when he least expects it, since he does not know the strange roads or the breaks in the mountains, and will light a lovely mile of his journey.

The traveler plodding through the dark yearns for light (and no doubt for water), and the surprise of the bright sky comes as consolation which Hopkins in *Poems,* No. 47, denotes as "tufts of consolation":

> Then though I should tread tufts of consolation
> Dáys áfter, só I in a sort deserve to
>   And do serve God to serve to
> Just such slips of soldiery Christ's royal ration.

These tufts make his pilgrimage more pleasant, since he walks like Moses with unshod feet, not like the trampling generations of "God's Grandeur."

The water and light of our image are operative in other comforting and life-giving activity in this sestet. The comfort which needs root-room also needs the light and water of God to grow. And He will give them, so that the joy which is at one with the comfort from the comfortless self of our image is, like peace and patience, an effect or a "fruit" of the Holy Ghost, the divine life of charity in the soul: "But the fruit of the spirit is love, joy, peace, patience . . ." (Galatians, 5:22). It was snatched away from Hopkins' soul together with peace, the dove, and he sends out his thoughts to find its scent or perhaps that of the thief. St. Thomas, in his discussion of this joy (*Summa Theologica,* II-II, q. 28, "De Gaudio") states in article 3 that "Gaudium autem comparatur ad desiderium sicut quies ad motum . . . ." Joy, in other words, is the end or goal of desire, so that as the desire is satisfied, joy grows. The desire so powerfully expressed in our image, especially in the analogy to thirst, is the prelude to the joy which will be full when that desire is fully satisfied by the possession of the desired object. And though joy is never *full* in the occasional smile of God in this life, the comforts of spiritual consolation, yet it sizes under that light and that water, the "fruit" of the life of Christ in the heart and the fostering care of the Spirit.

Bridges doesn't like "betweenpie." He could accept "intervariegates," but, like Alice, he wonders whether the one word (he should rather say "sound") "pie" can be made to mean such different things. The word "to pie" in Hopkins' sense does not exist, he says in his note to the poem. Bridges may never have heard of the expression "pie-eyed," though as a doctor he must have observed such effects. And someone must have pied the piper's coat before he became the Pied Piper. Hopkins' "Pied Beauty" (*Poems,* No. 37) might have prepared him for God as a pier of skies—"For skies of couple-colour as a brinded cow . . . ." And when the dark mountains are split open by the light and glorious color of a clear sky seen between them, what better word can express what those skies do (and what the Comforter does, and what Mary mother of us, our atmosphere and lovely sky, does) than "betweenpie"? Intervariegates?

In Sonnet 98, Shakespeare speaks of "proud-pied April," and in *Love's Labour's Lost* (V, ii) of "daisies pied." Milton's "Meadows trim with Daisies pide" in "L'Allegro" are familiar to everybody. No one ever thinks of pastry, surely, in reading those lines. I do not think it is altogether just and reasonable, therefore, to insist that Hopkins' use of the word *should* bring in the notion of pastry. If it does, it seems to me that it should come in in some such way as it does for Laura Riding and Robert Graves—who early insisted that Hopkins' words were used profoundly and exactly and that they had to be given their full rights in the text and context: "We must appreciate the accuracy of the term *Betweenpie.* Besides being again just the sort of homely kitchen language that the Jackself would use to describe how sky seems pressed between two mountains (almost as a smile is pressed between lips) it is also the neatest possible way of combining the patching effect of light . . . with the way this light is introduced between the mountains" (*A Survey of Modernist Poetry* [London: W. Heinemann, 1927], p. 92). To dapple or to pie the darkness of the way with a wedge of glorious sky between the mountains does not, to my mind, call in the thought of a piece of pie at all. Riding and Graves appear to me to advert delicately to such an influence in their "homely kitchen language," but they do not press the point, and their "smile pressed between lips" indicates a different shape from that of the pieces of pie I have known. It is the shape of the quarter-moon, like the "quaint moonmarks" which "scatter a colossal smile" out from the darkness of the stormfowl's wings in "Henry Purcell," *Poems,* No. 45. This sky which pies the darkness of the valley of the shadow is like that other colossal smile, here the smile of God which cannot be wrung from Him, but which, in His own time, is freely given. When He chooses, the lovely smile will light those unforeseen times.

In the relatively feeble imagery of "Nondum," *Poems,* No. 22, we heard the young Hopkins speak of the "chastening wand" of patience and ask God to lead him through the darkness and to whisper to his frightened and watching heart one word, to make him smile in confidence of love and protection. The patience we have seen in these last poems is no chastening wand, but a rack and a torment. The journey through the darkness is one of sterility, of whirling blasts on the mountainous cliffs, of utter blackness through towering mountains. And the whisper his heart echoes in horror is, "Our night whelms, whelms, and will end us." The foretelling of the young Hopkins was in a general way correct, but almost incredibly pale beside the violent and vigorous colors of the reality. And the wretch Hopkins—he judges himself a wretch, it should be noted; God does not—found these heights more formidable than men have found Mount Everest. Brave men have conquered Everest and have been honored with knighthood for their achievement. The glory owing to this knight of Christ who hung on, who kept on through storm and through torture and through darkness until he reached the goal, could not stem from the smile of an earthly monarch.

CHAPTER 8

The Good Earth

Earth, sweet Earth, sweet landscape, with leavès throng
And louchèd low grass, heaven that dost appeal
To, with no tongue to plead, no heart to feel;
That canst but only be, but dost that long—

Thou canst but be, but that thou well dost; strong
Thy plea with him who dealt, nay does now deal,
Thy lovely dale down thus and thus bids reel
Thy river, and o'er gives all to rack or wrong.

And what is Earth's eye, tongue, or heart else, where
Else, but in dear and dogged man?—Ah, the heir
To his own selfbent so bound, so tied to his turn,
To thriftless reave both our rich round world bare
And none reck of world after, this bids wear
Earth brows of such care, care and dear concern.
                    "Ribblesdale," *Poems*, No. 58

I remember a house where all were good
   To me, God knows, deserving no such thing:
   Comforting smell breathed at very entering,
Fetched fresh, as I suppose, off some sweet wood.
That cordial air made those kind people a hood
   All over, as a bevy of eggs the mothering wing
   Will, or mild nights the new morsels of spring:
Why, it seemed of course; seemed of right it should.

Lovely the woods, waters, meadows, combes, vales,
All the air things wear that build this world of Wales;
   Only the inmate does not correspond:
God, lover of souls, swaying considerate scales,
Complete thy creature dear O where it fails,
   Being mighty a master, being a father and fond.
            "In the Valley of the Elwy," *Poems*, No. 40

THE GOOD EARTH 163

> Earth, sweet Earth, sweet landscape, with leavès throng
> And louchèd low grass, heaven that dost appeal
> To, with no tongue to plead, no heart to feel;
> That canst but only be, but dost that long. . . .
> "Ribblesdale," *Poems,* No. 58

Man is not the only creature of God who gropes for Him, as the self of the desolate speaker of the previous image groped round its comfortless. Earth too, as Hopkins tells us in his lovely "Ashboughs" (*Poems,* No. 111), gropes through her living creatures, in this poem with the sweeping talons of the moving ash-boughs, toward God:

> . . . it is old earth's groping towards the steep
> Heaven whom she childs us by.

In our image above, earth appeals to heaven, and Hopkins makes the ambiguity of the verb operate fully in both its directions. The earth can be an appealing object in God's eyes because it is good and, in this poem, loving and pitiful. The earth can also state its appeal to God, and in this poem does, in the only terms in which it can state that appeal when its eye, tongue, and heart will not cooperate.

The formula of Genesis used after each element of the description of the creation of earth and all things upon it except man, "And God saw it, and found it good," contains the first Scriptural reflection of the appeal of earth for God. And the statement of St. Paul which Hopkins places in the manuscripts of the poem as the text upon which his thought is based indicates the active appealing and groaning of earth: "If creation is full of expectancy, that is because it is waiting for the sons of God to be made known. Created nature has been condemned to frustration; not for some deliberate fault of its own, but for the sake of him who so condemned it, with a hope to look forward to; namely, that nature in its turn will be set free from the tyranny of corruption, to share in the glorious freedom of God's sons. The whole of nature, as we know, groans in a common travail all the while" (Romans, 8:19-22). The interpretation of the passage is disputed among Catholic theologians, but Hopkins makes it clear enough in his poem how he interprets it. Nature is longing, yearning for that salvation which will come also to it through the "sons of God," the heirs of the previous verses of St. Paul's letter. Nature is not at fault, but it shares the condemnation put upon man by God, and it shares also in the hope of salvation through Christ. But the earth cannot cry out "Abba, Father" as the heirs can (Romans, 8:15), because man is its tongue and heart. And poor earth, that had to hear from the mouth of God those terrible words spoken to Earthy, Adam, its child, ". . . and now, through thy act, the ground is under a curse" (Genesis, 3:17), in Hopkins' poem both appeals to God for its children that it feeds with leaves and grass and, at the same moment that it yearns for its own freedom from the divine curse, worries over its child and its master, man, who will not work for that freedom either for himself or for his mother earth.

There is on some points a remarkable and illuminating analogy between the relations of earth to man and the relations of Mary to Christ. Hopkins hints at this analogy in "The May Magnificat" (*Poems,* No. 42), with its comparison of "mothering earth" with Mary magnifying the Lord. Mary, overshadowed by the Holy Ghost, brings forth a Son to Whom she really gives her human life and upon Whom she is totally dependent for her own salvation. Earth brings forth a child, too, under the *special* Breath of God added to that creative activity by which the divine Dove Who brooded over the waters formed the rest of material creation, and upon that child earth is totally dependent for her own fulfillment. She is given to that child fully by the Creator so that he may use her for his own good and for God's glory and so that through him she may share in the glorious freedom of God's sons. In this poem, earth in no sense is a wife to man, as Gardner thinks she is (". . . nature is like a devout woman married to a selfish waster" [2, p. 273]; if she is a wife, it is to God, as in "Ash-boughs."[1] She is a life-giving and life-preserving mother, like Mary, the Air, of *Poems,* No. 60, or like the "cordial air" and "mothering wing" of *Poems,* No. 40, which Hopkins calls the companion poem to the one we are considering.

Earth is sweet because, like all of creation except the sinful angels and sinful man, she says "Yes" to God in all things. Nothing of the sour "worst word" of man (cf. *Deutschland,* stanza 8) finds place in earth, except in so far as earth speaks in her child, man. And, as St. Paul indicates and Hopkins asserts, she does not want man to speak that sour word. She herself, in her own speaking, is pure. The only speech she has is her being, but that inarticulate speech she exercises, our image says, long and well. The state of being and the activities of earth and her infra-rational children, with their sounds and motions, are all *pure* speech, signifying their service and unknowing praise of God. Hopkins expressed this sweetness and pureness of earth perhaps most vividly in "The Sea and the Skylark" (*Poems,* No. 35). The imagery of that poem illuminates the sweet earth of our image.

The poet's right ear, as No. 35 opens, attends to the ancient noise of the sea, and his left ear hears the ancient pelting carol of the lark. These two sounds, founded in eternity and utterly incapable of direction toward evil, of impurity in service and praise of God, cry shame to the world of men, where activity is founded in time and tends toward evil, "shallow and frail town." The last splendid image throws a great deal of light on Hopkins' conception of the relations between man and earth. Hopkins includes all of the sons of Adam, "we," among those shamed by the sea and the skylark. And we are, all of us, the pride of all material creation, with our spiritual souls and activities, our ability to know and to love God, to serve Him and know that we are doing it. We are the crown of life, the peak of God's creative activity in the material universe, cared for by God and by earth and all other living things. We are, collectively, the crowned heir of which St. Paul speaks. And have we maintained that peak of cheer and charm which creation knew for that pitifully brief length of time in Paradise? God brought earth to that peak through so many aeons of forward-looking activity, and do we, the crowning achievement of earth under God, act purely for God's praise and service as all His creatures are made to do, as do the sea and the skylark all through time? No, we have lost that peak, and our activity, the things we make to love and to worship, the acts grounded in self-love by which we make them, are not keeping us at that peak, but are breaking us and all of creation with us down the slopes, down to the final dust to which we return, down to the first slime from which we were formed. And earth, which can be lifted up only in us, the bridge between matter and spirit, is also lost and sunk in her own dust and slime, ruined in our ruin.[2]

Earth is good in Hopkins' eyes, not evil, even though she bears the curse of God. And when man slides down toward earth instead of rising up toward God, earth is not pleased or happy. When man chooses himself above God, as he can, then he sinks into the matter from which he was raised—self-yeast of spirit cannot raise the mass; only God-yeast of spirit can do that, as St. Paul states in the verses preceding those which are the text of our image: "If you live a life of nature, you are marked out for death; if you mortify the ways of nature through the power of the Spirit, you will have life" (Romans, 8:13). And earth, which was created by God as good and given over to serve God through serving man, is concerned over the self-bent of man who is her child and her one means of reaching God. She grieves over the offense to the husband-Spirit for Whom she gropes by means of her trees and her grass, Whom she can reach only through man; but here her concern and care is centered upon the thriftless heir who ruins himself in ruining her.

The sweet earth of our image, in whose motherhood we find "all things sizing" in *Poems*, No. 42, here in No. 58 is thronged with leaves and covered with slouching low grass. Trees and leaves are most of all expressive to Hopkins of earth's good mothering function:

> Not of áll my eyes see, wandering on the world,
> Is anything a milk to the mind so, so sighs deep
> Poetry tó it, as a tree whose boughs break in the sky.
> (["Ash-boughs"] *Poems*, No. 111)

It is the aspens dear,

> ... whose airy cages quelled,
> Quelled or quenched in leaves the leaping sun, ...
> ("Binsey Poplars," *Poems*, No. 43)

which gave such beauty to the "Sweet especial rural scene." It is in the frame of an elm's arching boughs that Hopkins loves to see the splinters of light and ropes of shadow shift and pair in the great white clouds of heaven:

> Down roughcast, down dazzling whitewash, wherever an elm arches,
> Shivelights and shadowtackle in long lashes lace, lance, and pair.
> ("That Nature is a Heraclitean Fire ...," *Poems*, No. 72)

It is the chervil, literally the "rejoicing leaf," which is the symbol of nature's joy in motherhood in the "leaved how thick" banks and brakes of No. 74. The leaves give lovely shade and shelter in the "Epithalamion" (No. 121):

> ... We are leafwhelmed somewhere with the hood
> Of some branchy bunchy bushybowered wood. ...

THE GOOD EARTH

The leaves make the chosen pool "sweetest, freshest, shadowiest." Breaking up the summer light, they are of unearthly beauty:

> Rafts and rafts of flake-leaves light, dealt so,
>   painted on the air,
> Hang as still as hawk or hawkmoth, as the stars or
>   as the angels there,
> Like the thing that never knew the earth, never off roots
> Rose.

The trees in Paradise gave shade and food to man, as the grass gave comfort to the unshod foot and food to the beasts. On the first man and woman God pronounced His blessings, and through them, on the earth: "Increase and multiply and fill the earth, and make it yours; take command of the fishes in the sea, and all that flies through the air, and all the living things that move on the earth. Here are all the herbs, God told them, that seed on earth, and all the trees, that carry in them the seeds of their own life, to be your food; food for all the beasts on the earth, all that flies in the air, all that creeps along the ground; here all that lives shall find its nourishment" (Genesis, 1:28-30). The earth appeals to her Creator in bringing forth those lovely leaves which brood over man like "the beadbonny ash that sits over the burn" in Scotland, or truth-revealing leaves like those which speak to the heart of Margaret in No. 55 and to the heart of the poet in No. 62, or leaves that flash the beauty of God like those of the whitebeam and the abeles of No. 32. The grass which "clothes the mountainside" with food for man and beast and bird (cf. Psalm 146) and which offers to man's unshod foot "tufts of consolation" is the poor dumb speech of earth to the God Who created, or rather Who is now creating, her.

The *being* of earth of which our image speaks is elaborated in the next four lines. This is not a static or a mechanical being, not a product of the "Architect of the universe" notion of the deists. God does not start the machine and then withdraw to let it operate by itself. Creation is a continuous outpouring of being from God, as water pours from a fountain or light from the sun:

> Thee, God, I come from, to thee go,
> All day long I like fountain flow
> From thy hand out, swayed about
> Mote-like in thy mighty glow.
>   (*Poems*, No. 116)

Thus the long being of earth, which began "in the beginning" and which exercises itself now in the leafy dale and the winding motion of the river Ribble, was given by the hand of God at the moment of creation and is being given by the hand of God at this present moment too:

> ... who dealt, nay does now deal,
> Thy lovely dale down thus and thus bids reel
> Thy river. ...

God is giving earth her being, and earth in exercising it is pleading with Him both for herself and for the generations that have trod and are treading upon her; she is supporting and brooding over destructive and thriftless man, who should be heir both to the heaven to which earth appeals and to the renewed earth herself.

The tongue and the heart which our image finds missing in earth are discovered, in the opening lines of the sestet, in "dear and dogged man." Hopkins works the word "dogged" for all it is worth. In *Deutschland,* stanza 9, the idea of being hunted, harried by dogs, is strongly suggested:

> ... Wring thy rebel, dogged in den,
> Man's malice, with wrecking and storm.

In "Ribblesdale," it is man's sullen pertinacity which is primary, though the suggestion of his being hunted by God his Father, watched by Earth his Mother, is not absent from the word. He is dear to both of them, and they dog his footsteps even when he goes his own ruinous way.

This man, who is earth's eye, tongue, and heart, since he alone of all earth's children can see God, speak to God, love God, is the heir in the glorious Pauline sense found in the passage in Romans, 8, to which Hopkins refers us, as specifically was the nun of *Deutschland.* He is also heir in the sense of the Beatitudes, "Blessed are the patient; they shall inherit the land . . ." (Matthew, 5:4), and in the sense of St. Peter's second letter, "And meanwhile, we have new heavens and a new earth to look forward to, the dwelling-place of holiness; that is what he has promised" (3:13). But he will receive his inheritance only if he accepts the divine life through and in Christ, only if he shares in the glorious freedom of the sons of God which will come to earth through those human beings who receive it. And the heir is not accepting Christ's gift. Unlike the river and the dale, which are God-bent, which give themselves over fully to the use (rather to the abuse) of each generation, this heir binds himself to his own self-will, ties himself to his own selfish and evil inclinations.

The will bent to self rather than to God we have seen previously. The word "turn," however, offers here more than one possibility. Since it is a question of destroying the goods of the earth without care for those who come after, the word could mean that this heir considers only his turn in the unending cycle of generations, his time of life without regard to posterity. Since it is a question of his following his inclinations, his "selfbent," rather than following the commands of God and accepting the divine gift of "world after," the word could mean that this heir accepts only what appeals to his turn of mind, his disposition. Both meanings appear to me fully operative, the first developed in the "thriftless" activity which recalls the Prodigal Son, that heir who rejected his inheritance with no regard for his father or for his posterity, and the second developed in the "reck" which recalls the "reck his rod" of "God's Grandeur" and which refers to the rejection of God's authority in favor of one's own inclinations.

Over this self-centered and self-destroying child, Earth frowns in worried care. Gardner thinks that this frown does not appear on earth, but on the face of a just man: "The relationship of men to 'mute insensate things' had been even closer in *Ribblesdale,* in which the poet says that man is the 'eye, tongue, heart' of Earth; so that when a just man knits his brows with pain and sorrow at the sight of sin and ugliness, the Earth too appears to 'wear brows of such care, care and dear concern'" (2, p. 352). Gardner falters, I fear, before the vigor of Hopkins' metaphoric activity. It is the earth that frowns, not a just man. There is no just man in this poem, but only the selfish and thriftless heir, the Prodigal in the course of his prodigality. And the earth can frown because she is a mother, and mothers have brows and do frown over their unconcerned and careless children. The physical basis for the frown in the dale of Ribble is discussed by Hopkins in a letter to the journal *Nature,* printed on January 3, 1884, and quoted in *Letters* 2, pp. 162-66. After the detailed description of a remarkable sunset, Hopkins says: "While these changes were going on in the sky, the landscape of Ribblesdale glowed with a frowning brown" (p. 166). This is the sweet landscape of our poem which is frowning, and in the poem Hopkins supplies the reason for the frown. With an eye on the revelation of St. Paul in Romans, 8, as well as on the lovely, frowning landscape, Hopkins builds a rich and complex metaphorical structure which, well founded in physical reality, soars safely to spiritual heights. His lovely earth yearns metaphorically and, in a mysterious way, also literally, for the divine life, and she makes her appeal to God in her blind, dumb, insensate way, since her "pride and cared-for crown" will not speak for her. And as she faithfully travels the bend, the curve, the God-bent to which God determines her (recall "the bent world" of "God's Grandeur") and as she turns with the motion that God gives her, she feels deep concern for her child and God's, who bends his will away from its straight course to God, who chooses to rankle and roam in backwheels like a wagon churning in a muddy rut (cf. *Poems,* No. 47), rather than to roll forward with the turn God gives him. Earth serves God and at His command gives herself to her child, man, in spite of all "rack and wrong," and in her sweet unselfish love is filled with concern over the reaving of her rich round self bare and over the ignoring of the next world, not so much for her own sake, but because it is her child that is inflicting this loss not only on her but most of all on himself.

Both in imagery and in sound-structure our poem resembles its companion, No. 40, "In the Valley of the Elwy." That poem was written some five years before ours, but the concern with the goodness and the mothering quality of earth is the same. The imagery of No. 40 closely resembles the structure of "God's Grandeur," with the "mothering wing" and the "mild nights" fostering life as do the "warm breast" and "bright wings" of dove and sun. The movement and the rhythms of No. 40 are quiet like quiet and cordial air. *M*'s and *r*'s and *l*'s keep the flow of sound calm and continuous, rising to two pairs of quiet surges in the prayer at the end.

In that poem the earth is giving life and completing its God-given work, but man is not. In our poem, earth is involved in the hurt and havoc of the Fall. The sound-structure of our poem, too, is subtly different from that of its companion poem. The motion of the smoothly turning earth is brought out in our poem, in part, by the lack of pause at the ends of lines and by the emphasis on *l*'s and *r*'s in the building of the sound-structure.

The striking difference in sound pattern between the octet and the sestet of our poem can be most readily perceived, I think, by noting that the long *e* sound, first sounded and repeated in "sweet," is dominant with the pervading *l* in the octet. The *r*, with shorter vowels, takes over in the sestet. The effect seems to my ear to be that in the octet the sound expresses an upward curve or lilt, a lift, as of earth's appeal, and that the sound of the sestet expresses a downward curve, as of earth's brooding over man.

Certainly the rhythm of the octet is far more smoothly continuous than the rhythm of the sestet, with its pauses and its climactic catch in the "care, care" of the final line. The rhythm of the earth, smooth in its own response to God's dealing and bidding and giving, is hesitant and uncertain and broken in its concern over man's failure to respond to the direction and the motion God gives him.

Kind and perceptive Canon Dixon, in his response to Hopkins after receiving from him a copy of this poem, wrote, "I like the Sonnet on Earth the Creature, which you sent, very much, as I do all your work: it has the rareness, the sweetness that is in all: and could have been written by none other" (*Letters* 2, p. 110). Rare and sweet the poem is, and it reveals much of Hopkins' Pauline attitude toward nature. Nature is good, and its natural products, the "wildness and wet" of "Inversnaid" (*Poems,* No. 56), are good and priceless:

> What would the world be, once bereft
> Of wet and of wildness? Let them be left,
> O let them be left, wildness and wet;
> Long live the weeds and the wilderness yet.

This good wildness of nature is not found among human persons, except for Mary Immaculate, "World-mothering air, air wild. . . ." The curse of God, so vividly pictured by St. Paul, lies upon man (though in Christ that self-bent will can be straightened, if man wills) and through man on the good earth. Sin and death reach down even into the center of inanimate creation, since the pride and crown of the material universe has upset the relation of things to God, has broken off the flow of the divine life of the sons of God into the material universe. Nature too, as Paul states, shares in the frustration which man has brought upon himself. And the profound and mysterious truth that Paul sets forth, that through the infusion of divine life into man nature, too, can be set free from the tyranny of corruption, that even sweet earth, to the limit of its natural capacity, can find the bliss that the nun of *Deutschland* found "for the pain, for the patience"—this truth lies behind our image and gives it life.

CHAPTER 9

The Thread for the Maze

> . . . *lovely-felicitous Providence*
> *Finger of a tender of, O of a feathery delicacy, the breast of the*
>   *Maiden could obey so, be a bell to, ring of it, and*
> *Startle the poor sheep back!*
>   *The Wreck of the Deutschland, Poems,* No. 28, stanza 31

> *It will flame out, like shining from shook foil . . .*
>   "God's Grandeur," *Poems,* No. 31

> *Mary Immaculate,*
> *Merely a woman, yet*
> *Whose presence, power is*
> *Great as no goddess's*
> *Was deemèd, dreamèd; who*
> *This one work has to do—*
> *Let all God's glory through,*
> *God's glory which would go*
> *Through her and from her flow*
> *Off, and no way but so.*
> "The Blessed Virgin compared to the Air we Breathe,"
>   *Poems,* No. 60

> *My heart in hiding*
> *Stirred for a bird,—the achieve of, the mastery of the thing!*
>   "The Windhover: To Christ our Lord," *Poems,* No. 36

> *And so he does leave Patience exquisite,*
> *That plumes to Peace thereafter.*
>   "Peace," *Poems,* No. 46

> *Óur tale, O óur oracle! Lét life, wáned,*
> *ah lét life wind*

*Off hér once skéined stained véined variety upon, áll on
   twó spools . . . .*
>   "Spelt from Sibyl's Leaves," *Poems*, No. 62

*I cast for comfort I can no more get
By groping round my comfortless, than blind
Eyes in their dark can day or thirst can find
Thirst's all-in-all in all a world of wet.*
>   *Poems*, No. 71

*Earth, sweet Earth, sweet landscape, with leavès throng
And louchèd low grass, heaven that dost appeal
To, with no tongue to plead, no heart to feel;
That canst but only be, but dost that long—*
>   "Ribblesdale," *Poems*, No. 58

> ... that they may have life ....
> John, 10:10

We have examined in fairly exhaustive detail eight of Hopkins' images, both with regard to their essential elements and to their poetic environment. They are characteristic images, as our survey has attempted to demonstrate in indicating some of their relationships to other images and groups of images. They comprise, in oil-driller's terminology, a good "core," a sampling of the structures beneath the surface. And I shall attempt, in this concluding chapter, the geologist's job of analyzing that core, of stating the conclusions which may justly be drawn from these gleaming segments of poetic strata.

The words of the images reveal the exactness, the resources, and the ingenuity of the mind which employed them and which required of them a full day's work and often more. "Feathery," for example, in our first image expresses not only the exact quality of the delicacy involved, but encompasses the feathers of that Providence which would gather His children under His wings, refers back to the "O Father, not under thy feathers" of stanza 12 and in effect contradicts that statement, and above all (poetically considered) builds the sound and rhythm pattern which the poet here desires.

Again, the words, with their exact meaning, their full and complex emotional content, their references to other images, sometimes reach deep into history—not pedantically, not leaving the present world in which they operated when used by Hopkins, but vigorously and truly catching up in their living selves the meanings and responses of vanished ages. Examples from among our images are the "mastery" of image 4, which in its context pulls in the valorous knightly ideal of medieval times, and the "oracle" of image 6, which includes the richness and the dark mystery of the ancient rites.

These are living words. There is no dust upon them. They are words that people use. Sometimes, it is true, when he could not find a word with the exact meaning and sound that he wanted, Hopkins coined a term or built a new word on analogy with ordinary usage, like "leaf-meal." He did so because he knew, as Bridges and many others did not and do not, that language is a living instrument of acting minds and mouths, not a catalog of embalmed symbols. Like all great and original masters of language, Hopkins *employed* it. Like Humpty-Dumpty, though with better balance, he did not allow it to master him. In image 8, for example, he claims "louchèd" as a coinage for his own purposes, though he was mistaken in supposing the word was not previously in existence, as Bridges points out in his note to the poem. Hopkins wrote Dixon: "In the sonnet enclosed 'louched' is a coinage of mine and is to mean much the same as *slouched, slouching*. And I mean 'throng' for an adjective as we use it here in Lancashire" (June 25, 1883, *Letters 2*, p. 109). That Hopkins thought that the word was original with him indicates he had no fear of making up a word to serve his purpose. And since words, of course, proceed from the human mind in the first place and are formed and breathed forth from the human mouth for the purpose of communicating an individual and unique response to reality, word coinage would seem a natural thing for a poet to do. Only the victims of a dictionary-fixation and a standardized education, it seems to me, would deny him the right to do such a thing. At any rate, Hopkins did coin when he felt the need of doing so, and it is interesting to observe that terms which he originated, like "instress," "inscape," and "sprung rhythm," are beginning to show up in the dictionaries.

The predication of the words in the eight images indicates, and truly, that Hopkins' mind tends toward expression through metaphor rather than through simile. Five of the images are metaphors, three are similes. The proportion is representative of the thrust of Hopkins' creative mind into reality, which, as I see the matter, is the basis of metaphor. Simile is the expression of the detached mind observing and comparing beings. Metaphor is the expression of the mind thrusting itself into the white-hot center of one being and there fusing a new creation. It is this habitual involvement with being which makes it seem quite natural to Hopkins to speak of a "frowning landscape," because the metaphor which lies behind the statement is so vivid to him. To a mind which prefers the clarity and order of concept, simile is the natural expression. To a mind which hungers for the reality of being, even involved as being is in the darkness of unintelligibility, mystery, and confusion, metaphor is the natural expression. Bridges is a poet of simile, and Yvor Winters is his prophet. Hopkins is a poet of metaphor, and my whole effort, pitifully unworthy of his artistry, has been to make a bit straighter the way.

Yvor Winters has two articles titled "Gerard Manley Hopkins," in *The Hudson Review*.[1] They reveal Winters, as a critic, existing in a purely conceptual universe, or trying hard to do so. Winters, first of all, ignores the significance of a poem's rhythms, which, as Hopkins' definition of poetry (which I discuss later in this chapter) makes clear, is the formal element that basically effects the "framing" or patterning, the inscape, of the speech. Winters reasons that because language is primarily conceptual, and a poem is constructed of language, therefore a poem is primarily conceptual. A deeper application of the logic which appears to be his prime and ultimate good might lead him to perceive the fallacy of his argument.

Winters wants clear concepts and adequate predications (the material of simile, the opposite of metaphor), and of one of Bridges' bloodless lines he says admiringly, ". . . the concept and all its implications are clear." He goes on to say, "Hopkins has no such generating concept. . . ," as if he were identifying a fault. Since Hopkins is interested in beings, not in concepts, in reality as it is in itself, not in reality as it is in the mind, Winters is quite right in his statement, though quite wrong in his deductions therefrom.

Winters wants clarity in poetry above all else, and he says, in regard to Hopkins' and Mizener's statements that sprung rhythm holds the cadences of actual speech, "It is this kind of thing which often makes poetry and the criticism of poetry in our day so baffling a study." Being is baffling to the human mind, which must abstract, from actual being, the concept which expresses the intelligibility the intellect can receive. But the mind wants actual being, and metaphor is the mind's expedient to keep itself in touch with actual being. Metaphor is never clear, cannot be so, in a conceptual sense, and thus will never find favor with conceptualist critics. The cadences of actual speech, too, are non-conceptual things; Winters therefore dislikes discussing them: "This kind of thing is a violation of our integrity; it is somewhat beneath the dignity of man."

Winters can in apparent seriousness state that he is "fairly certain" that the moral character of his little Airedale is more admirable than that of Hopkins' bird! And he thinks that Hopkins "offers a poor perception of embers as such." And he finally states clearly his critical creed: "The poetic medium is simply a means to a finer and more comprehensive act of understanding than we can accomplish without it." Thus the final end of a poem is not to serve as an object for contemplation, as Hopkins states in his definition, but as an instrument for the perfection of the understanding. Thus Art is put to the service of Prudence, and *being* is totally and bloodily sacrificed to *concept*.

Most modern critics are, for various reasons, more aware of the power and importance of metaphor than critics of recent centuries have been. The renewed concern of science with the nature of the mind has been one of the factors, I presume, stimulating critics to look more closely at the central mystery of poetry. And in our own time, as John Crowe Ransom has made clear, the reaction against a "poetry of ideas" has brought poets and critics to a new appreciation of metaphor:

Clearly the seventeenth century had the courage of its metaphors, and imposed them imperially on the nearest things, and just as clearly the nineteenth century lacked this courage, and was halfheartedly metaphorical, or content with similes. The difference between the literary qualities of the two periods is the difference between the metaphor and the simile. (It must be admitted that this like other generalizations will not hold without its exceptions.) One period was pithy and original in its poetic utterance, the other was prolix and predictable. It would not quite commit itself to the metaphor even if it came upon one.[2]

Ransom proceeds less happily, in my judgment, when he attempts to discuss what the nature of that difference between metaphor and simile is: "Specifically, the miraculism arises when the poet discovers by analogy an identity between objects which is partial, though it should be considerable, and proceeds to an identification which is complete. It is to be contrasted with the simile, which says 'as if' or 'like,' and is scrupulous to keep the identification partial."[3]

I believe that Ransom is wrong in his discussion of the way metaphor is formed. He thinks that the mind of the poet, in producing that "miraculism" which rises from metaphor, sees a partial identity between two distinct and existent objects and then proceeds to identify them. I think that such a process is demonstrably impossible, and I hold that analogy does not enter into the formation of metaphor.[4] Rather, the mind of the poet, focused completely on one being, supplies for that being a nature that does not really belong to it. There is only one existent object involved. If there were two, the poet could never identify them, but would have to be content with simile.

However, that is a philosophical question and need not be threshed out here. While I believe that Ransom's philosophy is at fault, I judge that his criticism is solid and correct. Although he is, in my opinion, wrong about what metaphor is and the way in which it comes into being, he is profoundly right in his perception of what metaphor does. He makes, in his discussion of the point, one of the most penetrating statements of metaphor's activity that criticism can offer: "The poets therefore introduce the psychological device of the miracle. The predication which it permits is clean and quick but it is not a scientific predication. For scientific predication concludes an act of attention but miraculism initiates one. It leaves us looking, marvelling, and revelling in the thick *dinglich* substance that has just received its strange representation."[5] The predication of metaphor is indeed not a scientific predication, since it does not deal with the real thing as it is in reality. Simile does deal with two real things as they are in reality and compares them. Hence simile can be used to clarify. Simile is available to scientists. As Ransom so magnificently points out, scientific predication, which deals with real things as they are, concludes and sums up an act of attention and leaves the mind satisfied and comfortable with what it has seized. Metaphorical predication, on the other hand, deals with real things as they are not and leaves the mind peering into the unintelligible mysteries of real being, "looking, marvelling, and revelling in the thick *dinglich* substance." That is the aim and function of metaphor, which it alone among human predications can accomplish. All other predications reduce reality to the level at which they can be grasped by our abstractive intellects; they reduce the real to the conceptual and are clear. Metaphorical predication reduces the mind to the thick and dark unintelligibility of material being. Metaphor attempts to drag the intellect into the imagination. In order to force the intellect to peer into material being just as it is, the metaphor states that there is in that material being what is clearly not really there. This is the "strange representation" of which Ransom speaks, and, in its own order, this predication of metaphor is just as true as any other predication. Ransom points that out and gives the reason: ". . . it accomplishes precisely the sort of representation that it means to. It suggests to us that the object is perceptually or physically remarkable, and that we had better attend to it."[6] This is precisely what the metaphors of Hopkins aim to do, and do.

Hopkins' mature work has an organic unity, and that unity is founded, I believe, in his ultimate reliance on metaphor as his proper mode of expression. Rosemond Tuve makes this point in regard to the poems of Herbert:

This kind of organic unity will always characterize the work of a man who interprets life by the aid of metaphor, because metaphor does not 'compare' one thing with another, it states that one thing is another. Metaphor (and allegory, which is metaphor) deals not with likenesses but with essences. So, of course, do symbols, the extreme of metaphors. They can reconcile seeming contradictions because their terms can be 'different from' and 'the same as' simultaneously; nor is this in defiance of logic, for metaphors deal with reality at the level of universals. When, as Sydney says, particulars 'are seen in their universal consideration' every part can be the whole without ceasing to be itself.[7]

Hopkins' work too deals mainly "not with likenesses but with essences," or, as I would prefer to put it, not with likenesses but with beings. Miss Tuve's statement is fruitful critically, but again I believe I discern a philosophical weakness in her assertion that "metaphors deal with reality at the level of universals." Without hearing her definition of "universals," I cannot judge accurately what she means by the statement, but if she speaks in the same Scholastic terms that Sidney is employing in the quotation which she gives, then I would find it necessary to disagree. It is scientific discourse that deals with reality at the level of universals in the Scholastic sense and metaphor which deals with reality on the level of the imagination, and such metaphorical discourses, while lower than the discourse of science in so far as clarity is concerned ("lowest among sciences," St. Thomas states), are yet more satisfactory to a human animal whose intellect is made to contemplate *being,* not universals.

The union of mind with being, of intellect with, to use Ransom's words, ". . . things in their thinginess, or *Dinge* in their *Dinglichkeit* . . . ," which metaphor expresses, is effected through love. The mind can form an original and living metaphor only when it is utterly lost in the object which it contemplates. It is out of this passionate union that metaphor is born. I know of no more discerning critical statement on this point than that made by Cleanth Brooks following upon his consideration of Donne's "The Canonization": "For us today, Donne's imagination seems obsessed with the problem of unity: the sense in which the lovers become one—the sense in which the soul is united with God. Frequently, as we have seen, one type of union becomes a metaphor for the other. It may not be too far-fetched to see both as instances of, and metaphors for, the union which the creative imagination itself effects. For that fusion is not logical; it apparently violates science and commonsense; it welds together the discordant and the contradictory."[8] Metaphor apparently violates science and does violence to the universal, Plato's real objection to poetry. It does indeed weld together in perfect union the real being with a nature which does not in reality belong to it. And how does it accomplish this? Brooks goes on to suggest the answer in his original and illuminating discussion of "The Phoenix and the Turtle," which he considers as an allegory of the imaginative power which produces metaphor:

> So they loved as love in twaine,
> Had the essence but in one,
> Two distincts, Division none,
> Number there in love was slaine.

The paradox, like the phoenix, rises from the ashes of the separate two, i.e., in my own terminology, the real being and the mental universal, when they are joined in the metaphorical predication. The "essence" is in the one being which the two become, and number is slain in love.

In my own approach to metaphor, I hold that every metaphor can be reduced to three terms: the *noun* which is the subject of the predication, the *"is"* which expresses the act of existence of that subject, and the *predicate-noun* which is made to share in the existence of the subject. Whether or not one agrees with my philosophical arguments, I hope at least that this approach will be found useful, and, when properly understood, illuminating. As Ransom, Tuve, and Brooks agree, there is a fusion in metaphor which is quite different from the comparison (therefore the lack of fusion) in simile. For philosophical reasons, I disagree with the usual notion that the fusion in metaphor is between two beings. I hold that one real being is fused with a nature which is a concept and not a real being. The one real being exists and operates outside the mind, and in the metaphorical predication is expressed by the subject plus "is." The alien nature exists only in the mind, not in reality, and is expressed in the metaphorical predication by the predicate noun. The simple predication of an alien nature for a subject to which that nature does not, in reality, belong—"This being is a nature other than its real one," "This nun is a bell"—lies at the base of every metaphorical use of language. Each metaphor, too, is unique, because only *in* the metaphor (never in reality) does a real being operate by a nature that does not belong to it.

The first of our eight images, for example, is basically this predication, "The nun is a bell." The subject and verb there express the being, the real woman who is swinging back and forth with the motion of the waves and who is sending out the loud sound that pierces the elements. The predicate noun there expresses the alien nature supplied by the mind. The mind supplies that nature because such a nature (which is, in Scholastic terminology, "a principle of operation") can better express the quality of the nun's activity than can her real nature. Considered as a source of this sound, the nun is more properly a bell than she is a woman.

The poet's mind can form this predication only when it is fixed upon the real nun, when it is lost in love of the real existing being, so that it can supply out of its own substance another nature to express what it sees in that real existing being. The alien nature, the predicate noun, must proceed from the substance of the contemplating mind, not from reality. It got into the mind in the first place from reality, of course (unless one wants to accept the inborn ideas of the Platonists or to posit some sudden influx of ideas from God or an angel or Melpomene). But as far as this metaphor is concerned, the ultimate source of the predicate noun is the creative mind and imagination of the poet. And it is *this* union of mind with thing that carries the mind into "the thick *dinglich* substance" of the real being, leaving it marveling and reveling in the real being which it was made to contemplate. There is, however, no identity between objects here, no analogy drawn from the similarity of act of two existent beings, as Ransom supposes. There is here no real bell, no act of a bell. No comparison between the nun and a bell can be made, because there is no bell. There is only the nun and her act. The mind perceives her act as proceeding from the nature "bell" instead of the nature "woman," and it does so because as it focuses on her act, it perceives there qualities that seem out of proportion to the nature "woman" as source, but in perfect proportion to the nature "bell."

The call of the nun which Hopkins perceives is, for one thing, louder than one expects from a woman. It pierces the noise made by the raging elements so that all on the ship hear it. The contemplating mind, proffering a nature as source for that call, might tentatively state, "That nun, the source of that call, is a whistle." However, there are other considerations. The nun is swinging back and forth. The call emanates from a bell-like cavity and finds tongue in the nun's mouth. The call expresses what is in the nun (her union with Christ), and it is intended by her to reach the ears of

Christ. But it is also caused and produced by God and is intended by Him to reach the ears of His flock, to warn them of danger and to call them to the Sacrifice. For all these reasons and no doubt others, the nun's call is perceived as the sound of a bell. It is not *like* the sound of a bell, because if it were like such a sound we would have two sounds. Those two sounds would proceed from two different beings, and the individual nun could never become one with an individual bell. Two real beings would give analogy and the basis for simile, but they would destroy the possibility for metaphor. The only being the mind here perceives is the nun with her call and her environment, and out of its own substance the mind furnishes for her a nature that is not in reality there, and a metaphor comes into being. The new being that exists in the metaphor and no place else, the "nun-bell," binds the mind to the outer being in that paradox that springs from love, the unique union of the real being and the contemplating mind, in which the being gives its individual reality and the mind gives the alien nature.

If Hopkins had formed his metaphor expressive of the calling nun in the manner described by Ransom, so that he discovered "by analogy an identity between objects which is partial, though it should be considerable . . . ," he would have been forced to state, "The nun is like a bell." When there are two objects which can be compared, they each have their own real existence. It is impossible, in my view of things, to remove existence from a being by the activity of the mind. Once it has existence, only God can take that existence away from it. Hence my insistence that if metaphor is to be possible at all, the predicate noun must have no real existence of its own. In that case, the alien predicate noun can share in the existence of the subject in the metaphorical predication. If it once has its own existence, it can never share in that of another. To say that "The nun is like a bell" is to say that those two beings, in something that they *do* or *have,* resemble each other. In this case there would be four terms: the nun, her act, the bell, its act. These four terms that analogy requires make it possible to form a simile. Simile deals with relation between beings, not directly with being itself. Hence, since the two sides of the simile both exist outside the mind, simile can be used by the scientist. Metaphor, on the other hand, deals with being itself as that one being exists in its union with the mind. Science cannot use metaphor, because metaphor reduces the universal to the particular, because metaphor is essentially unclear—it does not bring reality into the mind in conceptual form, as science desires, but draws the mind into the non-conceptual mysteries of reality. In Ransom's inimitable statement, it does not conclude an act of attention, but initiates one.

Metaphor uses, then, three terms: the nun, her act, a bell. ("A bell," note, not "the bell," since I am dealing with a nature and not with an individual. The predicate noun of a metaphorical predication will necessarily be a universal, or if it is a word normally signifying an individual, like "Atlas," then that word in a universal usage, "George is an Atlas.") Simile uses five terms in all: the nun, her act, the bell, its act, and the preposition which expresses the relation or relations between them. Metaphorical predication consists, essentially, of a *subject,* the *verb* which expresses the existence of the subject, and a *predicate noun.* Simile consists of *two subjects, two verbs* (expressed or implied) signifying the acts of existence of each subject, and the *preposition* which signifies the relation on which the comparison is based. Our second image is a simile, "Grandeur is like shining (is)." Both the grandeur and the shining exist, and they are compared. The mind is not lost in its contemplation of grandeur so that it cannot remove its gaze. It takes its gaze from grandeur to find some other being that has a similar quality and finds that the shining from the foil is analogous to the grandeur from the earth. That discovery concludes an act of attention. It does not leave us reveling in the flame of grandeur. Our response to it is not a more intense gaze at grandeur, but an assent to the comparison. When we see the comparison, we say, "Yes, I see what you *mean.*" Our response to metaphor is (if we can see the real being, the subject, since metaphor can only point out to it, it cannot bring it into a concept), "Yes, I see what it *is.*"

Hopkins' simile which is our second image is a relatively simple affair, building up to the enormous metaphor in which "God's Grandeur" gloriously ends. Yet this simile also indicates the metaphorical tendency of Hopkins' mind, since the first of the two beings that compose the simile, grandeur, is treated metaphorically as a flame, with an implied reference to the tongues of fire which symbolize the Holy Ghost.

The third image, which deals with Mary's actions, is the second branch of a yet more complicated simile, whose first branch is air and its activity. The mothering, feeding, nursing qualities of air build a complicated metaphorical structure of air as a mother. That metaphor of the air-mother is the whole being which is compared to the real woman, Mary. And in the metaphor which closes the poem, all those elements merge when Hopkins' mind is lost in contemplation of the really important being of whom the poem treats, Mary. In order to compose the whole complicated simile which makes up the poem, except for the conclusion, both elements had to be of profound and passionate interest to the poet. He had to examine both exhaustively, be deeply interested in both. But when his mind concentrates on one and loses its hold upon the other being, he indicates that to him the one on which he concentrates is more important, more lovable than the other. He reveals with which being his mind chooses to be joined, when through the action of his mind Mary is no longer like the air that we breathe, but is herself life-giving air. We no longer know what he *means;* we see Mary as he sees her, we see what she *is,* as long as we are looking at her. The metaphor has meaning only as long as we are focused on the subject and its act or quality. The simile can have meaning whether we have the beings compared actually and fully before us or not; we can be made to *understand* the special point or points of comparison. Metaphor can have significance only when the acting and qualified subject exists actually and fully before us, because only there can we see the basis of metaphorical predication. To state that Mary is like air makes me look at both. To state that Mary is air makes me focus exclusively on Mary.

Simile, I say, requires that we understand the points of comparison, and we can do this even if the beings are not immediately present to us. The reason is that both beings are acting according to their proper natures, and therefore we can deduce what the point of comparison is through a study of those natures. If Mary is like air, we can, even without further discussion, deduce likenesses from the *characteristic* activities of the two beings, not as individuals but as the *kinds* of things they are. But if Mary is air, then we are helpless to proceed unless we can see the individual Mary, because her nature as woman will give us no clue. It will rather mislead us, since it is precisely as not-a-woman that she can be air. The basis for the metaphor, if it is a good one, must be an act or quality in Mary which is so much an individual note of her own that we can conceive it as not flowing from her proper nature as woman. It is that remarkable individual act or quality that makes it possible for us to see Mary as some other kind of thing, from which that extraordinary act or quality flows. We cannot deduce that act or quality from a consideration of her own nature. Only in the individual, existing, acting, and qualified Mary can we discover why it is true to say that *she* is air. And the point of Hopkins' final metaphor in "The Blessed Virgin compared to the Air we Breathe" is not that Mary is like all mothers, but that she is that absolutely unique Mother who actually is carrying off the poisons of sin and concupiscence, who feeds the soul with the life of Christ. Unless we see *that* Mary, we are not sharing in Hopkins' metaphor or in Hopkins' total poem. Up to the final metaphor, the poem may be adapted to the reader's own knowledge and taste, to some extent. Simile permits such adaptation, since we can see what we choose of relations between beings, up to a point. But metaphor is intransigent. Either you see and are joined with the one individual being as it individually and peculiarly exists in the metaphor, or you see either nothing at all or something totally different.

Hopkins' third simile among our images, image 7, is about as complex in structure, I suppose, as a simile can well be. It has three elements, rather than two: the protagonist, the eyes, and thirst are all compared on the basis of yearning, searching, and not finding. Each one of them is involved, within its own branch, in metaphor, so really three metaphors are compared among themselves to make up one simile. The speaker is a hunter, whose prey is comfort and whose thoughts are dogs, and further a prisoner or trapped person who gropes for something that is not imprisoned or trapped with him. The blind eyes, too, are personified as searching for that day that they cannot find in the prison or trap of darkness in which they find themselves. Thirst, too, is a searcher which cannot find in its parching prison the water it desires. Further, the delicate gradation which I discussed in chapter 8, of the completeness of the proportion between the thing that yearns and the thing for which it yearns—that is, the speaker is a whole self who will retain his individuality even when joined to the Comforter, the eyes are parts of the self which will be penetrated by and responsive to light but not swallowed up by it, thirst is a sheer longing which will lose its own being in that for which it longs—operates with tremendous power in the simile.

Hopkins' similes, penetrating and constructive as they are, do not operate apart from metaphor, and it is metaphor which is the core of his creative operation. With a mind well stocked with natures whose intimate properties were known to him from intense and loving observation, he was, as a poet who loved beings, ready to express the passionate joining of his mind with a loved being in the union of metaphor. The nun could be to him in such a full sense a bell because a bell in the mind of Hopkins was itself so full and rich a treasure of bell-qualities and bell-acts. His heart could be a knight in so complete a sense because the nature of knight, in Hopkins' mind, was so deeply a nature of beauty and valor and act. Patience can be so significant a fledgling because fledglings, in Hopkins' mind, were natures of depth and promise. Life could be a rich thread because threads, in Hopkins' mind, were themselves significant and important natures. The earth could be a speechless and worrying mother because mothers, in Hopkins' mind, were natures of loving care for their children. Metaphor could proceed from the mind and heart of Hopkins in such rich and deep profusion because he was himself so deeply involved with reality. He profoundly loved all reality that was worded by the Word and was word of Him. And in such love metaphor is grounded. Simile deals with reality as it is outside the mind, as observed by the mind. But metaphor plunges into the darkness of the real because of love and hunger for being. Observation is not enough, and metaphor is the embrace of mind and the real material being.

But that account is pitifully partial, because the basis of metaphor is not only the mind, but much more the love, the heart, of the poet. The meters and rhythms, that structure of sound which frames the speech into a poetic object, spring from the heart of Hopkins rather than from his brain. I believe that this is the case in every true poet and gives basis to the dictum that poets are born, not made. These rhythms and sounds are mysteriously born with the thought deep in the poet's being, "in the spiritual night of the preconceptual activity of the poet," as Jacques Maritain so expressively puts it.[9] I agree wholeheartedly with Maritain when he argues against supposing that a poet invests an argument with poetic trappings: "The poet does not have to invest any argument with emotional force, because he does not begin with any argument. He begins with creative emotion, or poetic intuition, and the argument follows. Donne forcefully and eloquently developed his theme—because the creative spark and power came entirely, not from his theme, but from his creative emotion, which I would designate as the wound suddenly produced by some incomprehensible contrast—*poisonous minerals,* and me—and by virtue of which the whole poem exists."[10] I should rather call that wound the thrust of real being into the mind, but I agree that out of that spiritual wound the whole poem proceeds, if it is to be a living poem. Rhythms and sounds cannot be added to an argument as ornament and produce a living poem. I believe that Bridges' poems are like corpses made lovely with cosmetics because he added "poetic" qualities to clear thought. No doubt a poet could operate by clarifying his thought first in prose and then "versifying" the thoughts, but I doubt whether the product would be a poem. In any case, the following quotation from a letter of Hopkins to Bridges indicates that Hopkins did not operate that way:

You speak of writing the sonnet in prose first. I read the other day that Virgil wrote the Aeneid in prose. Do you often do so? Is it a good plan? If it is I will try it; it may help on my flagging and almost spent powers. Years ago one of ours, a pupil of mine, was to write some English verses for me, to be recited: he had a real vein. He said he had no thoughts, but that if I would furnish some he would versify them. I did so and the effect was very surprising to me to find my own thoughts, with no variation to speak of, expressed in good verses quite unlike mine.

(January 4, 1883, *Letters 1*, p. 170)

Hopkins' own method was not so calculating, not so mechanical. His poems welled up from the depths of his soul—not without painful and exhausting effort on his part: "Then again I have of myself made verse so laborious" (*Letters 1*, p. 66)—and were formed by the exercise of what St. Thomas calls "a habit of art," a virtue to which the mind must be brought through training, guidance, effort, and exercise, but which works by its own laws and which must exist and operate if living works of art are to be produced. Hopkins indicates in a letter to Bridges how his magnificent habit of art operated, in such a manner that the poem appeared to him to be forming within him independently, to be tantalizingly just out of his grasp. He speaks of the inchoate beginnings of what developed into the lovely "Inversnaid," *Poems*, No. 56, something more than two years later:

I have two sonnets soaking, which if they should come to anything you shall have, and something, if I could only seize it, on the decline of wild nature, beginning some how like this—

> O where is it, the wilderness,
> The wildness of the wilderness?
> Where is it, the wilderness?

and ending—

> And wander in the wilderness;
> In the weedy wilderness,
> Wander in the wilderness.
> (February 22, 1879, *Letters 1*, pp. 73-74)

Hopkins, note, had to reach for the whole poem all at once, thought, rhythms, sound, everything. His testimony here about the nature of his own artistic activity is profoundly in accord with what is perhaps one of the most revealing studies of the creative process in literature, the picture Joyce gives of the formation of a poem in his *A Portrait of the Artist as a Young Man*. I quote the following lengthy passage both as a contrast to Bridges' careful writing out of the thought in prose first and as a basis for comparison with Hopkins' own poetic statement of the poetic process in his final sonnet:

> An enchantment of the heart! The night had been enchanted. In a dream or vision he had known the ecstasy of seraphic life. Was it an instant of enchantment only or long hours and years and ages?
> The instant of inspiration seemed now to be reflected from all sides at once from a multitude of cloudy circumstances of what had happened or of what might have happened. The instant flashed forth like a point of light and now from cloud on cloud of vague circumstances confused form was veiling softly its afterglow. O! In the virgin womb of the imagination the word was made flesh. Gabriel the seraph had come to the virgin's chamber. An afterglow deepened within his spirit, whence the white flame had passed, deepening to a rose and ardent light. That rose and ardent light was her strange and wilful heart, strange that no man had known or would know, wilful from before the beginning of the world: and lured by that ardent roselike glow the choirs of the seraphim were falling from heaven.
>
>> *Are you not weary of ardent ways,*
>> *Lure of the fallen seraphim?*
>> *Tell no more of enchanted days.*
>
> The verses passed from his mind to his lips and, murmuring them over, he felt the rhythmic movement of a villanelle pass through them. The roselike glow sent forth its rays of rhythm; ways, days, blaze, praise, raise. Its rays burned up the world, consumed the hearts of men and angels: the rays from the rose that was her wilful heart.
>
>> *Your eyes have set man's heart ablaze*
>> *And you have had your will of him.*
>> *Are you not weary of ardent ways?*
>
> And then? The rhythm died away, ceased, began again to move and beat. And then? Smoke, incense ascending from the altar of the world.

> *Above the flame the smoke of praise*
> *Goes up from ocean rim to rim*
> *Tell no more of enchanted days.*

Smoke went up from the whole earth, from the vapoury oceans, smoke of her praise. The earth was like a swinging swaying censer, a bell of incense, an ellipsoidal ball. The rhythm died out at once; the cry of his heart was broken. His lips began to murmur the first verses over and over; then went on stumbling through half verses, stammering and baffled; then stopped. The heart's cry was broken.[11]

Joyce lays bare here the activity of the habit of art in his young man in terms so vivid and so true and with prose rhythms so compelling that his prose, as often, approaches the condition of poetry. His statement of what goes on within the spirit and the imagination agrees point for point with Hopkins' own statement of the act of the spirit impregnated with the flame of reality for one flashing and glorious instant. Joyce compares the formation of the poem in the imagination with the formation of the human nature of the Word in the womb of Mary. Hopkins, too, compares the mind to a mother, a widow in whose womb the seed of a past and dead moment of inspiration, the "instant" of which Joyce speaks, grows to a perfect song. Joyce compares that instant to a point of light, Hopkins to a blowpipe flame. Both are aware that the real has penetrated into the dark and yearning womb of the artist's mind and imagination. Both are aware, too, that the artist's mind and heart work by their own laws in forming the poem, that the rhythms spring up with the thoughts and the colors and the sounds. A child forms in the womb by the law of its own nature, and the analogy has force in the formation of a poem, as Hopkins particularly indicates in "To R. B.," *Poems,* No. 75. The mother's nature knows what she is about and at what she aims, and her body and blood cooperate with the forming child without making mistakes:

> The fine delight that fathers thought; the strong
> Spur, live and lancing like the blowpipe flame,
> Breathes once and, quenchèd faster than it came,
> Leaves yet the mind a mother of immortal song.
> Nine months she then, nay years, nine years she long
> Within her wears, bears, cares and combs the same:
> The widow of an insight lost she lives, with aim
> Now known and hand at work now never wrong.

The strong spur that galvanizes the mind into activity, that delight that is the male element in forming thought, that lancing, piercing flame, is the thrust of reality in its full vigor into a mind with equal vigor to receive it, to become one with it. Behind the thought and imagery both of Joyce and of Hopkins lie the vigor and the beauty of Catholic philosophical and theological tradition, the Word and the word, the life-giving work of the Holy Ghost, the divine work effected through the womb of Mary, the divine poem which is the Word-made-flesh, the sharing by God of the rhythms of the human heart. We have seen these things behind our images: the Word which the breast of the nun rang out to the ears of the sheep; the reflected flame from the world and the life-giving flame of the sun, symbol of the Holy Ghost; the Word carried by Mary into our ears and souls; the heart which can beat with the life of God because He shared its beat; the dove, Peace, which forms life in the nest; the life dimmed by the self's rebellion; the dark and lonely soul waiting for the flame of comfort; the earth pleading for a higher life. Both Joyce and Hopkins know this world and this vast tradition. It is a part of both of them and a force in their works. Both magnificent artists, they work with what is in them to bring forth works of immortal beauty, and both of them know that works of great art proceed from the whole man, from the heart as from the brain.[12]

In *nature,* then, Hopkins' mature imagery is exact, profound, alive, predominantly metaphoric, with rhythms and sound which are components as essential as the meanings of word and sentence. The *function* of his imagery is primarily to contribute to the object of contemplation. That object is the poem, which Hopkins defines in the following terms: "Poetry is speech framed for contemplation of the mind by the way of hearing . . ." (*Journals,* p. 289). Hopkins here gives three of the Aristotelian four causes. The material object from which poetry is made is speech, connected words, by which Hopkins means both the concept signified by a word and the sound which embodies it. Since the speech involved includes more than one word, rhythms, pitch, vowels, consonants, physical movements of lungs, throat, tongue, and jaw are all involved, too. All of this material comes under the influence of the formal object, which Hopkins expresses in the verb "framed." This signifies the structure which is built from the material, the body with beginning, middle, and end, the object that mind and ear can receive. And the final cause, the reason for the thing, is as an object for the contemplation of the mind by way of hearing. The mind just looks at it, by way of ear. It is an object of mortal beauty, which keeps warm the wits with its lovely fire. Of itself, it does not teach, it does not enlighten, it does not mean. It just is, and its intent is just to be looked at. "Beauty is truth, truth beauty," it says.

I trust that it is clear from the preceding chapters, if from nothing else, that Hopkins is not belittling the element of meaning for words. He develops the definition quoted above thus: ". . . or speech framed to be heard for its own sake and interest even over and above its interest of meaning" (*Journals*, p. 289). *Even* over and above meaning. Speech is made up of words, and words are not mere sounds. They are sounds, but they are also the concepts signified by those sounds or the judgments expressed by those combinations of words. Speech cannot be had without meaning. In prose the meaning is primary, and all the embellishments of style and rhetoric are there to enhance the meaning. Hence prose allows of relatively satisfactory translation from one language to another. In poetry the structure, the pattern, in Hopkins' terms the "framing," is primary, and meaning is one of the elements that goes to make up that pattern, as do all the other elements of speech, sounds, and rhythms especially (which include timing, silences, stress, length, and so forth). Poetry, then, can never be translated from the particular speech in which it lives. That is of its essence, its body and soul. The meanings of its words and predications can be translated, and its other elements can perhaps be analogously approximated, but the result would no more be the poem than a statue is a real woman or a history book a war. The speech of prose aims at meaning; the speech of poetry aims at pattern, at structure. Prose intends to interpret reality, to carry being into the mind; a poem intends to take its place in reality, to be a being that the mind may contemplate by way of ear, to draw the mind out into real being.

Catholic thought and attitudes toward reality are founded upon and profoundly conditioned by the Incarnation. The fact that God entered into our universe as a part of it is the basic truth that makes all the difference for one who believes it. And a Catholic believes it as a fact, not as a "dogma" (as the word is ordinarily understood outside Catholic circles). The general attitude of critics of Hopkins and of most non-Catholic writers, as far as I am aware, is that the Catholic tradition embraces a number of ideas worked into a system and imposed, as carefully as possible, on reality. To a Catholic, his tradition is drawn from reality itself. It is an expression of reality, and the center of it is the fact of the Incarnation. If that is not a fact, then the whole Catholic tradition is based on an error and is at least open to any absurdity of development. If the Incarnation is a fact, however, then any tradition which does not take it into account as a basic fact is at least incomplete. Hopkins' world-view is basically conditioned by his complete belief in the fact of the Incarnation.

The most unfortunate tendency among Hopkins' critics in regard to his world-view is that many of them tend to furnish him with one drawn not from the text of his poems or other writings, but from what they think a Catholic world-view is. The general tendency to do this appears, I believe, in this quotation from a distinguished critic: "Similarly with Dante; with the cumulative disintegration, even for Catholics, of mediaeval Christianity as the ultimate convention of human life, the success of *The Divine Comedy* comes more and more to depend on the exhibition of character and the virtue of language alone—which may make it a greater, not a lesser poem."[13] Blackmur is speaking of the power of language to set up or to manipulate conventions. His statement appears to me to conceal a presupposition, however, which illustrates the tendency of which I am speaking. He states that Catholics no longer accept, as Dante did, medieval Christianity as the ultimate convention of human life. What he means by "mediaeval Christianity" he does not state, and I am unable to determine definitely his meaning from the context. If he intends to equate medieval Christianity with things like feudalism or a Ptolemaic cosmology, the statement is wholly correct, but not altogether rational, since then he could hardly say "even for Catholics," unless he had (as I know he does not have) an extraordinarily warped notion of modern Catholics, who have no tendency, at least as a group, to cling to the Ptolemaic system or to any remnants of feudalism. Hence I presume that he means by "mediaeval Christianity" the beliefs that Catholics as such held about reality at that time and that Dante employed in his poem. Catholics hold precisely the same beliefs now that they did then, and a Catholic of the twentieth century who hears or reads *The Divine Comedy* will find himself accepting its ultimate attitudes toward reality with precisely the same sincerity that characterized its acceptance by a comparable Catholic of the fourteenth century. The Catholic tradition has not disintegrated. A great many other traditions have sprung up in opposition to it, so that it exists in different circumstances from those of Dante's time. But it is the same tradition, and if I am correctly interpreting his statement, then it seems to me that Blackmur is presupposing a situation which in reality does not exist.

I can well understand why a reader of the critical studies of Hopkins' work might be confused in regard to the Catholic worldview. The present state of the Catholic tradition need not be a mystery, since there is no dearth of Catholic books and speakers. But, as Hopkins bitterly complains in his "To seem the stranger," they are not heard or, if heard, are not understood by those to whom that tradition has become strange. We have seen, particularly in the critics' discussion of "The Windhover," how men as influential as Richards and Empson supply to Hopkins a notion of the religious life which is completely foreign to the Catholic tradition and which fails to take into account such basic facts as the Incarnation, the true final goal of human beings (which in the Catholic view is a supernatural one), and the nature of the Mystical Body as interpreted by Catholics. They presume a purely natural goal for a man, as they indicate in their discussion of the frustration of nature which they think the religious life entails, of the opposition which exists (in their minds) between the joyous natural activity of normal men and the dark and intense frustrations of Jesuits. If man's goal is purely natural, then of course they are right in their implicit condemnation of Catholic religious life. But if man's goal is supernatural, then they are missing the main point.

Hopkins' poems without exception presuppose the opposite of the presuppositions of Richards, Empson, and some others, that is, that man's highest goal is to reach God and that his nature can best be fulfilled in attaining that aim. Nor is there anything natural that is bad, for Hopkins. But Richards and Empson and others think that he turns away from sense pleasures and natural joys because they are bad. Actually, in so far as Hopkins turns away from them, it is because they are good, but in the circumstances impede, or seem to impede, his progress toward something better.

Miss Phare illustrates the assumption of a world-view for Hopkins from the critic's personal notion of what the Catholic view is: "By his intellect everything is seen as tidy, orderly, part of a pattern; the world as viewed in the light of Catholic dogma is a riddle solved."[14] These reflections, combined with her confident picture of "the tidy, cut-and-dried mental world of the Jesuit," are based, I suppose, on a Protestant judgment of what the Catholic view and a Jesuit's mind *must* be, based not on experience with individual Catholics or Jesuits but on conclusions drawn from Protestant notions of medievalism and its superstitions, floating impressions of the work of St. Thomas Aquinas, recollections of the any-means-to-an-end caricature of a Jesuit in *Henry Esmond,* etc., etc. They are less excusable in that the work of Maritain and Gilson, among others, has brought at least the philosophical aspects of the Catholic tradition into general currency. Surely if Miss Phare had glanced at the volumes of Maritain which were then available, or indeed if she had stopped in at a Jesuit house, she could not have supplied that tight and well-categorized universe for the Catholic world or that tidy mental cabinet for the skull of a Jesuit. Such misapprehensions are funny, but the critical confusion they bring about when they are seriously employed as fundamentals of the criticism of a Catholic writer is not very funny.

More recently, James Reeves has discussed in detail what actually went on in Hopkins' mind and heart: "The motives and impulses which led him to sacrifice his life to the Jesuit ideal will never be fully understood. But there is a kind of temperament, as often found among Calvinists as among Catholics, which, in certain circumstances, cannot fulfil itself except through some form of self-chastisement."[15]

I don't know what Mr. Reeves would make of Gethsemane, but I can guess. This confident judgment on the masochism of the intimate spiritual experiences and motives of Catholics and Calvinists is based, like Miss Phare's, on deductions from what *must* be. And the principles which are the foundations for those judgments are not the most reliable principles to bring to a judgment of Hopkins' desolation sonnets, for example. Reeves, however, goes much further. He divides the attitudes of critics toward Hopkins between the rationalistic-aesthetic, which regards Hopkins' adoption of the Jesuit way of life as disastrous, and the extreme Jesuit view, which "is that his life and poetry form a harmonious whole in which everything is subordinate to the over-riding necessity of devotion to the glorification of God and the imitation of Christ . . . . That the renunciations and privations he endured maimed his genius and in the end killed him may be true; there can be little doubt of it. [The typhoid germ had some causality!] At the same time, it has to be admitted that some at least of Hopkins' finest poems are the result of this process of self-destruction."¹⁶ The term "self-destruction" reveals an attitude on Reeves' part which is, at least, not that of Hopkins, in so far as Hopkins' attitude appears in his writings. But somehow or other Reeves gets behind those writings and their statements and sees that "Hopkins' muse, I believe, never underwent conversion."¹⁷ Like Empson, he peers into the interior of this Jesuit, and sees wondrous sights that were evidently hidden even from Hopkins himself: "But there was much that Hopkins wrote—had to write—which he could never reconcile with the avowed aims of the Society, however ingeniously some of his successors have labored to do so. His life was dedicated to God, but many of his poems he must have dedicated, in his heart, to the poetic spirit that had been born in him, to his Muse, or to posterity."¹⁸ He "must have dedicated" his poems so, and hence there is no use arguing the matter, especially since "he could never reconcile" his poems with the aim of the Society. These assured judgments proceed from a settled conviction, not only about the interior of Hopkins, but about the Catholic tradition in which he operated. And I, who operate in the same tradition, find no grounds for those judgments in reality. If Reeves has any grounds besides his misconceptions, I would count it a kindness to be enlightened.

My view, as I have presented it in this study, is quite different from that illustrated by Phare and Reeves. I have sincerely attempted to present my view of Hopkins' attitudes as seen in his poems, not from what I could deduce from what those attitudes *must* be (though to do so I believe I am in an infinitely better position than Phare or Reeves), but from the text of the poems and from Hopkins' other writings in his letters, journals, and sermons. I cannot read Hopkins' mind and heart except as his mind and heart are reflected in his writings, but I don't believe that others can either, above all others who neither understand nor are sympathetic to the deepest motivations of his mind and heart.

In my judgment, the Catholic view of reality is presented in Hopkins' work with a depth, a fullness, and a sweep that English poetry has not known since the Reformation. The life-giving power of divine life as it pours from the Heart of Christ, the ultimate significance of the Incarnation, is the basic key to all of Hopkins' mature work, as I see it. The objective correlative of his intense emotions, the ultimate aim of all his imagery, and the sometimes hidden basis for the structure of all his mature poems, is the majestic and life-giving figure of Christ. We saw in our consideration of "Nondum" in the Introduction how the young Hopkins searched the "glories of the earth" but found no host in the lighted but empty hall. In *Deutschland,* with the Scriptural act of adoration that Job refused to give to creatures, Hopkins kisses his hand to the stars, because behind them and in them he sees the Host, the Word. And from there to his final poem, Christ is the one subject that engrosses his mind.

Our eight images indicate how pervasive is the life-giving presence of Christ in the mature imagery of Hopkins. The first deals with Christ in the nun, His complete union with her as His member, His exercise of His royal power and the carrying out of His doom in her, His use of her to call to His flock—the image, like the poem, deals with the perfect mastery of the Kingdom of Heaven's Dauphin. The second image deals with Christ in His Spirit, the Comforter Whom He sends to His members to carry out and complete His life-giving work. The third image deals with Christ in Mary and in us, His divine life coming to us through her. The fourth image deals with Christ Who should be in the heart, as Christ the Knight is revealed in the bird, as He could be more gloriously revealed in the heart of His member. The fifth and sixth deal with Christ's wrestling with the soul, His struggle not to the death but to His life. The seventh image deals with Christ's apparent desertion of the yearning soul, a further and deeper development of the Christ-life in the soul. And the eighth image deals with Christ the Word's relation to His world as well as to His member, with His life destined to reach even the world through His members.

It is the Catholic interpretation of the Mystical Body of Christ which most profoundly explicates the depths of Hopkins' words and predications and rhythms. The figure of Christ must remain in the picture if the result is not to be partial and misleading. Those who leave out Christ or reduce Him to merely human stature do not see the most important part either of Hopkins' poems or of his life. Eleanor Ruggles' biography of Hopkins is a good illustration. Happily, she did not intend to portray the whole picture, but only that portion of it which is explicable and available in human terms. Her treatment is both intelligent and refreshing, if at times somewhat misleading, but it leaves the major problems of Hopkins' life, poems, and imagery untouched, since it does not extend to the ultimate base of Hopkins' thought, the life-giving figure of Christ. It has the advantage, however, of avoiding the danger to which those who concentrate too much upon the divine elements of the picture are subjected, of taking human nature and human activity too seriously. There is a ridiculous aspect to human aspirations when they aim at the infinite, and to those like Jesuits, to whom the situation's serious aspects are never far away, Miss Ruggles' almost flippant (though not really so) treatment can serve as an antidote to a lugubrious solemnity.

One thing particularly that Miss Ruggles' book did, for which I am deeply grateful, was to occasion W. H. Auden's review, in which he approaches the subject as she does, but with a poet's insight and love carries on toward the depths of the subject in a way that Miss Ruggles could not do, nor could anyone else who is not a poet and seer, as Auden certainly is. He suggests the whole picture that he has in mind with his significant title, "A Knight of the Infinite," and though he dwells on the human elements in the foreground, the depths of his picture suggest the forces of human and divine love. He compares Hopkins to Don Quixote, and from his mind the comparison yields splendid insights. The three friends, Hopkins, Dixon, and Bridges, each of them a lovely person in certain lights at least, he groups in the picture, humorously and happily suggesting Bridges as a svelte Sancho Panza, Dixon as a minor Quixote wielding an umbrella rather than a spear against the world that will not see the beauty of Hopkins' poems (Auden's treatment of the dear Canon's "abrupt footnote" lies deep enough for tears), and Hopkins as an earnest Quixote: "Yes, like Don Quixote, his poems gloss over none of the suffering and defeat, yet when we read them, as when we read Cervantes, the final note is not the groan of a spiritual Tobacco Road, but the cry of gratitude which Hopkins once heard a cricketer give for a good stroke, 'Arrah, sweet myself!' "[19]

The true and total picture which Hopkins' amazingly unified work gives[20] infinitely deepens, however, and all the ridiculous elements are swallowed up, when the majestic figure of Christ is seen as operative throughout. There is nothing ridiculous about Christ, and the glory and nobility which He bestows by His presence are not that of an imposed idea, but that of a reality as real as earth and air and birds and Jesuits. He and his life-giving operations are the one sure thread through the maze of reality and through the maze of Hopkins' imagery as well, since that imagery follows and interprets the maze of reality by means of that thread. With Christ in the picture, the knight of the infinite is no longer a figure of fun, even of gentle and loving and deeply human fun, but a true and glorious knight, whose flame of exploit is really a divine and immortal flame, joined as it is in literal unity with the flame of the Divine Knight.

This literal union which the Catholic interpretation of the Mystical Body teaches profoundly affects Hopkins' imagery. The Catholic view does not picture an analogy between Christ and the Christian in the same way other views do, as a simile rather than an existential metaphor. The Catholic view does picture a literal union, so that the Christian and Christ are fused in one being like the Phoenix and the Turtle, sharing one life. The Incarnation itself can be viewed, analogously, as an existential metaphor, in which the Divine Word joins with a human nature in the perfect personal union of one divine act of existence. Again, the union of Christ with His member can be viewed analogously as an existential metaphor in which the God-Man shares with a human being His divine life, so that in a true and literal sense that human being, while remaining himself, becomes Christ. The mind of a Catholic poet, then, which is saturated with this view and most deeply motivated by it, inclines most naturally toward that metaphor which expresses the union of knowledge and love between the mind itself and some real object outside the mind. This is all the more true because for such a mind every object speaks of and reflects the Word. The Word is, in a true sense, in all of His creatures as their Creator, and also, since the Incarnation, among them as their co-Creature. And for the member who aims always at living union with his Head, the way through creatures is a normal and effective way to reach the Lord of creatures.

For Hopkins, all creatures are good, a fact that, if properly taken into account, would shift the structure which some of his images acquire in the minds of some of his critics. In my discussion of the image which is central to my study, image 4 from "The Windhover" (as the idea involved in that image is central to the thought of Hopkins and the poem is central in the works of Hopkins), I have attempted to show that those whom I listed as "pagan critics" are reading the poem, to some degree, in Manichaean and Pelagian terms, not in Catholic terms. William F. Lynch, S. J., in the course of his discussion of such influences in modern art has this to say:

The whole theology of the fact and mystery of Christ, it will be proposed, involves on His part a relation to the finite and concrete human situation that can be summed up under the terms of total and actual, positive and "athletic" penetration of the finite (*exultavit ut gigas*). As such, Christology stands as the model and enduring act of the healthy and successful human imagination which, if it really grasps the act of Christ, will be able analogically to transfer this act to its own plane of human life. But today, in so many ways, men adopt a startlingly different attitude toward the finite and human: their present attitude is profoundly manichaean and non-Christic, in what detail and with what consequences we shall see.[21]

Lynch later indicates that tragedy in the West suffers when: "1. existence is absurd, mean or flat (manichaean); 2. man becomes the romantic hero (the Pelagian), conquering mystically and irrationally by rebellion, resentment or exaltation in pain."[22] Lynch reveals, it seems to me, the exact contrast between the view which Hopkins' imagery expresses and the opposed view which some critics have derived from that imagery. In "The Windhover," for example, those whom I have called "pagan critics" confuse *limitation, finitude,* with *evil,* the Manichaean attitude to which Lynch refers. The bird for them, as crumpled, can be a symbol of sacrifice because they can suppose that something which is somehow evil is crumpled in the bird. In Hopkins' Christological view, there is nothing whatever evil in the bird, and hence it cannot, as crumpled, be the symbol of the destruction of any evil or the attainment of any good. Not only is there nothing evil in it, but in its finite natural good it is the reflection of the Word's infinite good.

Again, this Manichaean and Pelagian attitude shows up in the interpretations some critics give to the "desolation sonnets," in which they suppose that Hopkins' Jesuit ideal is working in him to crush his natural good so that a supernatural good can be attained. Hopkins' view of the matter again is that whatever is natural in himself is not only finitely good, but is a finite reflection of the Word's infinite good that is far greater than any non-spiritual finite good. Man himself, after all, is an *image* of God. But incredibly more than this, with the added gift of grace, of a sharing in divine life, Hopkins sees his nature as being raised up to a divine plane, in so far as nature is capable of that, so that he himself literally shares in the life and activity of Christ. Hence if he tried to crush anything naturally good in himself, he would be either sinful or insane. Further, the sublimation of sexual powers and of poetic gifts, the crushing of the vanity and pride which he thought he discovered in himself, while often in certain circumstances painful, is by no means the *ultimate* reason or objective correlative for the depth and intensity of his sufferings. To read them so is not only to read them under a Manichaean light but to make them ridiculous, to some extent at least. The ultimate reason for his suffering, as is clear not only from Hopkins' Christological view of the universe, not only from his repeated statements in letters and journals and sermons, but above all in the text of the poems themselves and in the images we have considered, is his personal human struggle against Christ, the struggle which every saint has known, the struggle which evidences, as St. Paul most powerfully reveals, the power of sin. Sin is the one evil in the universe, "man's malice," and it is this deep-seated and humanly ineradicable struggle against Christ and His life which Hopkins experiences within himself and expresses as no other poet has done in the English language. To be seen in focus and truly, Hopkins' sufferings must be seen in that Christological view which gives unity, depth, and life to the imagery and to the poems of Hopkins.

Hopkins is in the deepest sense of the word a Catholic poet, and it seems to me that his success in expressing the Catholic tradition in splendid poetry should make him all the dearer to those who love English poetry. The Catholic tradition, so vital in English literature for its first seven centuries of existence, almost disappeared with the Reformation and shows up in good poetry only spasmodically and with little strength. The reasons for that are many and complex, but one which weighed most upon Hopkins was the ever widening gap between the thoughts, attitudes, and values of English Catholics and English non-Catholics. The very presence in our language of words like "hocus-pocus" and "jesuitical" bears testimony to the separation which cut Hopkins to the heart, as we have seen in our discussion of his bitter "To seem the stranger. . . ."

Into this troubled atmosphere Hopkins has introduced a body of poems which revives the Catholic tradition with exact and profound expression of its deepest themes. English ears may be suspicious and cautious, but if they will listen they will find, I am convinced, that Hopkins has brought forth in lovely limbs, for English ears, the Catholic word. He is, for modern England, a new Dante. And not only for England, but for all those to whom the English tongue is native, familiar, and beloved.

The comparison of Hopkins with Dante is a natural one. Even Miss Phare, to whom Hopkins' Catholicism was such a barrier, a puzzle, and too often a critical stumbling-block, finds them allied as Catholic poets: "In spite of the peculiarities of his mind and circumstances, Hopkins in his best work comes as near as, say, Dante, to making his experience available to all: he merits the extreme of popularity which he himself, a critic as just as modest, thought his due."[23] Dorothy Sayers, in discussing Dante as a religious poet, finds it natural to quote (slightly to misquote, unhappily) from "The Windhover": "Out of some inexhaustible spring in his fierce heart this great fountain of happiness comes bursting and bubbling. The *stupor* that we share with Dante, thus 'from glory unto glory advancing,' is accompanied by a minor, yet not unworthy, *stupor* at 'the achieve, the mastery of the thing.' It is a marvel to watch mere poetry, mere words, thus go up and up, and to feel sure inner certainty that we can trust the poet to take them all the way, the song growing shriller and sweeter the higher it soars. . . ."[24] Maurice B. McNamee, S. J., who reveals what is to my mind a unique insight into the deep influence of the theme of divine life in Hopkins' work, compares Hopkins and Dante on this most basic characteristic of a Catholic poet:

If even the natural manifestation of God in the works of creation has found continual voice in the songs of poets, we would expect that the astounding condescension and generosity of this supernatural communication of God in the works of grace would be a perennial source of limitless inspiration to Christian poets. But the strange fact is that seldom has this been the sustained theme of a poet's song in any language. Dante has sung of it extensively and incomparably well in his *Divine Comedy;* Milton sang of it coldly and erroneously in *Paradise Lost* and *Paradise Regained;* Patmore sang of some phases of it in *The Unknown Eros;* other English poets, Crashaw for instance, have made it the subject of an occasional poem; but Hopkins sang of it more consistently and beautifully than any other English poet.[25]

With that final judgment I am in wholehearted agreement, and my study has aimed at supplying the evidence which Hopkins' imagery gives to show, at least, that the incomprehensible sharing of divine life, surely the most, immeasurably the most, important fact in the Catholic view of human life, is a basic theme in Hopkins' mature work. And it was so, as McNamee points out, in Dante. The two poets are much alike in this, and strikingly different from most other poets. It is for the introduction, or rather revival, of this basic Catholic theme in beautiful poetry that I think that English-hearing lovers of poetry should be grateful, because without Hopkins' work, they would have to turn to Italian to hear precisely those deep harmonies and soaring tones.

The effect of Hopkins' Catholic world-view on his poems does not escape Arthur Mizener:

What did make Hopkins almost unique in his time, was his Catholicism, not an emotional, antiquarian, or hedonistic Catholicism—these were fairly common in the period—but a precise, logical and deeply felt knowledge of Catholic doctrine to which, on the whole, he successfully disciplined both his thinking and his feeling. . . . The clearness of his thought, however odd his words, on the immanence and transcendence of God saved him from any of the jerry-built cosmologies to which the Victorians and Romantics had frequently to resort in trying to deal with their intense awareness of nature. . . .[26]

F. R. Leavis carries through this attitude toward Hopkins' Catholic world-view with a suggestive comparison of Hopkins with Dante:

The intellectual and spiritual anaemia of Victorian poetry is indistinguishable from its lack of body. Hopkins is a very different poet from Dante, but a remark that Mr. Eliot throws out in the discussion of Dante has a bearing here: 'That Hell, though a state, is a state which can only be thought of, and perhaps only experienced, by the projection of sensory images; and that the resurrection of the body has perhaps a deeper meaning than we understand.' The critical implications of this (they can be generalized and discussed apart from any theological context) deserve pondering.[27]

We have been pondering for a good many pages now the critical implications of Hopkins' basic concern with the Christ-life in himself and in the world. While I am not altogether certain what Leavis has in mind when he says that the critical implications of Eliot's remark can be removed from a theological context, I assume he means that the implications of the intellectual and spiritual vitality that a great religious tradition can give are as true in critical discussions as they are in theological textbooks, and perhaps as valuable.[28] The difference he has in mind is, I suppose, that the theologian deals with Hell and with resurrection as matters of belief, whereas the critic, as such, deals with them as matters of knowledge. The theologian deals with them in relation to reality; he asserts their presence or absence in the real universe. The critic deals with them in their relation to the work of literature; he analyzes their effect in the universe of the literary work. The critic need not believe, but he must *know*. The critic of Hopkins, as of Dante, must certainly aim at an understanding of the theological views which so deeply formed the imagery of those poets if he is to understand what those images are expressing, the spiritual realities that those images flow from, express, and symbolize.

Hopkins' world-view reaches from the inner life of the Trinity through the human heart down to the earth itself, as our eight images indicate. In image 1, the nun rings the call to that Sacrifice which carries man into a share of the inner Sacrificial Life of the Trinity. Images 2 and 3 express the flow of that divine life to us from God the Holy Ghost and from His human instrument, Mary. The great central image, 4, expresses the central truth of the Catholic view, the literal union of the divine Heart of Christ with the human heart of His member. In image 5 the human heart exercises that divine life in the virtues, the fruits of the Holy Ghost. In 6 the heart wills the suffering which the struggle of that life with "man's malice" entails, and in 7 the exhausted heart yearns for God's comfort. In image 8 that divine life which flows out from the Trinity reaches clear down to the sweet earth, or at least there is the promise of its reaching there, since the earth, too, yearns and appeals for the share that it can have in the freedom of the sons of God. This is a large view, and its rich inclusion of other traditions appears in our images, too: the Jewish (especially in image 2); the Classic, in image 6; the Medieval, in image 4; even to some extent the Darwinian, in image 8. The body of Hopkins' poetry can do much, I believe, not only to beautify, but also to enrich our literature.

The central theme of Hopkins' imagery and its main function is to express the double theme of St. Paul: the power of sin and death and the triumph of Christ and life. It is life that flows through every one of Hopkins' poems. Each of our images deals with life—with a call to life, with the source and fostering of life, with a living out and a suffering for and a yearning for life, with an appeal even from brute nature for life. In one of his sermons Hopkins states the great theme:

And what was to be man's reward and wages for his work done?—Eternal life, glorious peace and power and praise and satisfaction from his king and his angel companions and his own conscience, peace and the sense of life everlastingly in mind and body for the efforts made, the pains taken, the strength spent. For the natural reward of duty, as St. Paul tells us, is life—life in some shape or other, the continuance or the lengthening or the heightening of life, life here or life hereafter or the life of fame in others' minds or life in one's line and offspring or wages, food or money, which are the means of life—every way, for man or God, life is what answers to duty done.

(*Sermons*, p. 60)

The life of God in this world is the great theme of Catholic thought, and it is this tremendous theme which is most central to the imagery of Hopkins. As Dante gave that theme poetic life in Italy, so Hopkins, with power and with profound vision, has given it poetic life in modern England. The nature and function of his imagery, concerned most intimately with the deep reality of life, reveal him as a poet who discovered that the lighted hall of the world was not empty after all, who found the Host and gained the power to frame his vision, his love, his loneliness, his pain and his patience, his great hymn to life, in immortal song.

Notes

Notes

Introduction

1. (p. xi) For a philosophical approach to my theory, see my "The Nature of Metaphor," *The Modern Schoolman*, 31 (May, 1954), pp. 257-80, and "The Nature of Metaphor: Further Considerations," *The Modern Schoolman*, 34 (May, 1957), pp. 283-98.

2. (p. xii) The fine delight that fathers thought; the strong
 Spur, live and lancing like the blowpipe flame,
 Breathes once and, quenchèd faster than it came,
 Leaves yet the mind a mother of immortal song.
 Nine months she then, nay years, nine years she long
 Within her wears, bears, cares and combs the same:
 The widow of an insight lost she lives, with aim
 Now known and hand at work now never wrong.
 (Poems, No. 75)

3. (p. xv) Cf. Hopkins' "That Nature is a Heraclitean Fire and of the comfort of the Resurrection," *Poems*, No. 72:

 Both are in an unfathomable, all is in an enormous dark
 Drowned.

The graduated vowels with no full stops, prolonged by the *n*'s, *m*'s, and *r*'s, express the growing waves of overwhelming dark and in their openness suggest, like Milton's line, the depth and breadth of the darkness.

4. (p. xviii) Captain Brickenstein's testimony, *The Times* (London), December 10, 1875, p. 10.

5. (p. xxii) Hopkins corrected this error in German a few weeks later in another letter to Bridges: "That German word is *sache*, not *sach*, except in compounds: you should have set me right" (Aug. 14, 1879, *Letters 1*, p. 85). For another illuminating defense of his word-choice, cf. *Letters 1*, pp. 296-97.

Chapter 1

1. (p. 5) The most obvious of the Scriptural sources for the "feathers" of God is Christ's sad address to Jerusalem, "How often have I been willing to gather your children as a mother bird gathers her brood under her wings! But you refused it!" (Matthew, 23:37). In *Deutschland*, the "dovewings" of stanza 3 recall the "wings like a dove" which bear up the troubled heart of Psalm 54 and relate the activity of grace to the Third Person of the Trinity, the Holy Spirit Who is symbolized both by a dove and by a finger ("Digitus Dei"). This combination of Christian symbols to express the activity of the Holy Ghost with new and vigorous power will be fully discussed in chapter 2. The numerous references in the Psalms to the protecting wings of God also give depth to the imagery of the poem—most particularly Psalm 56, "And in the shadow of thy wings I seek refuge, till the disaster be past," and Psalm 90,

"He will shelter thee with his pinions, and thou shalt take refuge under his wings: his faithfulness is a shield and a buckler."

2. (p. 6) This insight was one of many I gained from the sensitive and competent study by Sister Mary Adorita Hart, B.V.M., "The Christocentric Theme in Gerard Manley Hopkins' 'The Wreck of the Deutschland,'" (Doctoral dissertation, Catholic University, Washington, D.C., 1952). In discussing "voel," Sister Adorita says: "As was pointed out, Mr. Gardner sees in the word an allusion to a mountain (The Voel) near St. Benuo's; Miss Schneider considers the word as used in 'The Deutschland' to mean 'any bare hill.' The interpretation made here is that 'the voel' refers to the 'bare hill' of Calvary. This is where the 'hero of Calvary' purchased the gift of sanctifying grace for all men. From the act of redemption on this 'bare hill,' men were once more given the opportunity of possessing in their souls that supernatural quality which makes them partakers of the divine nature and of the divine life in a real and formal, but *accidental* manner. Such a reading of the text underscores the precision of the narrator's use of 'pressure.' And since this is participation in *life,* he rightly speaks of it as a 'principle.' Finally, it is 'Christ's gift'—the gift of the Victim of Calvary, the gift of the Eucharistic Victim to Whom the narrator had fled for salvation and for sanctification" (p. 73).

3. (p. 6) There is an echo in these stanzas of the Hymn from the Breviary's Common of Martyrs:

> Sed corde impavido mens bene conscia
> Conservat patientiam.

The nun, a victim of the *Kulturkampf,* is regarded by Hopkins as a martyr since she willingly accepts death because of her faith. The German authorities intended her exile, not her death, and therefore she would not in the strictest sense be classified as a martyr. But her willing acceptance of death in union with Christ's sacrifice is worthy of a martyr, in Hopkins' eyes.

4. (p. 19) "In *cynghanedd,* the rules of alliteration are much stricter than in English. Words of more than one syllable alliterate when *all* their consonants, except the final ones, are the same and in the same order" (*Gardner* 2, p. 148).

5. (p. 20) One (rather minor) cause of the musical differences in stanzas 30 and 31 is the arrangement of stressed and unstressed syllables in each. In the first of the two stanzas, lack of motion and rest are indicated by the relatively small number of syllables and by the end-stopped lines. In the second, the many syllables and the run-on lines express motion and speed.

Stanza 30

```
       / x / /
       / x / /
     / x x / / x x /
       / x / x x x /
     / x x / / x x / /
   x / x / x x x x / / x /
     x / x / x / x x /
   / x / x / x x / x / x /
```

Stanza 31

```
         / x x / x x / x x
         / x x / x x x / x x
       / x x / x x / x x / x x
           / x x / x / x x
       / x x / x x / x x / x x / x x
   / x x x / x x x x x / x x / x x x x / x x
         / x x x / x x x / x / x x x
   / x x x / x x x / x x x / x x / x x x x / x x
```

NOTES

Chapter 2

1. (p. 27) It is interesting to note that another Jesuit, writing some twenty years later, sought an analogy for almost the exact notion that Hopkins expresses in this poem and hit upon precisely the same comparison. Poulain is speaking of those who feel that they are not exercising virtue, that they do not have the power of God in their souls, and to illustrate that those virtues may be in our souls without our knowledge of the fact, he says: "An electric machine may be charged, but the electric fluid is not visible. But if we approach it we get proofs of its existence by a sharp shock." *The Graces of Interior Prayer,* trans. Leonora Smith (London: Kegan Paul, 1910), p. 412.

2. (p. 40) *The Text of the Spiritual Exercises of Saint Ignatius,* trans. from the original Spanish (London: Burns, Oates, and Washbourne, 1936), p. 76. This book will hereafter be cited as *The Spiritual Exercises.*

3. (p. 41) Ed. Dom Bernard Orchard and others (London: Thomas Nelson, 1951), p. 1187. This work will hereafter be cited as *A Catholic Commentary.*

4. (p. 42) When three nouns focus on one adjective or verb, as in this case "Holy Ghost," "dove," and "sun" focus on "broods," then the complexity tends to trip the unwary reader. For example, Macbeth's naked babe and equestrian cherub (or cherubs) join with Pity in focusing on the two qualities of helplessness (from their own natures) and of unnatural powerfulness (from the upset caused by the "horrid deed"); the threefold image has puzzled generations of critics, as I indicate in "The Imagery of *Macbeth,* I, vii, 21-28," *MLQ,* 16 (June, 1955), 130-36.

Chapter 3

1. (p. 48) Cf. Eric Burrows, S.J., "The Doctrine of the Shekinah and the Theology of the Incarnation," in *The Gospel of the Infancy and Other Biblical Essays* (London: Burns, Oates, and Washbourne, 1940), pp. 101-10.

2. (p. 48) *Finnegans Wake* (New York: The Viking Press, 1947), p. 304.

3. (p. 54) Patristic and later treatments of the Word's entering into His members through their ears are numerous, though I have seen nothing which approaches the subtlety of Hopkins' use of air as conductor of sound. Modern physics contributes to the new use Hopkins can make of the traditional elements for the imagery. The following ancient text from Ephraem (*ca.* 306-373 A.D.) indicates how pervasive those elements are in Catholic tradition: "In the beginning, by the sin of our first parents, death passed into all men; today, through Mary, we have been transferred from death to life. In the beginning the serpent filled the ears of Eve, and from there the poison spread to the whole body; today Mary caught with her ears the restorer of eternal felicity. What was instrument of death, therefore, has become instrument of life as well." *De Diversis sermonibus 3: De laudibus Dei genitricis Mariae (Opera omnia syr. et lat. 3* [Rome: Salvioni, 1743], p. 607).

4. (p. 55) In all those exquisite poems of *The Temple* expressive of the meaning and function of the Church, Mary appears only in the doublet entitled "Anagram":

> How well her name an "Army" doth present,
> In whom the "Lord of hosts" did pitch His tent!

"The British Church" appears as "deare Mother," but Mary has no function in the Church whatever except as the physical mother of Jesus, the tent—Herbert evidently has in mind the literal Greek meaning of the verb in John, 1:14, "and pitched His tent among us," and perhaps the verbal tie-up between ἐσκήνωσεν and *Shekinah,* which would give more point to his reference to the "Lord of hosts," Who appeared as the Shekinah. The contrast between Mary's position in *The Temple* and her position in English religious poetry before the Reformation is striking and deeply significant.

5. (p. 56) An excellent source of information on the depth and ubiquity of English devotion to Mary before the Reformation is "The Assumption in the Early English Pulpit," by Noel J. Ryan, S.J., in *Theological Studies,* XI (Dec., 1950), 477-524. Another informative article on the subject is "The Origins of Devotion to our Lady's

Immaculate Conception," by H. Francis Davis, in *The Dublin Review*, Fourth Quarter (1954), pp. 375-92. The main thesis, that the doctrine flourished on English soil and was rather imposed upon Rome than vice versa, is not, to me, altogether convincing, but the material advanced to sustain the point is revelatory of the background of Scotus' defense of the doctrine, as Davis points out.

6. (p. 56) "It is plain that by denying the reality of sanctifying grace the Reformers struck at the very heart of the Christian religion. The rejection of that doctrine carried with it the rejection of such truths as our sonship to God, our membership in Christ, our deliverance from the power of sin. The old phrases might still be retained, and in fact were retained in very large measure, but they had been evacuated of all meaning." G. H. Joyce, S.J., *The Catholic Doctrine of Grace* (New York: Benziger, n.d.), pp. 47-48.

7. (p. 57) The "L" stanza of Chaucer's "A.B.C." indicates this traditional Catholic view of Mary's sharing in Christ's salvific Sacrifice—"that ye *bothe* have bought so deere" (italics, of course, mine).

A full and clear statement of the position of the Catholic Church on Mary's function in the Mystical Body can be found in *Mary in Doctrine*, by Emil Neubert, S.M. (Milwaukee: Bruce, 1954).

8. (p. 59) Illustration of differences between Protestants and Catholics in regard to Mary's position in the Church may be found in the *Dublin Review*, New Series VI (April, 1866), 412-49; N.S. VII (July, 1866), 142-99; and *ibid*. (October, 1866), 455-514. There is evidence in *Letters 3*, p. 28, that Hopkins had read at least the July article, and it is probable that he had read them all. Mary is represented as a goddess for Catholics. Faber's translation of de Montfort in the *Review* offers imagery strikingly similar to that of Hopkins' poem: "She is good, she is tender, she has nothing in her austere or repulsive, nothing too sublime and too brilliant. In seeing her, we see our pure nature. She is not the sun, who, by the vivacity of his rays, blinds us because of our weakness; but she is fair and gentle as the moon, which receives the light of the sun, and tempers it to render it more suitable to our capacity" (July, 1866, p. 170). The anonymous *Review* writer describes de Montfort's analogy in words which apply exactly to the first part of Hopkins' development of our text: "The concluding extracts occur in an analogy, which to some may seem far-fetched, but which to us appears singularly beautiful; an analogy between that joint office, on the one hand, whereby the Holy Ghost and Mary produced Christ Himself, and that joint office, on the other hand, whereby they form Christ in the individual soul" (July, 1866, p. 197).

9. (p. 60) Hopkins' imagery is based on the fact that both Mary and Christ, though in infinitely different ways, are sources of grace. Thus Gardner's note on the lines, "Yet no part but what will / Be Christ our Saviour still," is doubly unfortunate. He states (*Poems*, p. 241) that Hopkins means "The grace all comes from Christ, not from Mary herself." In the first place, Hopkins is not speaking about the *source* of grace in those lines, but about the *product*, which is Christ-in-us, Christ in His member. When Mary shares her life with us, the product is Christ. In the second place, Gardner's statement, in this context, is simply wrong and removes all meaning from the life-giving function of Mary which Hopkins is describing. If one were speaking of the absolute source of grace, Gardner's statement is true. But if one is speaking of a relative source of grace, as Hopkins is, then Gardner's statement is wrong. Relative to us and dependent on Christ, the grace we receive does come from Mary herself, and it is this extraordinary and mysterious fact which Hopkins is imaging.

10. (p. 62) The terms used above are those of my own definition of metaphor, which I discuss at length in "The Nature of Metaphor," *The Modern Schoolman*, 31 (May, 1954), 257-80, and 34 (May, 1957), 283-98. The definition is: "Metaphor is an identification by means of direct predication of an individual being with an alien nature on the basis of a quality or act which is characteristic of the individual as such and of the nature as such." I shall have occasion to enlarge on this matter in my final chapter.

NOTES

Chapter 4

1. (p. 76) As I shall have occasion to discuss later, "To own my heart" is an inversion, for rhythmic reasons, of "to my own heart." The voice, I think, could do whatever is necessary to bring out this meaning, but on the page, at least, the inversion is hard on the sense. The device is like the one in *Deutschland*, stanza 6, where I am convinced (though with no decisive objective evidence) that "like riding a river" is an inversion for "like a riding river." The rhythmic demands are much like those in the inversion above from "Peace," the inversion is the type that Hopkins has a weakness for (e.g., "And frightful a nightfall folded rueful a day" in stanza 15 of *Deutschland*), and most of all, the image of Christ's procession into time giving it direction compared to the river Jordan giving motion and direction to the Sea of Galilee is developed in *Sermons*, p. 196. (Father Devlin, in his note on this passage, reaches a conclusion similar to mine.) Hopkins seems, engrossed as he was with the rhythms and sound, not to have realized the extent of the puzzlement inversions like that in "Peace" could cause from the printed page. Or perhaps he did realize it, but considered such problems irrelevant, since he composed for the ear, not for the eye.

2. (p. 79) That it is Christ who *stirs* his heart Hopkins tells Bridges: "Feeling, love in particular, is the great moving power and spring of verse and the only person that I am in love with seldom, especially now, stirs my heart sensibly and when he does I cannot always 'make capital' of it, it would be a sacrilege to do so" (Feb. 15, 1879, *Letters 1*, p. 66).

3. (p. 82) Facing p. 80 of *Some Eminent Victorians*, by J. Comyns Carr (London: Duckworth, 1908). The background in Emblem Books, as for example in *Schola Cordis*, of Benedict Haeften (Antwerp: 1629), in *Cardiomorphoseos*, of Francis Pona (Verona: 1645), in Quarles's *Emblemes*, etc., is familiar to scholars and is echoed in a recent edition of *The Verse in English of Richard Crashaw* (New York: The Grove Press, 1949), where, on p. 196, a flaming and winged heart prepares for some of Crashaw's imagery.

4. (p. 83) G. F. Lahey, S.J., *Gerard Manley Hopkins* (London: Oxford, 1930), pp. 116-17.

5. (p. 83) W. A. M. Peters, S.J., *Gerard Manley Hopkins, A critical Essay toward the Understanding of his Poetry* (London: Oxford, 1948), pp. 85-86 and 105-6.

6. (p. 83) *Gerard Manley Hopkins* (London: Longmans, Green, 1955), p. 29.

7. (p. 83) "The Bird as Symbol," *Studies*, 44 (Autumn, 1955), 295.

8. (p. 84) *Selected Poems of Gerard Manley Hopkins*, ed. James Reeves (London: W. Heinemann, 1953). The paraphrase quoted is taken from the note on "The Windhover," pp. 85-86.

9. (p. 84) *The Dial*, 81 (July-Dec., 1926), 197.

10. (p. 84) *Seven Types of Ambiguity* (2nd ed.; London: Chatto and Windus, 1947), pp. 224-26.

11. (p. 85) *The Poetry of Gerard Manley Hopkins, A Survey and Commentary* (Cambridge, England: The University Press, 1933), pp. 130-33.

12. (p. 85) Empson states in a footnote (*Ambiguity*, p. 226) that Hopkins intended, or rather *thought* he intended, only the "heroic action" idea and "would have denied with anger that he meant 'like a bicycle wheel,' and then after much conscientious self-torture would have suppressed the whole poem." My own suspicion is that the young Empson was taking his criticism far more seriously than Hopkins would have taken it. His picture of Hopkins seems to me, too, to have little resemblance to the real man. I myself believe that there would have been no self-torture in Hopkins' reaction, if he indeed would have had any other reaction than amused surprise at Empson's notion of a Jesuit's interior. He would more probably have asked him, as he asked Bridges, "Did you ever see one?" (*Letters 1*, p. 40). Nor do I believe that any amount of Freudian (or pseudo-Freudian) dogmatizing would have persuaded Hopkins to suppress one of his successful poems. He was not a fool.

That the tendency to suppress things was not part of his character in reality (as opposed to Empson's imaginative picture) is evidenced by his later sorrow over his inability to produce more.

13. (p. 85) Her remark seems to me a wise one which deserves more attention than it has received from the majority of writers on Hopkins' work: "I sometimes suspect that we are many of us so certain that becoming a Jesuit must involve some unnatural and undesirable deformation or repression that we are prepared to see oddities in a Jesuit poet where there are none" (Phare, *Survey and Commentary*, p. 141).

14. (p. 85) In *Four Independents* (New York: Sheed and Ward, 1935), p. 148.

15. (p. 85) *New Bearings in English Poetry* (London: Chatto and Windus, 1942), pp. 181-82.

16. (p. 86) Hugh Kelly, S.J., "The Windhover—and Christ," *Studies*, 45 (Summer, 1956), 192.

17. (p. 86) *Times Literary Supplement*, 54 (June 24, 1955), 349.

18. (p. 86) *The Unmediated Vision, an Interpretation of Wordsworth, Hopkins, Rilke, and Valery* (New Haven: Yale, 1954), p. 61.

19. (p. 87) *Ibid.*, p. 67.

20. (p. 87) *The Shaping Vision of Gerard Manley Hopkins* (London: Oxford, 1958), p. 53.

21. (p. 88) *Gerard Manley Hopkins, A Study of his Ignatian Spirit* (New York: Bookman Associates, 1959), p. 103.

22. (p. 88) *Ibid.*, p. 157.

23. (p. 88) "The Creation of the Self in Gerard Manley Hopkins," *ELH*, 22 (1955), 307. Miller well treats of Hopkins' use of the verb "catches." He refers to its use in *Journals*, p. 231, "I caught as well as I could while my companion talked the Greek rightness of their (the bluebells') beauty . . ." and states that the verb is "Hopkins' special term for the strenuous activity of perception" (p. 304).

24. (p. 88) *Ibid.*, p. 316.

25. (p. 88) *Ibid.*, p. 318.

26. (p. 89) *Gerard Manley Hopkins, A Life* (New York: Norton, 1944), pp. 155-57.

27. (p. 90) "A Note on Hopkins' Windhover," *Studies*, 45 (Spring, 1956), 88.

28. (p. 90) "An Analysis of *The Windhover*, an Experiment in Structural Method," *PMLA*, 60 (Dec., 1955), 977.

29. (p. 91) "The Analogical Mirrors," in *Gerard Manley Hopkins by the Kenyon Critics* (Norfolk, Conn.: New Directions, 1945), pp. 15-27.

30. (p. 91) "What does the Windhover Mean?," in *Immortal Diamond: Studies in Gerard Manley Hopkins*, ed. Norman Weyand, S.J. (New York: Sheed and Ward, 1949), pp. 275-306.

31. (p. 91) I attempted to express this in "A Footnote on 'The Windhover,'" an article which appeared in *America*, 82 (Nov. 5, 1949), 129-30. At that time I had not perceived the deep significance of the "heart" imagery in the poem or the ultimate key to the poem's unity, which is its expression of the theology of the Sacred Heart—the significance of the union of the human heart of Christ with the Verbum on the one hand, and of that human-divine Heart with the hearts of His members on the other.

32. (p. 92) "The Windhover," in *Interpretations: Essays on Twelve English Poems*, ed. John Wain (London: Routledge, Kegan Paul, 1955), p. 144.

33. (p. 92) *Times Literary Supplement*, 54 (May 6, 1955), 237.

34. (p. 92) "The Windhover de G. M. Hopkins," *Études Anglaises*, 9 (1956), 15.

35. (p. 95) By "knightly meaning" I refer to the manner in which the words operated during the era of knighthood. In this sense "sillion" too has a knightly meaning, since during that era it existed in that form ("selion" is the modern form)

and meant a field for plowing. "Dangerous," with its derivation from the Latin word for "Lord" and its meaning in knightly times of power and mastery, is most significantly operative in the poem. These serve to place the poem in the knightly era in time, looking backward to Christ the Knight in His historical achievement, labor, and death, looking forward to Christ the Knight in His Jesuit member in modern Wales.

36. (p. 99) Hopkins' imagery in speaking of a fellow Jesuit on January 1, 1882, indicates further his attitude toward the plow imagery as it is connected with the dedicated service of Christ our Lord: "One of our Fathers, who was for the best part of two years my yokemate on that laborious mission, died there yesterday night after a short sickness, in harness and in his prime" (*Letters 3*, p. 162). The yoke of Christ on those who labor with Him is straightforward and conventional enough, but the ambiguity of harness—that of the yoked beasts and that of the minions of Christ, the seeming versus being of "Alphonsus"—might escape one who did not know the tradition of knightly imagery in the Society of Jesus. Hopkins' note on "The Kingdom of Christ" unites the desertion-of-the-plow imagery with the cowardly knight imagery: ". . . substituting . . . the disgrace of putting the hand to the plough and looking back in the kingdom of heaven for the recreant knight . . ." (*Sermons*, p. 163).

37. (p. 105) E.g., in the story of the Prodigal Son: "But, while he was still a long way off, his father saw him and took pity on him; running up, he threw his arms round his neck and kissed him" (Luke, 15:20). "Fell on his neck" is the more familiar, if less idiomatic, translation.

Chapter 5

1. (p. 116) ". . . per patientiam animus praeservatur ne obruatur tristitia" (*Summa Theologiae*, II-II, question 136, article 1, ad 3). For a useful background to Hopkins' attitude toward peace and patience as virtues in the exercise of divine life, see *Summa Theologiae*, I-II, q. 70, "De Fructibus Spiritus Sancti"; II-II, q. 29, "De Pace"; II-II, q. 136, "De Patientia."

2. (p. 117) For similar imagery, see *Purgatorio,* canto 6, in which Christ as "highest Jove" is questioned about apparently forsaken Italy. Hopkins' "wilder beast from West" is perhaps remotely allied to the "lawless Shepherd from westward" of *Inferno,* canto 19.

3. (p. 121) Peters is at his best in such matters: " 'Began' is a noun, and as such properly preceded by an attributive adjective. But it is the past tense of the verb 'to begin' that is used as a noun; a verbal form expressing activity is thus used to indicate a quality of the poet. The poet calls himself a 'began,' not a beginner; for 'beginner' would express a permanent static quality and would not be the perfect expression of the inscape of the poet whose essential quality here and now is 'I once began,' and that is what he is left now: from that aspect his essence is left unaltered. 'Lonely began' as descriptive of the essence is indeed a terrible expression and well fits the terrible sonnet of which it is the closing phrase" (W. A. M. Peters, S.J., *Gerard Manley Hopkins, A Critical Essay towards the Understanding of his Poetry* [London: Oxford, 1948] p. 131). "Terrible," I suppose it is superfluous to note, has no pejorative intentions here.

Even more pointed and revealing is the comment of Sister M. Laurentia Digges, C.S.J. (in "Gerard Manley Hopkins's Sonnets of Desolation, an Analysis of Meaning" [Doctoral dissertation, Catholic University, Washington, D.C., 1951], p. 53): "The word *hoard* mitigates somewhat the loneliness of the last line . . . and helps to explicate the puzzling use of *began* as a substantive. One does not hoard a thing which has never come into existence, and so what the speaker says here is that the heart possesses and still holds the thoughts that might have reached friends, the poems which might have honored England, the pleading that might have influenced others."

4. (p. 123) "If you do not like 'I yield, you do come sometimes,' (though I cannot myself feel the weakness you complain of in it, and it has the advantage of being plain) will 'I yield, you foot me sometime' do?" (*Letters 1*, p. 196).

Chapter 6

1. (p. 134) Reeves's view of Hopkins' poetic end is quite different from mine: "This was Hopkins' last poem. It is doubtful if any great poet has ended his poetic life on a note of deeper hopelessness and desolation" (*Selected Poems*, p. 98). Ignoring both the poem's assumption of a former autumn and harvest when the "arch and original Breath" inspired Hopkins and the magnificent poem's own refutation of what it states, Reeves can yet say, "In to R.B. he makes his final admission of total failure" (p. xxvi). I judge from Reeves's other remarks that he arrives at this reading impelled by a powerful conviction that it *must* be so, that the masochism which led Hopkins to "sacrifice his life to the Jesuit ideal" would necessarily lead to some such end.

2. (p. 134) "I do not ask the Irish to see this, but I should like the English dupes and dullards to see it. If you knew the world I live in! Yet I continue to be a Home Ruler: I say it must be, and let it be." To his brother Lionel (March 1, 1889, *Letters 3*, p. 194).

3. (p. 136) The original version of lines 3-8 was this:

>By flood, by fall, low-lull-off or all roar
>Frequenting there while moon shall wear and wend;
>Left hand, off land, I hear the lark ascend
>With rash-fresh more, repair of skein and score,
>Race wild reel round, crisp coil deal down to floor,
>And spill music till there's none left to spend.

Joyce's image for the birds Stephen watched and heard is so strikingly similar to Hopkins' that I have wondered (without, alas, hope of verification) whether Joyce might have seen or heard Hopkins' poem from one of Hopkins' colleagues at University College: "But the notes were long and shrill and whirring, unlike the cry of vermin, falling a third or a fourth and trilled as the flying beaks clove the air. Their cry was shrill and clear and fine and falling like threads of silken light unwound from whirring spools" (*A Portrait of the Artist as a Young Man* [New York: Modern Library, 1928], p. 263).

4. (p. 137) Inter oves locum praesta,
>Et ab hoedis me sequestra,
>Statuens in parte dextra.

5. (p. 142) The rack is a Christian image in the light of the Roman Martyrology, which is read daily in religious communities and which constantly describes the racking of the martyrs. Hopkins' own English Jesuit brothers, Campion, Southwell, and others, brought the image even closer home for Hopkins, in their prolonged tortures on Elizabethan racks.

Chapter 7

1. (p. 150) "But what some of the contemporary poets are trying to do is to use words in patterns quite irrespective of the meaning" (David Daiches, *The Place of Meaning in Poetry* [London: Oliver and Boyd, 1935], p. 59). The author goes on to attribute this aim to Gertrude Stein. Something like this appears to be what Hartman thinks Hopkins is aiming at: "The final tendency of Hopkins is toward pure speech, what he might call the inscape of speech. And 'buckle' therefore, is in the nature of a pure speech movement, an 'explosive,' that cares little about grammatical precision" (p. 188).

2. (p. 150) This "changeless note" expresses the Trinity in its repetition.

3. (p. 156) Cf. St. Ignatius' statement on spiritual desolation in the fourth of the Rules for the discernment of Spirits for the First Week in the *Spiritual Exercises,* and particularly, "For as consolation is contrary to desolation, so the thoughts that spring from consolation are contrary to those that spring from desolation." St. Ignatius is concerned merely with categorizing the two types of thoughts as evidence for determining the state of soul, but his statement indicates something of that basic tension in the soul expressed in opposing thoughts. And the opposition between consolation, when

the soul is filled with the increase of "all interior joy" and is "quiet and tranquil in its Creator and Lord" (Rule 3), and desolation, when the soul is filled with "darkness and disquiet of soul, an attraction towards low and earthly objects, the disquiet of various agitations and temptations, which move it to diffidence, without hope and without love, when the soul finds itself slothful, tepid, sad, and, as it were, separated from its Creator and Lord" (Rule 4), indicates both the comfort which the Jesuit poet wants and the terrible aloneness and aching desire which, in the literal sense of the word, desolate him.

4. (p. 157) A misreading of these lines, I suspect, led to the following statement of Marshall W. Stearns, in the course of his commentary on one of Dylan Thomas's sonnets: "Mary's reference to Jesus as 'Jack Christ' (a phrase found in Gerard Manley Hopkins) suggests Christ's relation to common humanity" ("Unsex the Skeleton: Notes on the Poetry of Dylan Thomas," *The Sewanee Review,* 52 [1944], 432). The phrase does not occur in Hopkins.

5. (p. 158) "We take heart, then, continually, since we recognize that our spirits are exiled from the Lord's presence so long as they are at home in the body, with faith, instead of a clear view, to guide our steps" (II Corinthians, 5:6-7).

Chapter 8

1. (p. 164) In one of the extant versions of the poem, Hopkins says that "Earth childs *us* by heaven" and in another, "Earth childs *things* by heaven." Gardner thinks that Hopkins changed "us" to "things" ". . . as though he had feared the monistic or pantheistic implications of 'us'" (2, p. 351). Unless I am badly mistaken, the fear is totally Gardner's. In the one case, Hopkins speaks as one of earth's children; in the other, he speaks objectively as any speaker, man, angel, or God, might do. Since man is a thing that springs in part from earth, the second statement is as "monistic" as the first—that is, neither one is either monistic or pantheistic.

2. (p. 165) In supposing that Hopkins is talking about a Welsh town in particular and in failing to read the "we," Gardner misreads the image: "To stigmatize as shallow and frail a whole townful of dear and dogged Welsh folk seems almost a sin against the brooding presence of the Holy Ghost" (2, p. 248).

Chapter 9

1. (p. 175) I (Winter, 1949), 455-76, and II (Spring, 1949), 59-93.

2. (p. 177) *The World's Body* (New York: Scribner's, 1938), p. 137.

3. (p. 177) *Ibid.,* pp. 139-40.

4. (p. 177) I indicate the philosophical arguments from which I derive my conclusions in my articles on metaphor in *The Modern Schoolman,* 31 (May, 1954), and 34 (May, 1957). My study of the matter indicates the importance, in my opinion, of the "is" of the predication, which expresses the incommunicable act of existence in the subject. It is that act of existence that makes it impossible for that subject to be another thing which has *its* own incommunicable act of existence. Hence identity between two distinct and existent objects, each with its own "is," is impossible.

Analogy requires two distinct and existent objects, because analogy involves unlikeness of act or quality as well as unlikeness of nature. For this reason I hold, as I attempt to develop in my article, that while analogy is the basis of simile, it has nothing whatever to do with metaphor.

5. (p. 178) Ransom, *The World's Body,* p. 142.

6. (p. 178) *Ibid.*

7. (p. 179) *A Reading of George Herbert* (Chicago: University of Chicago Press, 1952), p. 202.

8. (p. 179) "The Language of Paradox," in *Criticism, The Foundations of Modern Literary Judgment,* ed. Mark Schorer *et al.* (New York: Harcourt, Brace, 1948), p. 365.

9. (p. 186) *Creative Intuition in Art and Poetry* (New York: Pantheon, 1953), p. 312.

10. (p. 187) *Ibid.*, pp. 363-64.

11. (p. 189) (New York: Modern Library, 1928), pp. 255-56.

12. (p. 190) This is the reason for an artist's not being in a necessarily privileged position in interpreting his own work. It may be dark to his mind because he doesn't know why he did it right or because his mind cannot probe as deeply as his heart can send her roots. He may judge quite wrongly about the product of his habit of art's perfect judgment.

Bridges' own rationalistic approach to poetry led him to alter the octet of No. 75 for clarity's sake. In the first two editions, the sixth line reads, "Within her wears, bears, cares and moulds the same."

Not only is the pattern of sound seriously disturbed, but the wonderful analogy between the cells of honeycomb, the ordered arrangement of the parts of the child's body, and the ordered arrangement of words into lines and stanzas is totally lost. The idol "clarity" is not a benignant deity for editors or critics.

13. (p. 192) R. P. Blackmur, "The Later Poetry of W. B. Yeats," in *Critiques and Essays in Criticism, 1920-1948*, ed. R. W. Stallman (New York: Ronald Press, 1949), p. 369.

14. (p. 193) Elsie Elizabeth Phare, *The Poetry of Gerard Manley Hopkins, A Survey and Commentary* (Cambridge, England: The University Press, 1933), p. 10.

15. (p. 194) James Reeves (ed.), *Selected Poems of Gerard Manley Hopkins* (London: W. Heinemann, 1953), p. xi.

16. (p. 195) *Ibid.*, p. xv.

17. (p. 195) *Ibid.*, p. xvi.

18. (p. 195) *Ibid.*, p. xxviii.

19. (p. 197) The review originally appeared in *The New Republic*, 111 (1944), pp. 223-24. It is reprinted in *Literary Opinion in America*, ed. M. D. Zabel (New York: Harper, 1951), p. 255.

20. (p. 197) Miss Tuve, speaking of the unity of Herbert's work, indicates a fact which applies also to Hopkins' mature poems: "The poems are not 'organized around the same idea'; in fact my necessarily purely conceptual analysis has done them violence, and they grew, rather than were organized, out of the same pattern of symbols" (*A Reading of George Herbert*, p. 201).

A further observation of hers in regard to the tradition in which Herbert wrote has a pointed application in regard to the Catholic tradition in which Hopkins wrote: "Herbert writes within a symbolic tradition, to him familiar, accepted and significant. . . . If we are willing to learn Herbert's language we shall hear what he says, or most of it, being made able to experience the beauty and the power which are inextricably part of it. Since he says it in the language of metaphor, it did not stop being true when certain meanings it may have had to him ceased to exercise power over men's minds. Metaphors cheat time in ways beyond a poet's foresight. The meanings we find still true, even in ways he did not foresee, are yet his meanings, but at a level so deep that no man knows or could say in cold conceptual formulation the reach and scope of them" (*ibid.*, pp. 202-3).

21. (p. 199) "Theology and the Imagination," *Thought*, 29 (1954), 61.

22. (p. 199) *Ibid.*, p. 63.

23. (p. 201) Phare, *The Poetry of Gerard Manley Hopkins*, p. 150.

24. (p. 201) "'. . . And Telling You a Story,' A Note on *The Divine Comedy*," in *Essays Presented to Charles Williams* (London: Oxford, 1947), pp. 34-35.

25. (p. 201) "Hopkins: Poet of Nature and of the Supernatural," in *Immortal Diamond: Studies in Gerard Manley Hopkins* (New York: Sheed and Ward, 1949), p. 238.

26. (p. 202) "Victorian Hopkins," in *Gerard Manley Hopkins by the Kenyon Critics* (Norfolk, Conn.: New Directions, 1945), p. 101.

27. (p. 202) *New Bearings in English Poetry* (London: Chatto and Windus, 1942), pp. 186-87.

28. (p. 202) A valuable remark of Gardner's, made in the course of a review of Pick's and Reeves's collections, is worth repeating here: "Finally, it is worth reflecting that such renunciations as Hopkins made derive from, and give additional validity to, that Christian ethic and universal *mystique* which underlie much great religious poetry besides his own. The values he asserted increase and strengthen the significance of Dante, St. John of the Cross, Donne, and Mr. T. S. Eliot" ("Hopkins's Harvest-Home," *The Month,* N.S. 10 [1953], 308).

Select Bibliography

Index

Select Bibliography

Arendzen, J. P. *The Holy Trinity*. London: Sheed and Ward, 1937.
Auden, W. H. "The Knight of the Infinite," *The New Republic*, 111 (August 21, 1944), 223-24. Reprinted in *Literary Opinion in America*, ed. M. D. Zabel. Rev. ed. New York: Harper, 1951.
Augustine. "De sancta virginitate," *Enchiridion Patristicum*, ed. M. J. Rouet de Journel. Barcelona: Herder, 1951. Also in *Patrologiae Cursus Completus, series Latina*, ed. J.-P. Migne, 40, 399. Paris, 1844-55.
Bede. "Homilia in lib. 4, cap 49 in Luc. 11," in "Commune Festorum B. Mariae Virginis," *Breviarium Romanum*. Rome: Marietti, n.d. Also in *Patrologiae Cursus Completus, series Latina*, ed. J.-P. Migne, 92, 480. Paris, 1844-55.
Beeching, H. C. *A Book of Christmas Verse*. New York: Dodd, Mead, 1895.
Bischoff, D. A., S.J. "The Manuscripts of Gerard Manley Hopkins," *Thought*, 26 (Winter, 1951), 551-80.
Blackmur, R. P. "The Later Poetry of W. B. Yeats," in *Critiques and Essays in Criticism, 1920-1948*, ed. R. W. Stallman. New York: Ronald Press, 1949.
Boyle, Robert, S.J. "A Footnote on 'The Windhover,'" *America*, 82 (Nov. 5, 1949), 129-30.
———. "The Thought Structure of The Wreck of the Deutschland," in *Immortal Diamond: Studies in Gerard Manley Hopkins*, ed. Norman Weyand, S.J. New York: Sheed and Ward, 1949.
———. "The Nature of Metaphor," *The Modern Schoolman*, 31 (May, 1954), 257-80.
———. "The Imagery of *Macbeth*, I, 7, 21-28," *MLQ*, 16 (June, 1955), 130-36.
———. "The Nature of Metaphor: Further Considerations," *The Modern Schoolman*, 34 (May, 1957), 283-98.
Britt, Dom Matthew, O.S.B. *The Hymns of the Breviary and Missal*. New York: Benziger, 1952.
Brooks, Cleanth. "The Language of Paradox," in *Criticism, The Founda-

tions of Modern Literary Judgment, ed. Mark Schorer *et al.* New York: Harcourt, Brace, 1948.

Burrows, Eric, S.J. *The Gospel of the Infancy and Other Biblical Essays.* London: Burns, Oates, and Washbourne, 1940.

Daiches, David. *The Place of Meaning in Poetry.* London: Oliver and Boyd, 1935.

Davie, Donald. *Purity of Diction in English Verse.* New York: Oxford, 1953.

Davis, H. Francis. "The Origins of Devotion to Our Lady's Immaculate Conception," *The Dublin Review,* 228 (October, 1954), 375-92.

Devlin, Christopher. "Time's Eunuch," *The Month,* N.S. 1 (January-June, 1949), 303-12.

———. "The Image and the Word," *The Month,* N.S. 3 (January-June, 1950), 114-27, 191-202.

———. Correspondence, *The Month,* N.S. 4 (July-December, 1950), 210-15.

Digges, Sister M. Laurentia, C.S.J. "Gerard Manley Hopkins's Sonnets of Desolation, an Analysis of Meaning." Unpublished doctoral dissertation, Catholic University, Washington, D.C., 1951.

Donoghue, Denis. "The Bird as Symbol," *Studies,* 44 (Autumn, 1955), 291-99.

Downes, David A. *Gerard Manley Hopkins, a Study of His Ignatian Spirit.* New York: Bookman Associates, 1959.

Doyle, Francis G., S.J. "A Note on Hopkins' Windhover," *Studies,* 45 (Spring, 1956), 88-91.

"Dr. Pusey on Marian Doctrine—Peace through the Truth," *The Dublin Review,* N.S. VI (April, 1866), 412-49; N.S. VII (July, 1866), 142-99; N.S. VII (October, 1866), 455-514.

Ellman, Richard. *Yeats: the Man and the Masks.* New York: Macmillan, 1948.

Empson, William. *Seven Types of Ambiguity.* 2nd edition. London: Chatto and Windus, 1947.

Ephraem. "De laudibus Dei genitricis Mariae," in "De diversis sermonibus, 3," in *Opera omnia quae exstant Graece, Syriace, Latine, in sex tomos distributa.* Vol. 3. Romae: Salvioni, 1743.

Fairchild, Hoxie. *Religious Trends in English Poetry.* New York: Columbia, 1949.

Gardner, W. H. *Gerard Manley Hopkins (1844-1889), A Study of Poetic Idiosyncrasy in Relation to Poetic Tradition.* 2 vols. New Haven: Yale, 1948.

———. Correspondence, *The Month,* N.S. 4 (July-December, 1950), 210-15.

———. "Hopkins's Harvest-Home," *The Month,* N.S. 10 (July-December, 1953), 308.

Gilson, Etienne Henry. *Jean Duns Scot, Introduction à Ses Positions Fondamentales.* Paris: J. Vrin, 1952.

Grigson, Geoffrey. *Gerard Manley Hopkins.* London: Longmans, Green, 1955.

Hart, Sister M. Adorita, B.V.M. "The Christocentric Theme in Gerard Manley Hopkins's 'The Wreck of the Deutschland.'" Unpublished doctoral dissertation, Catholic University, Washington, D.C., 1952.

Hartman, Geoffrey H. *The Unmediated Vision, an Interpretation of Wordsworth, Hopkins, Rilke, and Valery.* New Haven: Yale, 1954.

Hesiod. *Hesiod, the Homeric Hymns and Homerica.* Translated by Hugh G. Evelyn-White. London: W. Heinemann, 1936.

———. *The Greek Poets.* Translated by Moses Hadas. New York: Modern Library, 1953.

Heuser, Alan. *The Shaping Vision of Gerard Manley Hopkins.* London: Oxford, 1958.

Hopkins, Gerard Manley. *The Correspondence of Gerard Manley Hopkins and Richard Watson Dixon,* ed. Claude Colleer Abbott. London: Oxford, 1935.

———. *The Letters of Gerard Manley Hopkins to Robert Bridges,* ed. Claude Colleer Abbott. London: Oxford, 1935.

———. *Poems of Gerard Manley Hopkins,* ed. W. H. Gardner. 3rd edition. London: Oxford, 1948.

———. *Further Letters of Gerard Manley Hopkins,* ed. Claude Colleer Abbott. 2nd edition. London: Oxford, 1956.

———. *The Journals and Papers of Gerard Manley Hopkins,* ed. Humphry House. London: Oxford, 1959.

———. *The Sermons and Devotional Writings of Gerard Manley Hopkins,* ed. Christopher Devlin, S.J. London: Oxford, 1959.

Hill, Archibald A. "An Analysis of *The Windhover,* an Experiment in Structural Method," *PMLA,* 60 (December, 1955), 968-78.

The Holy Bible. Translated by Ronald Knox. New York: Sheed and Ward, 1956.

Ignatius Loyola. *The Text of the Spiritual Exercises of St. Ignatius.* Translated from the original Spanish. 4th edition. London: Burns, Oates, and Washbourne, 1936.

Joyce, G. H., S.J. *The Catholic Doctrine of Grace.* New York: Benziger, n.d.

Joyce, James. *A Portrait of the Artist as a Young Man.* New York: Modern Library, 1928.

———. *Finnegans Wake.* New York: Viking, 1947.

Kelly, Hugh, S.J. "The Windhover—and Christ," *Studies,* 45 (Summer, 1956), 188-93.

LaFarge, John, S.J. "Ignatius Loyola and Our Times," *Thought,* 31 (Summer, 1956), 165-86.

Lahey, G. F., S.J. *Gerard Manley Hopkins.* London: Oxford, 1930.
Leavis, F. R. *New Bearings in English Poetry.* London: Chatto and Windus, 1942.
Lynch, William F., S.J. "Theology and the Imagination," *Thought,* 29 (Spring, 1954), 61-86.
McLuhan, Herbert Marshall. "The Analogical Mirrors," in *Gerard Manley Hopkins by the Kenyon Critics.* Norfolk, Conn.: New Directions, 1945.
McNamee, Maurice L., S.J. "Hopkins: Poet of Nature and of the Supernatural," in *Immortal Diamond: Studies in Gerard Manley Hopkins,* ed. Norman Weyand, S.J. New York: Sheed and Ward, 1949.
Maritain, Jacques. *Creative Intuition in Art and Poetry.* New York: Pantheon, 1953.
Martz, Louis L. *The Poetry of Meditation, A Study in English Religious Literature of the Seventeenth Century.* New Haven: Yale, 1954.
Mary Humiliata, Sister. "Hopkins and the Prometheus Myth," *PMLA,* 70 (March, 1955), 58-68.
Miller, J. Hillis. "The Creation of the Self in Gerard Manley Hopkins," *ELH* [A Journal of English Literary History], 22 (1955), 293-319.
Mizener, Arthur. "Victorian Hopkins," in *Gerard Manley Hopkins by the Kenyon Critics.* Norfolk, Conn.: New Directions, 1945.
Morris, David. *The Poetry of Gerard Manley Hopkins and Thomas Stearns Eliot in the Light of the Donne Tradition, A Comparative Study.* Bern: A. Francke, 1953.
Neubert, Emil, S.J. *Mary in Doctrine.* Milwaukee: Bruce, 1954.
The New Testament, rendered from the original Greek with explanatory notes. Translated by James A. Kleist, S.J. Milwaukee: Bruce, 1952.
Peters, W. A. M., S.J. *Gerard Manley Hopkins, A Critical Essay towards the Understanding of his Poetry.* London: Oxford, 1948.
Phare, Elsie Elizabeth. *The Poetry of Gerard Manley Hopkins, A Survey and Commentary.* Cambridge, England: The University Press, 1933.
Pick, John. *Gerard Manley Hopkins, Priest and Poet.* London: Oxford, 1942.
Poulain, August, S.J. *The Graces of Interior Prayer.* Translated by Leonora Smith. London: Kegan Paul, 1910.
Ransom, John Crowe. *The World's Body.* New York: Scribner's, 1938.
Read, Herbert Edward. *The True Voice of Feeling, Studies in English Romantic Poetry.* London: Faber and Faber, 1953.
Reeves, James (ed.). *Selected Poems of Gerard Manley Hopkins.* London: W. Heinemann, 1953.
Richards, Ivor Armstrong. "Gerard Hopkins," *The Dial,* 81 (July-December, 1926), 195-203.
———. *Coleridge on Imagination.* 2nd edition. New York: W. W. Norton, 1950.

Riding, Laura, and Robert Graves. *A Survey of Modernist Poetry.* London: W. Heinemann, 1927.
Ritz, Jean-George. "The Windhover de G. M. Hopkins," *Études Anglaises,* 9 (1956), 13-22.
———. Correspondence, *Times* (London), *Literary Supplement,* 54 (May 6, 1955), 237.
Ruggles, Eleanor. *Gerard Manley Hopkins, A Life.* New York: Norton, 1944.
Ryan, Noel J., S.J. "The Assumption in the Early English Pulpit," *Theological Studies,* 11 (December, 1950), 477-524.
Sargent, Daniel. *Four Independents.* New York: Sheed and Ward, 1935.
Sayers, Dorothy L. "'. . . And Telling You A Story,' A Note on *The Divine Comedy,*" in *Essays Presented to Charles Williams.* London: Oxford, 1947.
Scheeben, Matthias Joseph. *The Mysteries of Christianity.* Translated by Cyril Vollert, S.J. St. Louis: Herder, 1946.
Schoder, Raymond V., S.J. "Spelt from Sibyl's Leaves," *Thought,* 19 (December, 1944), 633-48.
———. "What does The Windhover Mean?" in *Immortal Diamond: Studies in Gerard Manley Hopkins,* ed. Norman Weyand, S.J. New York: Sheed and Ward, 1949.
Speaight, Robert. "The Price of Poetry," *The Dublin Review,* 227 (1953), 371-80.
Stearns, Marshall W. "Unsex the Skeleton: Notes on the Poetry of Dylan Thomas," *The Sewanee Review,* 52 (1944), 424-40.
Theissen, A. "The Epistle to the Romans," in *A Catholic Commentary on Holy Scripture,* ed. Dom Bernard Orchard *et al.* London: Thomas Nelson, 1951.
Tuve, Rosemond. *A Reading of George Herbert.* Chicago: University of Chicago Press, 1952.
Ward, Dennis. "The Windhover," in *Interpretations: Essays on Twelve English Poems,* ed. John Wain. London: Routledge, Kegan Paul, 1955.
Winters, Yvor. "The Poetry of Gerard Manley Hopkins," *The Hudson Review,* I (Winter, 1949), 455-76; II (Spring, 1949), 59-93.

Index

Aaron, 33
Accents, speech, xiv; verse, xiv
Adam, 58, 76, 79, 98, 127, 165
Adorita, Sister Mary, B.V.M., 208n
Aeschylus, 141
Alphonsus Rodriguez, St., 80, 104, 152, 213n
Arendzen, J. P., *The Holy Trinity*, 38
Aristotle, 73
Atkinson, Brooks, 127
Auden, W. H., "A Knight of the Infinite," 197
Augustine, St., 7; quoted by M. J. Rouet de Journel in *Enchiridion Patristicum*, 61

Bede, St., Lectio 9, *Commune Festorum Beatae Mariae Virginis*, 8; imagery, 9
Beeching, H. C., *A Book of Christmas Verse*, 63
Being vs. concept, 176
Blackmur, R. P., 192, 216n
Blessed Virgin Mary, 8, 10, 17; sinlessness of, 8, 52, 57, 171, 209n; spiritual motherhood of, 51-54, 56-61 *passim*, 63-65, 153, 164, 185; poets' treatment of, 54-56, 209n; and Redemption, 57, 210n; Mother of God, 58, 59, 60, 63, 65, 164; and the Mystical Body, 59-62 *passim*, 203, 210n; intercessory power of, 64; second Eve, 64; mediatrix of all graces, 65
Bischoff, D. A., S.J., xxi
Bridges, Robert, xviii, xx, xxi, 18, 19, 23, 26, 50, 120-21, 131-35 *passim*, 147, 159, 174, 175, 187, 188, 197
Britt, Dom Matthew, O.S.B., *The Hymns of the Breviary and Missal*, 14, 39
Brooks, Cleanth, "The Language of Paradox," 179-80

Brown, John Mason, 127
Burne-Jones, Sir Edward, xxiii, 82
Burrows, Eric, S.J., 209n

Carroll, Lewis, *Alice*, 149; Humpty Dumpty in *Looking Glass*, 47, 174
Catholic Commentary on Holy Scripture, A, 40, 102
Catholic tradition, 190, 191-93, 195, 216n
Chaucer, Geoffrey, 46, 54
Christ, as Source of divine life of grace, xi, 60; the Good Shepherd, 4, 5, 6, 15, 16, 23, 24; the Lamb of God, 5, 6, 12, 15, 23; the Redeemer, 6, 23, 57, 208n; the Host, 6, 23; the Light of the World, 6-9 *passim*, 24, 52, 67, 68, 74, 156; the Word of God, 7-12 *passim*, 22, 23, 51, 52-54, 59, 61, 63, 64, 65, 68, 70, 119, 190, 196, 198, 199; the King, 24, 80, 100, 105; and the Second Coming, 27; in Gethsemane, 32; the Second Adam, 37; dual nature in, 60; as Paraclete, 79; the Knight, 80, 94, 196, 198, 213n; Resurrection of, 102; the Living Water, 156. *See also* Sacred Heart of Jesus, Mystical Body
Coleridge, 149
Colombiere, de la, Claude, S.J., 99
Concept, 150; as opposed to being, 176
Crashaw, Richard, 201
Critics, of "Windhover," *simpliste*, 82, 83-84; "pagan," 82, 84-88, 199; Christian, 82; conceptualist, 176
Cynghanedd, 19, 208n

Daiches, David, 214n
Dante, Alighieri, 6; *The Divine Comedy*, 3, 45, 145, 192, 201, 204, 213n
David, 129
Davis, H. Francis, 209-10n

Devlin, Christopher, S.J., 211n
Dies Irae, 129, 137
Dixon, Canon R. W., xx, 139, 171, 175, 197
Donoghue, Denis, 83, 89
Downes, David A., 84, 87-88
Doyle, Francis G., 89-90
Dunbar, William, "Of the Nativity of Christ," 46

Ellman, Richard, *Yeats: the Man and the Masks,* 49-50
Empson, William, 83, 84-85, 89, 193, 195, 211n
Ephraem, 209n
Evelyn-White, Hugh G. (trans.), *Hesiod, the Homeric Hymns and Homerica,* 135

Fairchild, Hoxie, *Religious Trends in English Poetry,* 54-55
Fortunatus, "O gloriosa Domina," 45
Free will, 17

Gardner, W. H., xx, 11, 17, 18, 19, 50, 66, 84, 85, 86, 107, 112, 122, 128, 129, 147, 148, 149, 153, 158, 164, 169, 217n
Gertrude, St., 15
Gilson, Etienne, 194
Graves, Robert, and Laura Riding, *A Survey of Modernist Poetry,* 160
Greene, Graham, *The Living Room,* 127
Grigson, Geoffrey, 83

Hartmann, Geoffrey H., 84, 86-87, 89, 107, 214n; *The Unmediated Vision,* 149-50
Herbert, George, 12, 55, 209n, 216n
Hesiod, *Theogony,* 129, 134, 140
Heuser, Alan, 84, 87, 88
Hill, Archibald A., 89, 90
Holy Ghost, 4, 17, 40, 95, 96, 100, 133, 164, 203; "Finger" of God, 4, 10, 11, 15, 24; the Paraclete, 5, 28, 79, 153, 196; symbolized by dove, 5, 37, 38, 41, 42, 78, 111-24 *passim,* 207n; indwelling of, 37, 113; the Life-Giver, 38, 42, 190, 196; Spirit of Light, 38, 41, 44, 130; Spirit of Love, 40, 43; Spiritual Unction, 38, 40; Spirit of Patience, 115-16, 123
Hopkins, imagery, xix, 22, 62, 73, 150, 161, 169-70, 174-204 *passim;* choice of words, xxii, 150-51, 156-57, 174-75, 207n, 213n, 214n, 215n; treatment of Blessed Virgin, 54-56; the Jesuit, 99, 100, 193, 194, 195, 197; influenced by St. Paul, 154, 171; conception of nature, 165; organic unity of the work of, 178, 197; definition of poetry, 190; world-view of, 192-204 *passim;* and the Catholic tradition, 190, 191-93, 195, 216n; compared to Dante, 200-2
Poems: "Ad Matrem Virginem," *No. 138,* 53; "The Alchemist in the City," *No. 10,* 34; "Andromeda," *No. 49,* 117; "Ashboughs," *No. 111,* 163, 164, 166; "As kingfishers catch fire . . . ," *No. 57,* 10, 19, 20, 97, 104, 105; "Barnfloor and Winepress," *No. 18,* 32; "Binsey Poplars," *No. 43,* 36, 166; "The Blessed Virgin compared to the Air we Breathe," *No. 60,* xix, 9, 17, 21, 47-70 *passim,* 117, 164, 171, 172, 183-85; "Brothers," *No. 54,* 78; "The Bugler's First Communion," *No. 47,* 80, 159, 170; "The Candle Indoors," *No. 50,* 74, 75, 96, 100, 156; "Carrion Comfort," *No. 64,* 77, 99, 115, 116, 139, 142, 152, 154; "Easter Communion," *No. 13,* 34; "Epithalamion," *No. 121,* 166-67; "The Escorial," *No. 1,* xv; "Felix Randal," *No. 53,* 117; "God's Grandeur," *No. 31,* xix, xxi, 25-44 *passim,* 137, 141, 155, 159, 169, 170, 172, 183; "The Habit of Perfection," *No. 24,* 77; "The Handsome Heart," *No. 51,* 80, 82, 144; "Harry Ploughman," *No. 67,* 98; "Henry Purcell, *No. 45,* xxii, 160; "Hurrahing in Harvest," *No. 38,* 66, 78, 82, 150; "In honor of St. Alphonsus Rodriguez," *No. 73,* 80, 117; "In the Valley of the Elway," *No. 40,* 20, 162, 164, 170; "Inversnaid," *No. 56,* 63, 171, 187; "I wake and feel the fell of dark . . . ," *No. 69,* 77, 145-46, 151, 154; "The Lantern out of Doors," *No. 34,* 20-21, 78; "Let me be to Thee as the circling bird . . . ," *No. 16,* 150; "The Loss of the Eurydice, *No. 41,* xxiv, 142; "May Lines," *No. 139,* 58; "The May Magnificat," *No. 42,* 42, 164, 166; "Morning Midday and Evening Sacrifice," *No. 48,* 73; "My own heart . . . ," *No. 71,* xx, xxi, 95, 142-43, 145, 147-61 *passim,* 173, 185; "Nondum," *No. 22,* xi, xii, xxiv, 31, 161, 196; "No worst, there is none . . . ,"

INDEX

No. *65,* 21, 142, 151, 152-54 *passim;* "On the Portrait of Two Beautiful Young People," No. *119,* 36-37; "Oratio Patris Condren . . . ," No. *132,* 70; "Patience, hard thing! . . . ," No. *70,* 78, 113-14, 119, 121-22, 137, 153; "Peace," No. *46,* xx, 76, 111, 112-24 *passim,* 172, 211n; "Pied Beauty," No. *37,* 28, 29, 160; "Ribblesdale," No. *58,* xx, xxi, 162, 163-71 *passim,* 173, 174, 175; "Richard," No. *87,* 10; "Rosa Mystica," No. *27,* 61; "S. Thomae Aquinatis: Rhythmus ad SS. Sacramentum," No. *131,* 156; "St. Winefred's Well," No. *105,* 138; "The Sea and the Skylark," No. *35,* 29, 30, 104, 135, 165, 214n; "The shepherd's brow . . . ," No. *122,* 132-33, 134, 157; "(The Soldier)," No. *63,* 76-77, 104, 105, 140, 151; "A Soliloquy of One of the Spies left in the Wilderness," No. *5,* 31-32; "Spelt from Sibyl's Leaves," No. *62,* xiv, xx, 34-35, 76, 114, 121, 125, 127-44 *passim,* 151, 152-54 *passim,* 167, 172-73, 174; "Spring," No. *33,* 28, "Spring and Fall: to a young child," No. *55,* 76, 93, 167; "The Starlight Night," No. *32,* 21, 99, 114, 117, 150, 167; "That Nature is a Heraclitean Fire . . . ," No. *72,* 6, 65, 75, 79, 97, 102, 151, 157, 166, 207n; "Thee, God, I come from . . . ," No. *116,* 167; "Thou art indeed just, Lord . . . ," No. *74,* 99, 120, 132, 151, 166; "The times are nightfall . . . ," No. *112,* 120, 126; "Tom's Garland," No. *66,* 36, 151; "To R. B.," No. *75,* xii, 133-34, 189, 207n; "To seem the stranger . . . ," No. *68,* 78, 117-19 *passim,* 122, 134, 135, 193, 200; "To what serves Mortal Beauty?," No. *61,* 77; "A Vision of Mermaids," No. *2,* xvi; "A Voice from the World," No. *77, 35;* "The Windhover: To Christ our Lord," No. *36,* xx, 9, 71, 73-110 *passim,* 128, 130, 154, 172, 174, 193, 198, 199, 201; "Winter with the Gulf Stream," No. *3,* 34, 37; *The Wreck of the Deutschland,* No. *28,* xvii, xix, xxi, xxiii, xxiv, 4-24 *passim,* 27, 28, 44, 49, 52, 53, 57, 60, 68, 74, 75, 78, 80, 81, 82, 86, 87, 93, 99, 101, 106, 115, 133, 142, 143, 144, 150, 153, 164, 168, 171, 172, 174, 180-83, 196, 207n, 211n

Humiliata, Sister Mary, "Hopkins and the Prometheus Myth," 153

Ignatius of Loyola, St., "The Contemplation for Obtaining Divine Love" in *Spiritual Exercises,* 40, 103; *Spiritual Exercises,* 79, 91, 139, 158; "Anima Christi," 138
Image, 24, 150
Imagery, xxi, xxii, xxiii, xxiv, 24
Incarnation, 75, 191-92, 193, 195; existential metaphor, 198

Jesuits, 193, 194, 195, 197; life of, 85; ideals of, 80, 106, 139
John, St., the Evangelist, light and darkness imagery, 38, 44, 52, 127, 136, 141
Joyce, G. H., S.J., *The Catholic Doctrine of Grace,* 56, 210n
Joyce, James, *A Portrait of the Artist as a Young Man,* 188-89, 214n

Keats, John, *Endymion,* 158
Kelly, Hugh, S.J., 84, 85-86
Knighthood, terminology of, 95-96, 212n. *See also* Christ, the Knight

LaFarge, John, S.J., "Ignatius Loyola and Our Times," 103
Lahey, G. F., S.J., 83-84
Laurentia, Sister Mary, C.S.J., 213n
Leavis, F. R., 84, 85; *New Bearings in English Poetry,* 202
Lightning, 11, 24, 26-28 *passim. See also* Metaphor
Luther, Martin, 15
Lynch, William F., S.J., "Theology and the Imagination," 198-99

McLuhan, Herbert M., 89, 90-91, 107
McNamee, Maurice B., S.J., "Hopkins: Poet of Nature and of the Supernatural," 201
Manuscript sources, xxi; MS A, xx, xxi, 19, 26; MS B, xx, xxi, 18; MS D, xx; MS H, xxi
Maritain, Jacques, *Creative Intuition in Art and Poetry,* 186; and the Catholic tradition, 194
Mary. *See* Blessed Virgin Mary
Melpomene, 181
Metaphor, xi, xii, xix, 5, 175-80 *passim,* 183-86 *passim;* compared with simile, 91, 175-78 *passim,* 180, 183; nature of,

180-83, 207n, 209n, 210n, 215n; *in Hopkins:* nun-bell image, 4, 5, 10-12, 20, 21, 24, 180-83, 190, 203; "Finger" of God images, 4, 10, 11, 15, 24; sheep images, 4-17 *passim,* 21, 24, 136-37; heart images, 5, 6, 73-76 *passim,* 78-80, 134, 190, 203, 212n; feather images, 5, 17, 174, 207n; fire images, 6-9 *passim,* 24, 28, 30-31, 41, 73-75 *passim,* 78-82 *passim,* 83, 84, 86-102 *passim,* 106, 190; harvest images, 9, 16, 20, 99; life-giving light-and-water images, 23, 24, 156, 159; sun images: Christ, 24, 65-69 *passim,* God, 30, Holy Ghost, 30, 37, 38, 40, 42, 190; gold-foil images, 26, 29, 30, 33, 38; lightning images, 28-29, 33; oil images, 31-36 *passim,* 41; Mary-air image, 66-69, 190, 209n; chevalier image, 81, 82, 90, 92, 93, 95, 96, 105-8 *passim,* 114; plow images, 83, 84, 89, 98-101 *passim,* 213n; dove-peace images, 113, 115-16, 190; skein-of-life image, 134, 135-36, 137; mother-earth images, 164-70 *passim*

Meter, xiii-xviii, 186
Metrical conflicts, xiv
Miller, J. Hillis, 84-88, 107, 212n
Milton, John, xiv, xvi, xvii, xxii, 54, 135; *Paradise Lost,* xiii-xv *passim,* 41, 56, 139, 201; "On the Morning of Christ's Nativity," xvii, 67; treatment of Blessed Virgin, 56, 58-59; "L'Allegro," 160; *Paradise Regained,* 201
Mizener, Arthur, "Victorian Hopkins," 201-2
Moses, 31, 33, 159
Mystical Body, xi, 51-52, 53, 54, 59, 70, 97, 102-4, 106, 110, 118, 193, 196, 198, 199, 203; inspiration of Hopkins' finest imagery 70, 102; existential metaphor, 198

Neubert, Emil, S.M., 210n

Oppenheimer, J. Robert, "Man's Right to Knowledge," 127
Original sin, 76

Parmenides, 73, 74
Patience, 111-24 *passim,* 129, 130, 134, 137, 141, 161, 213n; fruit of Holy Ghost, 159
Patmore, *The Unknown Eros,* 210

Paul, St., 37, 154, 164, 165, 171, 200, 203; military imagery of 79, 91, 93-94; and doctrine of the Mystical Body, 102; and the inner struggle, 141. Texts from: Epistle to the Hebrews, 4-5, 97, 98, 111; to the Ephesians, 17-18, 93-94; to the Romans, 30, 51-52, 68, 72, 102, 143-44, 163, 164, 165-66, 168, 170; First Epistle to the Corinthians, 69, 71, 137; Epistle to the Philippians, 71; to the Colossians, 110; to the Galatians, 112-13, 114, 159; Second Epistle to the Corinthians, 215n
Peace, 111-24 *passim,* 213n; fruit of Holy Ghost, 159
Peters, W. A. M., S.J., 83-84, 213n
Phare, Elsie Elizabeth, 84, 85, 193, 194, 195, 200, 212n
Pick, John, 84, 85
Plato, 129, 179
Poulain, August, S.J., *The Graces of Interior Prayer,* 144
Prodigal Son, 169
Providence, 4, 20, 174

Ransom, John Crowe, *The World's Body,* 177-83 *passim*
Read, Herbert, 84, 85
Reeves, James, 83-84, 194-95, 214n
Religious life, 99-100; misconceptions of, 84-89 *passim,* 193-95
Rhythm, xii, xiii-xviii *passim,* xxiv, 19, 24, 186-89 *passim;* metaphorical, xii, xv, xvii, 10, 18-20, 42-44, 66, 69, 93, 98, 106-10, 123-24, 136, 151-53, 170-71, 174, 190, 207n, 208n; sprung rhythm, xiv, 176; inversion of words for, 123, 211n
Richards, Ivor A., *Coleridge on Imagination,* 41-42; 84-85, 92, 108, 193
Riding, Laura, and Robert Graves, *A Survey of Modernist Poetry,* 160
Ritz, Jean-George, 89, 92
Roman Breviary, Common of Virgins: "Jesu Corona Virginum," 12; "Virginis Proles Opifexque Matris," 13
Ruggles, Eleanor, 89, 196-97
Ryan, Noel J., S.J., 209n

Sacred Heart of Jesus, 17, 24, 75, 76, 88, 91, 92, 96, 97, 99, 100, 101, 103, 105, 154, 195, 212n
Sacrifice, 3-6 *passim,* 12, 15, 20-23 *pas-*

sim, 57, 80, 86-89 *passim*, 95-96, 105-6, 137, 139, 194-95, 208n
Sanctifying grace, 21, 24, 52, 56, 58, 80, 98, 104, 113, 123-24, 195, 203, 208n, 210n
Sargent, Daniel, 84, 85-86
Sayers, Dorothy, 201
Scheeben, Matthias, *The Mysteries of Christianity*, trans. Cyril Vollert, S.J., 22-23
Schoder, Raymond V., S.J., 89, 91, 92, 107, 128, 130-31, 140-41
Shakespeare, William, *Midsummer Night's Dream*, xiii; *Troilus and Cressida*, xiii; *Antony and Cleopatra*, xvi; *Hamlet*, xvi; *King Henry VIII*, 15; Sonnet 73, 100; *King Lear*, 124; *I Henry IV*, 148; Sonnet 98, 160; *Love's Labour's Lost*, 160
Shekinah, 48
Simile, xi, xix, 183, 184, 185; compared with metaphor, 91, 175-78 *passim*, 180, 183
Spiritual desolation, 149, 152, 154-56, 158-59, 161, 203, 214n
Sophocles, 129
Sound structure, 18, 186-87, 190
Stearns, Marshall W., 215n

Suffering, 110, 114, 127, 130, 132, 137, 138, 203
Supernatural destiny of man, xiii, 193. *See also* Mystical Body, Sanctifying grace
Symbol, 99, 103, 105, 106, 207n

Thiessen, A., in *A Catholic Commentary*, 102
Thomas Aquinas, St., *Summa Theologiae*, 58, 116, 159, 187
Trinity, The Blessed, 24; self-donation in, 88
Tuve, Rosemond, *A Reading of George Herbert*, 178-79, 180, 216n

"Veni Creator," 39
Vows of religion, 114, 122. *See also* Religious life

Ward, Dennis, 89, 91-92
Winters, Yvor, 83, 175-76
Wordsworth, William, 54; "Ode to Immortality," 41; "The Virgin," 54-55

Yeats, W. B., 54; treatment of Blessed Virgin, 55

www.ingramcontent.com/pod-product-compliance
Lightning Source LLC
Chambersburg PA
CBHW021400290426
44108CB00010B/317